Especially for

_____

From

_____

Date

_____

© 2011 by Barbour Publishing, Inc.

ISBN 978-1-61626-391-1

Scripture quotations are taken from the *Holy Bible*, New Living Translation, copyright © 1996, 2004. Used by permission of Tyndale House Publishers, Inc. Wheaton, Illinois 60189, U.S.A. All rights reserved.

Published by Barbour Publishing, Inc., P.O. Box 719, Uhrichsville, Ohio 44683, www.barbourbooks.com

Our mission is to publish and distribute inspirational products offering exceptional value and biblical encouragement to the masses.

Member of the
Evangelical Christian
Publishers Association

Printed in China.

The Greatest Gift

BARBOUR
PUBLISHING

Good news from heaven
the angels bring,
Glad tidings to
the earth they sing:
To us this day a
child is given,
To crown us with
the joy of heaven.

MARTIN LUTHER

We spend so much time wrapping our gifts for each other in just the right paper, ribbon, and bow. For what? So we can have a trash bag full of pretty colors on December 26?

God wrapped His Gift—the Greatest Gift—to us not in beautiful foil or sparkly glitter, but in something everlasting: *Love.*

Christmas gift suggestions:

To your enemy, forgiveness.

To an opponent, tolerance.

To a friend, your heart.

To a customer, service.

To all, charity.

To every child, a good example.

To yourself, respect.

Oren Arnold

This is the Christ,

our God and Lord,

Who in all need shall aid afford;

He will Himself your Savior be

From all your sins to set you free.

MARTIN LUTHER

*But even greater is
God's wonderful grace and
his gift of forgiveness to many
through this other man,
Jesus Christ. . . .God's free gift
leads to our being made right
with God, even though we are
guilty of many sins.*

ROMANS 5:15–16

Ring out, ye bells!
All Nature swells
With gladness of
The wondrous story,

The world was lorn,
But Christ is born
To change our
sadness into glory.

PAUL LAWRENCE DUNBAR

Two things upon this changing
earth can neither change nor end;
the splendor of Christ's humble
birth, the love of friend for friend.

UNKNOWN

Raise, raise a song on high,
The virgin sings her lullaby.
Joy, joy for Christ is born,
The Babe, the Son of Mary.

WILLIAM CHATTERTON DIX

Only a manger,
cold and bare,
Only a maiden mild,
Only some shepherds
kneeling there,
Watching a little Child;

*And yet that maiden's
arms enfold
The King of heaven above;
And in the Christ Child
we behold
The Lord of life and love.*

UNKNOWN

Now let us all with
gladsome cheer
Go with the shepherds
and draw near
To see the precious
gift of God,
Who hath His own
dear Son bestowed.

MARTIN LUTHER

Remember the Greatest Gift. . .

*This Christmas season,
may you find time to quietly reflect on
the love of the Savior.*

The holly and the ivy

When both are full well grown,

Of all the trees that are in the wood,

The holly bears the crown.

The holly bears a berry

As red as any blood,

And Mary bore sweet Jesus Christ

To do poor sinners good.

ENGLISH FOLK CAROL

There's room in my heart, Lord Jesus, There's room in my heart for You.

GOSPEL CHORUS

For a child is born to us,
a son is given to us.
. . . And he will
be called:
Wonderful Counselor,
Mighty God
Everlasting Father,
Prince of Peace.

ISAIAH 9:6

One moment in time held
incomparable joy.
One moment in time held
perfect love.

One moment in time held
eternal significance.
One moment in time held
the promise of hope.

Joy to the world,
The Lord is come!
Let earth receive her King;
Let every heart
Prepare Him room,

And heaven and nature sing,
And heaven and nature sing,
And heaven, and heaven,
And nature sing.

ISAAC WATTS

Christmas is. . .

A season of love
A season of peace
A season of giving
A season of thankfulness

A season of beauty
A season of miracles
A season of joy
A season of hope

"If you sinful people know how to give good gifts to your children, how much more will your heavenly Father give good gifts to those who ask him."

MATTHEW 7:11

Praying you'll

experience the

Light of Christ in

an unexpected way

this Christmas.

Star of wonder,
star of night,
Star with royal beauty bright,
Westward leading,
still proceeding,
Guide us to the perfect light.

JOHN HENRY HOPKINS JR.

May each
Christmas star
you see, whether
in the sky or atop
your tree, fill you
with the wonder of
Christmas.

O come, O come, Emmanuel,

And ransom captive Israel,

That mourns in lonely exile here

Until the Son of God appear.

Rejoice! Rejoice! Emmanuel

Shall come to thee, O Israel.

JOHN MASON NEAL

This year, as you celebrate Christmas, may every holly branch you see remind you of the Christ Child, the true Root of any merry Christmas.

A Gift of Love. . .

A Gift of Joy. . .

A Gift of Hope.

All poor men and humble,

All lame men who stumble

Come haste ye, nor feel ye afraid;

For Jesus, our treasure

With love past all measure,

In lowly poor manger was laid.

OLD WELSH CAROL

"*Let's go to Bethlehem!
Let's see this thing that has
happened, which the Lord
has told us about.*"

LUKE 2:15

Love came down at Christmas,

Love all lovely, love divine;

Love was born at Christmas,

Star and angels gave the sign.

CHRISTINA ROSSETTI

What child is this who laid to rest,

on Mary's lap is sleeping?

Whom angels greet with anthems sweet,

While shepherds watch are keeping?

This, this is Christ the King,

Whom shepherds guard and angels sing:

Haste, haste to bring Him laud,

the Babe, the son of Mary.

WILLIAM CHATTERTON DIX

The simple shepherds
heard the voice of an
angel and found their
Lamb; the wise men saw
the light of a star and
found their wisdom.

FULTON J. SHEEN

Glory to God in highest heaven,

Who unto us His Son hath given!

While angels sing with pious mirth

A glad new year to all the earth.

MARTIN LUTHER

For Thyself, best Gift Divine
To the world so freely given,
For that great, great love
of Thine, Peace on earth
and joy in heaven:

Lord of all, to Thee we raise

This our hymn of grateful praise.

FOLLIOT S. PIERPOINT

This Christmas, bring to the Christ Child your heart's greatest treasures, laying them down at His feet with worship and love and wonder.

The magi, as you know, were wise men—wonderfully wise men who brought gifts to the Babe in the manger. They invented the art of giving Christmas presents.

O. HENRY

The free gift of God

is eternal life through

Christ Jesus our Lord.

ROMANS 6:23

Christmas is based on an exchange of gifts: the gift of God to man—His Son; and the gift of man to God—when we first give ourselves to God.

ANONYMOUS

A little child
A shining star,
A stable rude
The door ajar,

Yet in this place,
So crude, forlorn,
The Hope of all
The world was born.

ANONYMOUS

And is it true? And is it true,
This most tremendous tale of all,
Seen in a stained glass window's hue,
Baby in an in ox's stall?
The Maker of the stars and sea
Became a Child on earth for me?

SIR JOHN BETJEMAN

Whatever is good and perfect comes down to us from God our Father, who created all the lights in the heavens. He never changes or casts a shifting shadow.

JAMES 1:17

Christmas, my child, is love in action. Every time we love, every time we give, it's Christmas.

DALE EVANS ROGERS

What can I give him, poor as I am?
If I were a shepherd,
I would bring a lamb;
if I were a wise man,
I would do my part;
yet what I can I give him:
I give my heart.

CHRISTINA GEORGINA ROSSETTI

God grant you the light in Christmas,

which is faith;

the warmth of Christmas, which is love;

the radiance of Christmas, which is purity;

the righteousness of Christmas,

which is justice;

the belief of Christmas, which is truth;

the all of Christmas, which is Christ.

WILDA ENGLISH

"*We saw his star as it rose, and we have come to worship him.*"

Then be ye glad, good people,
This night of all the year,
And light ye up your candles:
His star is drawing near.

TRADITIONAL CAROL

A Christmas candle is
a lovely thing;
It makes no noise at all,
But softly gives
itself away.

EVA LOGUE

God's gifts put man's
best dreams to shame.

ELIZABETH BARRETT BROWNING

O Father, may that holy star

Grow every year more bright,

And send its glorious beams afar

To fill the world with light.

WILLIAM CULLEN BRYANT

O come, let us adore Him,

O come, let us adore Him,

O come, let us adore Him,

Christ, the Lord!

JOHN FRANCIS WADE

Gift better than Himself

God doth not know—

Gift better than his God

no man can see;

God is my Gift, Himself
He freely gave me;
God's gift am I, and none
but God shall have me.

Christ was born in the first century, yet He belongs to all centuries. He was born a Jew, yet He belongs to all races. He was born in Bethlehem, yet He belongs to all countries.

GEORGE W. TRUETT

* *

Great little One! whose
all-embracing birth
Lifts earth to heaven,
stoops heaven to earth.

RICHARD CRASHAW

So the Word became human and made his home among us. He was full of unfailing love and faithfulness.

JOHN 1:14

Christmas began in
the heart of God. It is
complete only when it
reaches the heart of man.

UNKNOWN

Morning Star, O cheering sight!

Ere thou cam'st how dark earth's night!

Jesus mine, in me shine,

Fill my heart with light divine.

MORAVIAN HYMN

'Tis the season to remember when
God came down to walk with men.
The Gift was not wrapped
in boxes and bows
For mercy came in swaddling clothes.
So when you think of Christmastime
It isn't about trees and tinsel shine.

Love stepped down from heaven's height
And was born on earth that blessed night.
So pause sometime in December
For 'tis the season to remember.

UNKNOWN

No matter how dark the night, the star of Christmas shines on, undimmed by human despair. May that same star fill your heart with light.

What are we to make of
Jesus Christ? . . . The real
question is not what we are
to make of Christ, but what
is He to make of us?

C. S. LEWIS

✳ ✳ ✳ ✳ ✳ ✳ ✳ ✳ ✳ ✳ ✳ ✳ ✳ ✳

Though wise men
who found Him
Laid rich gifts around Him,
Yet oxen they gave
Him their hay;
And Jesus in beauty
Accepted their duty;
Contented in manger
He lay.

OLD WELSH CAROL

Though wise men
who found Him
Laid rich gifts around Him,
Yet oxen they gave
Him their hay;
And Jesus in beauty
Accepted their duty;
Contented in manger
He lay.

OLD WELSH CAROL

Jon remained rooted in his position. Droplets of sweat drenched his face, his soaked shirt clinging to his body. *In the distance he could hear the cheering. Then the screams of adulation faded away and Jon could hear the pounding of his own running feet. Plunging headlong through the familiar dream forest, he could feel his wildly beating heart. His body and seared lungs ached.*

Jon shrank back from the people grabbing at him with emaciated fingers, their sallow faces deformed with loathing. The fog parted and he saw the figure of the blond woman motioning for him to join her. Knowing the people pressing about him would not impede his course, he began approaching the indistinct form. The blond woman now lay at his feet. He tried vainly to repel the cajoling pantomime of the pressing crowd. He shook his head furiously but knew he could not resist.

He would obey.

Slowly he raised the dream gun to his temple, at the same time squeezing the trigger. Jon felt the burning headache begin . . .

Trina inserted the key in the lock of their apartment. She turned the knob as Jon screamed. Throwing the door open, she saw him fall from his chair. The sight of blood flowing from his eyes, nose, mouth and ears transfixed her in the entryway, unable to move. . . .

Other Leisure Books by John Tigges:

UNTO THE ALTAR
THE GARDEN OF THE INCUBUS
KISS NOT THE CHILD
HANDS OF LUCIFER
THE IMMORTAL
AS EVIL DOES
VENOM
VESSEL

EVIL DREAMS

JOHN TIGGES

LEISURE BOOKS ■ NEW YORK CITY

*For my darling Kathy, whose voice kept me going
when the going was difficult.*

A LEISURE BOOK

MARCH 1989

Published by

Dorchester Publishing Co., Inc.
276 Fifth Avenue
New York, NY 10001

EVIL
DREAMS

PROLOGUE

THE DREAM

Anytime between
February 3, 1946
April 20, 1979

Sleep quickly captured Jon Ward's consciousness.

His eyes barely closed, the cheering began. It sounded like a soft whisper in the distance, as though separated from him by miles. Gradually, inevitably, the applause, the cries, grew louder and louder until he thought his eardrums would burst. Screams of adulation, fanatical cries of worship washed over him, sending his senses reeling with but one thought—one predominating idea—*HE* was a *GOD!*

A shouting rhythm flooded over the cacaphony, building to an intense tempo until thousands of voices cried out in unison: *Dee-Hah! Dee-Hah! Dee Hah!* For some inexplicable reason, he felt he should understand the call, but the words never were clear.

The dissonance stopped suddenly, the familiar deadly silence filling the void. Nothing. No sound of any type. Then he heard it. The

9

click, click, click of running feet. His lungs throbbed. Breathless. Exhausted. Looking down, he saw only his own feet, clad in boots, running as fast as he could. One desire, one obsession hammered at the surface of his sleeping consciousness—escape! He must get away! Flee! But from what? Who or what was pursuing him? Why should he fly from this unknown terror? There were no answers. Intensifying his efforts, he ran all the harder.

Alone! He was alone. Alone against everyone and everything awful and deadly. He found himself in a black vacuum, totally cut off from all society, all creation, devoid of any color except the ever present blackness. No friends! No enemies! Nobody!

Wait! There *were* enemies. Of course there were. He could feel their hatred, their loathing, suddenly concentrated, suddenly focused at him until it became a tangible weight about to smother him, to force him to the ground.

As quickly as the clamor of voices had changed to the awful quiet, he found his surroundings alter, taking on the shape of the dark, foreboding woods where the light of day never penetrated. He hated this area, this forest, but had no choice except to hurry through the dense underbrush, to run soundlessly, his feet barely striking the soft earth. His lungs begged for oxygen as he dashed blindly through the undergrowth. The prickly sensation of his neck hair moving of its own accord, told him something was about to happen and he knew it could not be avoided. The sequence never changed.

It loomed in front of him, the large root of a tree, blocking his path. Gathering himself as he ran, he prepared to hurdle it. When he jumped, the root of the tree, leaping from the ground, tripped him. He fell heavily, rolling out of the way just as the tree's branches swept down to strike him. Scrambling to his feet, he resumed his flight. His legs, barely moving, seemed to be made of lead. As he bolted forward, more branches waved, reaching out to grab him, to hold him. Trees shouldn't do this! *Trees couldn't do this!* Leafy arms dashed past his face, trying to scratch him. Vines and creeping ground vegetation writhed, attempting to snare him, to stop him, but somehow, miraculously, he kept to his staggering run.

A thick mantle of fog slowly swirled about, drifting in to enfold the trees. He raced ahead hide within its opaque embrace. Once more, he ran blindly through a vacuum, only a gray one this time. He slowed his pace to avoid falling again. If he stopped, for any reason, the awful trees would catch him and then he would be lost. When he settled on a frenzied walk, the fog began thinning.

Instead of dissipating completely, the haze moved apart, creating a misty corridor. Rushing along, he stopped short when the vaporous wall scudded to either side, exposing the shadowy figure of a woman off in the distance. Trina? Could it be Trina? He tried to fix his eyes on the silhouette before him, only to have her slither out of focus. It had to be Trina! But Trina didn't wear a leather coat or shoes like that—not low heeled oxfords. And the woman's hair seemed all wrong as well. Trina had auburn hair, long and flowing—not shoulder length and blond. But it *had* to be her. Only she could help him! Maybe this time it might be Trina. He tried calling out. Instead of a cry, he gurgled, choking when his throat tightened. Moving hesitantly toward the form, he could see her face taking on shape and structure: a nose—eyes—a mouth. Gradually, the woman, familiar in a strange way, came into sharp definition. He sobbed. It was someone else! Not Trina!

While he stood gaping at the strange figure, the cloudlike walls receded into the distance, disappearing, and he found the strange trees on both sides of and behind him. With only the pathway in front unobstructed, he had to move forward in the direction of the woman. Did the trees want him to go this way? Could this strange woman be his sole way out? Could a woman whom he had never met be his only means of escape? There had to be another way. Still, he knew he could not turn back. *No turning back! No other way!* As always, he would go to her when she called.

A low moaning from behind him snapped him about. He found the trees slowly transforming into people. Men, women, children. Sad faced people. All dressed alike. He tried desperately to fix his eyes on their wearing apparel but could not tear his gaze from their tortured features as they surrounded him. Many wept, moaning, grieving, as they shuffled toward him, extending their bony hands, opening, closing, grasping at the air that separated them from him.

He tried to scream but nothing happened. Falling back two steps, he shook his head, wildly trying to dissuade the living skeletons from their murderous intent. Something struck his cheek and he turned to catch the full impact of two young women spitting at him. The spiteful venom running down his cheek seemed to burn his flesh. Countless lips moved, mouthing curses. Unable to hear the words being spoken, he nevertheless understood the expressions of hate and revulsion on their cadaverous faces. Cowering until he squatted on his heels, he trembled as though experiencing a severe chill. Would this never end? Could this be the last time he would have to suffer?

Then, like the clear peal of a singular trumpet note, a new sound penetrated the grieving wall around him. Looking in the direction from which the call came, he saw the yellow-haired woman beckoning him with slow movements of her arms, to hurry to her side. Why would she want him there? If it were Trina, he could understand. Trina would be able to help him. But who could she be if not Trina? He knew! He knew it could *never* be Trina! If it were his wife, instead of this stranger, he felt this endless misery would be over for all time.

The shadowy figure of the woman motioned for him to hurry. He stood on shaky legs, taking a furtive step toward her. The throng fell back, waving bony fists at him. They continued spitting, mouthing their silent condemnations, but did nothing to impede his progress.

He understood they would not stop him now, and he ran the hundred feet separating him from his saviour. As he neared her she called out to him again. *But what had she called him? Had it been his name? It didn't sound right.* He tried to repeat the one word she had uttered for the second time. *What was it?*

Something pulled at his right arm, something weighing heavily against his shoulder. Bringing his hand up, he discovered a strange looking pistol in his grasp. Studying it dumbly for several long seconds, he slowly leveled it at the woman as though this were the proper and correct thing to do. She lowered her head, waiting for the blast of the gun.

He squeezed the trigger but nothing happened. No sound issued. He pulled it again. Muffled footsteps from behind brought him around to face the mass of people, resolutely closing their ranks about him. He turned to face the woman, taking aim once more.

No bullet or blast or smoke erupted from the muzzle. Nevertheless, the woman clutched at her abdomen with one hand, raking her breasts with the other. Slothlike, she brought both hands to her throat, clawing at it, her tongue lolling to one side of her open mouth. Eyes bulging, she threw her head back in a silent scream. She staggered forward in slow motion to crumple at his feet, her face contorting in death.

He turned to the people again. Would they be satisfied this time?

Ghastly smiles animated their vengeful faces. The throng made motions with their forefingers jutting out like pistol barrels, thumbs cocked like hammers waiting to fall on a live shell. Some were put against temples, others placed in open mouths.

He fell back, vigorously shaking his head, but submissively raised the pistol to his temple. An acutely violent paint seared both sides of his head as though his skull had split. He grabbed his face with both hands, the gun slipping from his fingers. His eyes burned intensely, his jaw and teeth buzzing with pain as though countless dentist drills bored through live nerves. His ears hummed insanely in a hissing wheeze. He could feel his legs buckling. The trees, which had become people, burst into flames, wavering in his sight as he collapsed.

Then Jon Ward screamed—long and loud—and awoke.

*"The dream
is its own interpretation . . ."*

The Talmud

PART ONE

THE DREAM CONTINUES

CHICAGO, ILLINOIS
April 27, 1979
to
May 1, 1979

CHAPTER ONE

Jon Ward strode energetically through the Fuller Building lobby toward the bank of elevators. For some reason he could not quite understand, he felt almost happy to be on his way to meet Dr. Samuel Dayton. Ever since he had been discharged from Presbyterian Medical Center, where they had convinced him to meet with the psychiatrist, he had experienced a sense of trepidation whenever he thought of the impending appointment. Now that the time was here, a sense of relief eased his anxiety.

After pressing the button, he stepped back to wait for the car and ran a hand through his black hair. He could not help questioning his sudden involvement with Chicago's medical community over the last seven days.

It had been at his wife's insistence that he visit a doctor the day after their second wedding anniversary. Trina's concern had totally overwhelmed his air of forced indifference following the recurrence of his nightmare after they had retired for the night. The next day, Saturday, she had maintained her conviction, insisting that he keep the promise he had made during the night.

Could the dream really be a threat to his well being? Ever since he had been a small boy, he remembered having it. So far, nothing adverse had happened to him. Still, to satisfy Trina, to please her because he loved her, he had agreed to see the doctor who, after a thorough physical examination, suggested that he have more tests taken in the hospital. If only he had gone to that appointment alone, without Trina, he could have told her everything was fine and that would have been the end of it. But, because she had been there, he had had no choice and consented to spending three days in the hospital. The doctors there, after nothing out of the ordinary had shown on the tests administered to him, suggested that he talk with Samuel Dayton, psychiatrist.

Fortunately, Trina could not find a substitute teacher and Jon had promised he would keep the appointment alone. Could knowing the meaning of the dream be that important? That vital to his existence? How would his life change if it suddenly left?

When the elevator doors opened, he boarded after the last passenger hurried away. Absently rubbing his elbow, he reprimanded himself. For someone who disliked doctors and had been apprehensive during the last twenty four hours, he tried to comprehend how he could feel so relaxed, so calm. Knowing he would be talking about the dream with an expert had brought him an air of uneasiness he had never before experienced. Lying wide awake the previous night, he had tossed and turned, finding it difficult to fall asleep. Normally, he drifted off within minutes after going to bed and seldom had difficulty sleeping. But last night, he had actually been afraid to close his eyes and had lain awake for hours thinking about his dream.

The elevator bumped to a stop and when the doors slid open, Jon stepped into an antiseptically clean hallway. Once he found the door bearing the words: SAMUEL DAYTON, M.D.— CONSULTATIONS, he pushed the heavy door in and approached the small blonde sitting behind the receptionist's desk.

"Yes?" she asked, an efficient crispness ringing in the single word.

"I'm Jon Ward," he said. "I have an appointment with Doctor Dayton at three." He was amazed at he ease with which he stated his reason for being there. During the last week, he'd been behaving like the worst type of hypochondriac. Reacting to his new role of perpetual patient, he smiled grimly.

"Yes, Mr. Ward," the woman said. "The doctor will see you in a few minutes. Would you please fill this out for our records while you wait?" She handed him a printed form, gesturing toward a small table across the room where he could write comfortably.

Crossing the outer office, he sat down, perusing the sheet of paper. Medical background?

He could give them something there, all right. All kinds of tests and doctors' names. A week ago, the form would have been virtually blank. He jotted in the necessary information but hesitated when he came to the bottom of the page. *Reason for seeking Doctor Dayton's assistance.* What should he put there? *My wife is upset because I have a dream and occasionally wake up screaming.* Or, *everyone who hears about it is fascinated but doesn't know the cause of it.* He felt as if he had been telling anybody and practically everybody about his dream during the last seven days. Why shouldn't this doctor hear about it as well? He wrote, *Recurring nightmare.*

After returning the form to the girl, he took a chair opposite the desk and noticed her covertly reading the form. Her heavily lashed eyes flitted across the page, arched brows giving her oval face an expression of indecisiveness. He wondered if she read everything about the patients. His eyes dropped from the woman to the desktop where he spotted a name plate— Miss Worthington. *Well, Miss Worthington,* he mentally scolded, *you're a sexy number but you're a nosy little bitch. Read on, 'cause you'll get an earful if you hear about my dream.*

After several minutes, a buzzer broke the silence and Miss Worthington pressed a button before picking up the phone. Looking quickly at Jon, she spoke softly into the mouthpiece. When she hung up, she stood, leaving the room through the doorway opposite the entrance, and carrying the form he had filled out. In seconds, she returned. "This way, Mr. Ward," she said, holding the door for him.

When he entered the plush office, the psychiatrist raised his head. "Thank you, Tory," Samuel Dayton said before she left quietly.

Jon felt trapped. He wanted to run. Why should this man be able to do something those other doctors, and Trina, and even he, could not do? Could this man, this doctor, solve the riddle of the nightmare, if indeed it held a solution?

Sam Dayton came around the wide mahogany desk, extending his right hand as he approached his visitor. Jon took it hesitantly, feeling himself loosen a little when he found a sincere quality to the manner in which the doctor grasped his.

Once they were seated in easy chairs facing each other, Jon took the opportunity to study the doctor in his own element. An inch shorter than Jon's own six feet, Sam was heavier in build, his broad shoulders and narrow waist indicating an athletic background and a well maintained condition. He appeared to be in his late thirties or early forties and dark brown, curly hair surrounded his round face. A long, straight nose separated piercing eyes while his wide, expressive mouth subtly displayed a slight overbite. Jon concluded he could, if necessary, trust this man who appeared self assured, almost cocky. Sam moved his hands very little when he spoke and at first, Jon found his steady gaze unnerving. While they talked, the doctor's attitude brought Jon to a point where he began giving more than monosyllabic answers to the psychiatrist's questions. When Sam smiled, his teeth flashed from a well tanned face, which Jon learned had been acquired during a four week vacation in Florida and the Bahamas the previous month.

"I understand, Mr. Ward," Sam said, "that doctors are not your favorite people."

"Who—?" he began.

"Presbyterian Medical Center sent over a complete file on you. It says your dislike has something to do with the death of your mother. Is that correct?"

"Well, the sonofa—, I mean, the doctor who attended her, refused to try any drugs on her when she was dying of cancer." Jon bit his tongue. He had promised Trina after he had become angry at the doctor's office last Saturday, not to let the memory of his mother's death and its circumstances bother him to the point of using foul language. Why take his wrath out on this man?

"When was that?"

"I was nineteen. About fourteen years ago."

"And as a result, you've more or less avoided doctors since then?"

He nodded. "It was my wife's idea to go to a doctor now."

"I also read in your file that you're an author?"

Jon smiled, his face reddening. "Not really. I've taken a year's leave of absence from teaching and am giving it the old college try."

"How do you feel about your wife supporting you? I see she's also a teacher."

Shaking his head, he said, "You know everything, don't you? Trina inherited a sizeable amount of money from her mother. She decided I should take the year off and write my novel."

Sam made a notation on his pad and looked up. "She decided?"

"It's not the way you think, Doctor. I didn't want to, but she pointed out that it should be looked on as an investment in our future."

"Have you ever had anything published?"

"Some articles. A few short stories. Not enough to say I could make it as a full time writer."

"I see," he said, adding to his notes. "I believe the course we'll follow will be one of associating different aspects of your dream to certain, if not all, areas of your present life as well as those of your past. Would you have any objection to the use of hypnotism if it became evident that the solution to your dream lay in its use?"

Jon's eyes widened. Hypnotism? Parlor tricks in a psychiatrist's office? "I—I don't know. Is that normal?"

"Not in all cases. However, considering the length of time you've been having the same dream, it might become necessary to unlock certain memories stored in your subconscious mind. Without help of some type, you may never be able to recall them. I believe hynotism could be the key in your case."

Jon quietly wondered about the element of doubt where any acceptable conclusion was considered. Would baring his soul, unlocking his memories to be examined in minutest detail by someone he hardly knew, really rid him of his nightmare? "Do you really believe that, Doctor?" he asked.

"I believe it completely, Jon," he said sincerely. "I've seen some very quick results occur through the use of hypnotism, cutting through all the incidentals of the problem right to its core. I also believe as an aspiring author—a creative person—you will be amazed at the hidden thoughts you'll pour out when you're 'under.' "

"Can I be hypnotized?" Jon asked, his curiosity slowly awakening despite his nagging doubts.

"We'll find out when we try, and that could be at our next session, if you're willing. I believe, for now, you can rest assured with the knowledge that I am medically and psychiatrically conservative and will not at any time put you in danger." He smiled reassuringly. "I'd like to add that I'll need your full cooperation, not only to place you in a deep hypnotic state, but during any of our meetings when you're just talking."

"I—I understand." A rueful expression crossed Jon's face. It was not unlike agreeing to love, honor and obey when one married or promising one's mother to be home at midnight. He caught himself when the thought of his own mother flashed across his mind. This was not the time. He had to go along with this man. If he did, the doctor might really be able to help him. If he got rid of the stupid dream, Trina and he would be better off. No doubt of that existed in his mind.

"Jon?" Sam asked when his last question had not been answered by his patient.

"Ah—what?" Jon stammered, recognizing the almost urgent sound to the psychiatrist's voice.

"I said I would like to get the dream, as you have experienced it, down on tape today. Then I can play it back several times to acquaint myself with it before we meet again."

With the moment of truth at hand, Jon squirmed uncomfortably in his chair. Uncertain, he waited. Would the next move be up to him or did the doctor have something else to say?

"I understand your reluctance at being here. You'll be defensive for a while until we get into the subject more and you can start treating it objectively."

"Just how much do you know, Doctor?"

"I know quite a bit about you and your wife, Trina. The dream however, was explained rather sketchily in the file."

"I don't particularly like people talking about me and my problems behind my back," Jon said, a touch of bitterness in his voice.

"Let's get one thing straight, Jon," he said evenly. "You're here to be helped. Hopefully, we'll be able to build the type of relationship and rapport necessary for an ultimate solution to your problem."

Jon nodded, waving one hand through the air as though to say, *I know when I'm whipped.*

Let's get on with it.

"Do you want to tell me about the dream?"

He smiled. "The sooner I tell you, the quicker we'll be finished."

Sam fixed his almond-shaped eyes on him before speaking again. "Let me clarify one thing. This isn't exactly like having a pain in your head that can be cured with an aspirin. I wish it were that simple. Helping you will depend on many things; your willingness to talk about yourself and your relationship with other people in your life; being perfectly honest about the dream and everything we'll talk about; how quickly you can accept certain things about yourself. Consequently, *you* will determine more than anyone or anything, how long we'll be working together."

"I'll be a good guy and cooperate," he said, flashing his best smile.

"As I mentioned before, I use a tape recorder during my consultations." Standing, Sam crossed the room to a console built into the wall separating the two offices. "You won't mind, will you?" he asked, fully opening the louvered doors which had been slightly ajar.

"I assume the tapes will remain confidential —that is, between you and me?" Although questioning the privacy of such a method, he admired the efficiency of the procedure.

"You, me, and my secretary," Sam answered.

"Miss—ah, Worthington?"

"Yes. Tory has been with me almost two years. She's very reliable, I assure you."

Did Jon have any choice other than accepting

his judgment? "I don't have any real objections to the recorder." He sighed resignedly.

Flipping a couple of switches, the doctor pressed a button to activate the tape recorder before returning to his chair. "I have a remote control for the recorder here on the desk, which I'll use from time to time, in case you wonder what I'm doing when I reach over and press a button. Incidentally, microphones are concealed in different areas of the office. Some of my patients are unable to talk freely if the mikes are in the open. Now, tell me, in as explicit detail as possible, about your dream."

In a detached, almost impersonal manner, he recounted his nightmare as he had experienced it for the last twenty-eight years, to the point where he would awaken.

When he finished speaking, the psychiatrist waited for a moment. "Is that it?"

"In all its glory," Jon said lightly. Perhaps if he kept his own attitude indifferent toward the dream, the doctor might decide there was no problem.

Sam peered at him, his brown eyes unblinking. For several minutes he remained silent and then said, "That's some dream. Is it always the same?"

Jon nodded. "Always."

"Never any deviation from what you've just told me?"

"Only in the degree of pain."

"Explain that."

"Sometimes my head feels as though it really has burst. Other times, it's relatively mild and I won't even wake up."

"How do you know you've experienced it when the dream doesn't awaken you?"

"I usually recall it later during the day."

"What would you say is the percentage of times you awake with the headache?"

Jon hesitated. "Maybe sixty percent of the time—I'm not certain."

Sam slowly nodded, dropping his attention to the pad where he had jotted notes to generate questions. "The span of time you've experienced the dream is quite unusual. What's the earliest age you can recall having it?"

Jon pursed his lips for a moment before answering. "About five, I guess."

Sam shook his head, failing to conceal his amazement. "You're thirty-three now, which means you've been having the same dream for twenty-eight years."

Jon nodded.

"I'm going to ask you a few questions concerning it to see if we can come to any conclusions about some of the symbolism."

Jon brightened and said, "Do you feel now it isn't as difficult as you made it sound at first?"

Sam's head jerked up. "No. Nothing of the sort. Knowing what I do about you, I want to see if there's a deep seated reason for the long standing repetition. But then, like all dreams, it's a jumble of symbols that probably mean something to you. In future sessions we'll work backward in your life. Now," he hesitated before consulting his pad, "the crowd noises, this could be related to a desire for acclaim as an author. Would you enjoy a public image as a recognized author?"

"I don't know. I might," he said. "Actually, most authors receive very little public recognition."

"How do you mean?"

"Their names are known, not their faces."

"Do you think you might have a desire to have yourself known and recognized as a celebrity?"

Jon shrugged. "I feel if I can finish the novel I'm working on by the end of the year, I will have accomplished my goal. I'll also have proven Trina's belief in me. Beyond that, if I can sell it and begin a career as a novelist, I'd be happy. But I don't think I'm doing it to gain a celebrity status."

"All right, Jon," he said, "we'll leave that particular aspect for now and move on to the running. Is anything annoying you, something you're trying to avoid?"

"No," he answered, after reflecting on the question for several minutes.

"What about your dislike for the medical profession? Do you feel perhaps you've tried to avoid being ill so you wouldn't have to consult a physician?"

"I've just been to a battery of doctors, *Doctor*," Jon icily reminded him. "I'm positive that has nothing to do with it."

"Are you happily married?"

Trina's image popped into Jon's mind. How could he be anything but happily married to someone like her? She constantly amazed him with her insight where he was concerned, overlooking his stubbornness in certain matters and being able to make him see the logic of her own arguments. After all, it had been Trina's idea to have him seek the cause of his nightmare. He would have plodded through life accepting the dream and the resulting headaches without question. Not that he had not wondered and thought about it over the years. He had come to almost accept it, but Trina's inquisitive mind and tenacious approach to the problem it represented had finally convinced him to seek help.

He smiled whenever he envisioned her. Trina, beautiful and charming like her mother, had fallen in love with him, and when he discovered her virginity the first night they went to bed, he wondered about his own good fortune in finding such a prize as she. Flawless in his eyes, she would complain about gaining weight while standing naked in front of the full length mirror in their bedroom, pointing out the indiscernible bulge of her tummy. Her breasts were a source of disgruntlement as well, she would complain, because they were not the right size for her tall frame. But Jon felt they were magnificent and knew she would tease him like that, trying to get him to compliment her. It worked every time.

"Of course," he said simply.

"Do you have any children?"

"No."

"Do you want children?"

"Someday we'd like to have at least one child."

The psychiatrist continued making marks on

the pad and Jon wondered if he were taking notes. If he were, why the recorder?

When he finished, Sam found his patient closely watching him. "I find the fog—both black and gray—interesting. That could be a desire for isolation so you could write undisturbed. What do you think?" He fixed an unblinking gaze on Jon, waiting for his answer.

"I don't think so, Doctor," he said. "Everything you've mentioned so far is way out in left field. The dream has always been the same, ever since I began having it. I wasn't writing then, had no idea I wanted to be a writer, or that I could be one. Nor was I trying to avoid anything."

Nodding slowly, Sam said nothing. A puzzled expression crossed his face as he looked away. "The trees turning into people could represent your desire to have an adoring public grow out of your loneliness as a writer."

"Hardly as a child," Jon said, an edge of irritation clinging to each word. "Besides, I've only been trying to be a full time writer for a few months."

"Remember, I said *could*. Sometimes a wish or desire can be so dominant in our lives, it becomes an obsession without our being aware of it. As we work together, we could discover you had an overpowering desire at the age of five to be known as a writer."

Jon chuckled to himself. Nothing could be solved if they took this approach. Hadn't he asked himself questions like this hundreds of times? The answers never made sense. If for no other reason, he would play the game for a little while—just for the experience. And, to satisfy Trina.

"What are you thinking right now?"

Jon suddenly realized the doctor had been studying him while he silently chortled. "Nothing, really. Just puzzling over the same thing you are," he lied.

"The woman, as you describe her, is most interesting. Has she always been the same?"

"Yes."

"Your description sounds as though her style of clothing might not be contemporary. What period would you say she's from?"

Jon thought for a moment. "Late thirties or early forties."

"What makes you say that?"

"Different movies I've seen."

"From the thirties or forties?"

"Yes. And movies depicting stories about those years."

"You were born in—" Dayton began but stopped to reach for a file on his desk. Thumbing through it, he pulled out a sheet and continued, "1946."

"February third," Jon said. "I've thought about that, too. I wasn't around when clothing like that was worn."

"How do you feel about your wife?"

"How should I feel?" Jon asked, smiling slyly.

"Do you love her? Are you jealous? Do you feel secure?"

"I was just about to the point of deciding I was going to be a bachelor when I met her.

Trina is probably the best thing that's ever happened to me. I love her and I'm not the least bit jealous.''

Jon still held the fact that Trina and he were married as somewhat of a marvel—his own personal Ninth Wonder of the world. They had met at a meeting of the Teacher's League and at first, he had thought a few dinner dates and movies or whatever, would be in keeping with his chosen state of bachelorhood. He had taught in Chicago for seven years, earning his Masters degree during summer classes at Loyola. By the age of twenty-nine, he had decided single life was for him—at least until he made up for all the playtime he had lost while working toward his advanced degree.

When Jon met her mother, he understood from whom Trina had inherited her beauty. Charlene Benson, barely fifteen years older than Jon, could have passed for Trina's older sister. Standing side by side, the statuesque women had taken his breath away.

Trina's father, Meredith, had died during her first year of teaching. Jon tried to understand their ready acceptance of what he interpreted as a tragedy, hoping to better reconstruct his own attitudes about death. Charlene adjusted well to her husband's untimely death and spent most of her time in Florida, until she died.

"Do you feel you own your wife—possess her?" The strange question broke into Jon's chain of thought. "Does she own you?"

"We love each other. We like each other," he answered, "but we don't own one another. We came to that conclusion long before we married."

"Does that knowledge make you feel secure?" Sam pressed.

"Of course. We're both mature enough to know we can go our separate ways if our feelings change."

"Do you ever feel threatened by her?"

Jon stared at him. "No way! Never!" he said simply. How could he possibly feel intimidated by Trina?

"How about your mother."

"How about her?"

"Is she a threat?"

"Hardly. She's been dead a long time."

"I know," Sam said quietly. "Her dying triggered your dislike for the medical profession. But could her memory be a threat to your well being now?"

"I loved my mother very deeply. I guess I went bananas when she died. But no, my relationship with her was a good one."

"Tell me a little about her."

"She met my dad in Germany right after World War II was over. The day after, to be exact. They got married before Dad was sent home and she came to this country about eighteen-months later. I was born in Germany. When I was old enough to understand, she told me about her home and how she grew up."

"Did she ever push you in school or say she wanted you to be a writer?"

"She wanted me to be a priest," Jon said. A tear, begging to form, was blinked away. How long would they concentrate on his mother? Jon had been extremely close to Helga Ward. Closer than to his father, Milton. For some peculiar reason, he had always felt that his father disliked him. At best, the older Ward's attitude remained aloof, almost indifferent toward his son. Jon seemed to favor his mother in personality, demeanor and mannerisms. There, however, the resemblance ended. Helga's flaxen hair and fair complexion contrasted sharply with her son's dark, handsome features. He often wondered, once he had reached adulthood, about his relatives in Germany. He had never met any of them but she had told him more than once that he had inherited his dark good looks from her forebears. Then, she would grow morose and say something about his own father's reddish-brown hair possibly showing up in Jon's children one day.

"Did she mention your becoming a priest often?" Sam asked.

"Not really. You'd have had to know her to understand how beautiful a person she actually was."

"How about your father?"

"Dad was like most fathers—stern, strict. He wanted my mother to do everything in the house, which included raising me."

"You said 'was.' Is he deceased?"

"Yes."

"When did he die?"

"1960. He was killed in an auto accident."

"Did you feel sorry when he died?"

"Of course."

"Did you love him?"

Jon's voice wavered before answering. "I guess I did. I know I was afraid of him."

"Did you respect him?"

"I had to."

"Did he ever hurt your mother?"

"Not to my knowledge. I think they really loved each other."

Before the doctor could pose another question, his wrist watch buzzed and Jon knew his first appointment had come to an end. He breathed deeply only to shiver, suddenly conscious of the fact his shirt, damp with perspiration, stuck to his body.

"That'll do it for today, Jon," Sam said, pressing the tape recorder's remote control button on his desk. "We'll continue the next time and begin moving a little further into your past."

"Do you think we'll find anything?" he asked, standing.

"I'm certain you'll know yourself better, and perhaps at the same time find the reason for your dreams. Make an appointment with Tory on your way out," he said, approaching his patient.

They shook hands before Jon turned to leave. Limping across the room, he rubbed his elbow before opening the door to the outer office.

CHAPTER TWO

Trina Ward hurried up the steps of the front porch stretching across the front and side of the turn-of-the-century mansion. After their marriage, she and Jon had moved into the front apartment on the first floor of this once elegant monument to some forgotten financier's millions. The calm, passive appearance of the brownstone in some ways mirrored their own existence, one she liked more as each day passed. But today, she experienced a certain anxiety that seemed foreign to her. Had Jon kept his appointment with the psychiatrist? What would have happened by now? She looked at her watch again for what seemed the thousandth time. Just three-thirty. If only she could have found a substitute teacher to take over her class, she could have gone with Jon.

Entering the front hallway, she first checked their mail box, withdrawing several envelopes which she stuck between her purse and briefcase. She fingered her chain of keys, selecting the right one with her free hand, before unlocking the door to their apartment. Why did she imagine Jon would be sitting there, waiting for her? He had promised he would keep the three o'clock appointment.

"Jon?" she called timidly when she stepped into the front room and breathed easier, relieved there was no answer.

During the day, she had planned their evening. It would have to be a pleasant one to make him comfortable. She knew full well that he had been unhappy with his hospital stay and the tests. Then, when she had sided with the doctors about his seeing a psychiatrist, she had felt his sense of aloneness. She would make up for everything this weekend.

She quickly changed clothes and hurried to the kitchen, glancing at the antique school clock hanging above the refrigerator. Perhaps she had been too blatant and pushy about his visiting a doctor to have the physical examination. She had accepted the dream, or nightmare, or whatever it was, just as Jon had, but for some reason she could not explain, it suddenly had grown ominous, seeming to pose a threat to their happiness. The last thing in the world she wanted was any type of conflict with her husband, especially over something as silly as a dream. But that nightmare was anything but silly.

Opening the freezer compartment, she took out two small rib eye steaks. Baked potatoes and a salad would complete their dinner. A smile changed her face to radiant beauty from the pensive expression she had worn most of the day. She crossed to a small pantry and selecting a bottle of Beaujolais, broke the seal. Inhaling its bouquet, she placed the wine on the counter to breathe. It would complement their meal and, since it was his favorite, put Jon in a good mood.

Why did it irritate her that she felt it necessary to bother with his mood? She wished she could analyze her feeling of dread where he and his nightmare were concerned. Usually, she could be most logical about any problem or situation confronting her, but her emotions ruled her mind when her husband was involved. She recalled her apocalyptic feelings when she awoke the night of their second wedding anniversary. A film of sweat formed on her forehead when she replayed Jon's screams in her mind.

Trina had bolted to a sitting position, wide awake at the first sound. Turning on the lamp next to the bed, she had blinked her sleep-filled eyes, automatically placing her arms around his naked shoulders to comfort him in soft, reassuring tones. That goddamn dream! Why did it have to happen? Almost six months had passed since he had last experienced it and for a while she thought it might be gone for good.

Jon had trembled, his lids undulating as his eyes rolled back and forth in the safety of their own private darkness. Perspiration glistened on his well muscled body, his side of the bed damp from the excessive sweating brought on by the nightmare.

"Are you awake darling?" she asked quietly.

His face drawn into a mass of worry lines, he opened his eyes, staring at her. Grabbing her arm, he squeezed until she squealed in pain. Startled by her cry, he released his grip and nodding in answer to her question, coughed to clear his throat.

Trina jumped from the bed, racing to the bathroom for a glass of water. From past experience, she knew he would be unable to utter a word until his parched mouth and throat had been wetted.

"I'm making an appointment for you with a doctor first thing in the morning," she said, returning with the water and a large towel draped over one arm.

Jon frowned, taking the glass to gulp the water. He coughed once more. "Come on, Trina," he said thickly. "I'm fine. So I have a nightmare once in a while. So what? Probably something I ate or drank at the restaurant." He peered at her through pain-filled eyes.

"I let you talk me out of it the last time you had the dream," she said sternly. "I'm not giving in this time. How do you feel?"

Rubbing his temples, he said, "It hurts like hell." He swung his legs over the edge of the bed. "I'll take a few aspirins and be fine in the morning." Standing, he toweled his body dry.

"Aspirins won't do the job, darling."

"I said I'll be fine in the morning."

"That may be, but I still think we'd better let a doctor take a look at you."

"Come on, Trina. I'm not going to tell some stranger about my dream. Christ, he'd think I'm wacko or something. Maybe he'd call the boys in white jackets."

"I think it's an excellent idea," she persisted, ignoring his lame protestations. "It's about time you have a physical anyway."

"I'm not going," he said, stubbornly.

"Look Jon, once someone's past thirty, it doesn't do any harm to know everything is working all right. You're thirty-three and I don't even know the last time you had an examination."

"When I bought life insurance, just before we got married."

"That's not what I mean. That exam wasn't extensive and you know it."

"Well, I still saw a doctor."

"Did you tell him about your dream?"

"Why the hell should I have told him? You know how I feel about doctors," he said vehemently. "Ever since that quack messed up with Mom and—"

He had launched into his tirade against the medical profession and Trina had carefully worked the conversation away from the subject.

Tearing lettuce and spinach for their salad, Trina shook her head in dismay. Jon could be so obstinate at times. A shudder ran through her when she thought of how she had learned of the dream. Shortly before their marriage, they had spent a weekend at Lake Geneva and Jon started screaming at the top of his voice after they had been asleep for several hours. She had been petrified. After he recovered, he explained, fascinating her with the narrative manner in which he related the details. Despite her initial fright, she believed him when he said that it never bothered him and shouldn't be a source of worry.

"Lots of people have dumb dreams that occur on a regular basis," he had said, chuckling.

Because she loved him so much and felt his love in return, she had dismissed the incident. But each time it happened, she became more concerned, until now it had given her an instinctive feeling of impending dire consequences if the nightmare were allowed to continue unchecked.

At least he had consented to the first appointment and now, one week later, they knew it was not caused by something physical or organic. At least the tests gave her hope that the dream could not harm her husband bodily. Perhaps it was nothing to be concerned about and the psychiatrist would give him a clean bill of mental health to go along with the other results.

The mantel clock in the living room struck the half hour past four and she finished tossing the salad. If the baked potatoes were to be done on time, she'd have to put them in the oven now.

A sudden chill swept over her. *Please, God, don't let anything happen to him*, she awkwardly prayed to herself.

At five-fifteen, the front door swung open and Jon strode in.

Looking up from the table where she had just lighted two candles, Trina said, "Hi, darling."

Closing the door, he answered simply, "Hi."

"How was it?" she asked, crossing the room to greet him more intimately. She kissed him deeply, wrapping her arms about him. Her tongue demandingly darted in and out of his mouth, eloquently hinting of the evening and weekend she had planned.

He returned the kiss with equal ardor, smiling when they parted. "If that's the kind of welcome I get when I come home from the shrink, I think I'll ask if he wants to see me every day."

"So, how was it?" she repeated, leaving the room for the small kitchen.

"I suppose it could have been a lot worse than it actually was," he began, and told her about the meeting while she finished preparing their meal.

When he finished, she slid the two steaks from the broiler. "When do you see him again?"

"A week from Monday, the seventh of May."

She left the room with the plates, her husband following closely. "That's it? No other comment or questions?"

"What's there to say?" She returned to the kitchen for the wine and poured the crimson liquid into tulip shaped glasses already on the table. Looking up, she found him scowling. "What's the matter, darling?"

"Get rid of that wine! You should know

better!" His guttural voice sliced the air separating them.

She stared at him. "What should I know better?" she asked quietly.

"I don't drink wine!" He growled the words in a voice Trina barely recognized.

"You don't drink—! Since when?" she demanded, a puzzled frown creasing her forehead.

"I never have. Oh, maybe an occasional glass, years ago when I was a youth. I know better now. It's not good for a person—especially me. I must be careful of what I take in the form of food and drink. I may even stop eating meat altogether." His face contorted, a satisfied grimace twisting his features. "It could," he continued, "affect my decisions . . . my ability as a leader . . . I mean, my powers of concentration . . . my creative abilities."

"Jon Ward!" Trina said sharply. "This is your own choice! Your favorite Beaujolais. You've always liked it."

His eyes glowing like coals, he said nothing, as if waiting for her to wilt under the pressure of his stare.

She returned his baleful look with one of bewilderment and curiosity. What could be wrong? Hadn't he always preferred this wine? Lowering her eyes to the table, she reached for the glasses. It would be senseless to argue over something so foolish. What he had said was totally out of character for him, but not worth an argument.

"Hey," he said quickly as Trina turned to take

the glasses to the kitchen, "where are you going with the wine?"

Trina almost dropped the goblets but recovered and bit her lower lip. What the hell was going on? What kind of game was this? She turned to find her husband smiling broadly.

He held her chair before taking his own place across the small table. With too much competition from the light of dusk filtering through the drawn blinds, the candles' flames danced feebly on their wicks, biding time until they would be the only illumination.

"Did I tell you," he said, "that he wants to hypnotize me?"

She shook her head, still perplexed over the momentary change in her husband's personality. Should she tell Doctor Dayton about this? Or was she merely being foolish? Had she placed herself under a degree of intensity today by worrying about Jon and the appointment? An intensity that suddenly twisted things out of perspective? Maybe she should be the one seeing the psychiatrist.

"I think it might be quite an experience," Jon continued between bites of meat. Glancing at his wife, he found her studying him, her face frozen in a baffled expression. "Are you all right, honey?" He reached for his glass, downing a third of the wine. "Mmmm! Delightful taste!"

Trina stared. "I have—have, some rather interesting plans for this evening," she offered tenuously. "Some that I hope will prove to be as intriguing as being hypnotized." She wondered if he caught the hesitancy in her voice.

Smiling, he leered at her.

The rest of the meal was consumed in silence. Their sense of anticipation rose, heightened by the wine and the occasional leg contact beneath the table.

When they finished, he stood and said, "I'll clear the table. You were the chef, I'll be the scullery maid—er, man— er, person. Right, scullery person. You got to the bedroom and prepare yourself, my fine wench." Precariously balancing the dishes in a shaky stack, he limped to the kitchen.

"You're—" Trina stopped. Had he hurt his leg? Should she call his attention to it? But why set him off again? She didn't want him thinking she was looking for things out of the ordinary. If she did that, he might completely shut her out. She resolved not to mention anything he did that might be interpreted by her as being abnormal. More than likely, his leg had fallen asleep during dinner.

"I'm what?" he asked, hobbling back to the living room. He rubbed his elbow as though it bothered him.

"You're not going to be too long, are you?" Trina asked, feigning seductiveness. She did her best to pretend she hadn't noticed his lameness and unconscious attention to his arm. The question and her attitude apparently escaped detection. She sighed inaudibly.

He scooped her into his arms. "I'm ready when you are," he chuckled.

Carrying her, he limped toward the bedroom.

* * *

Tory Worthington paused before the old door which opened to her private world, to the stairs leading to the fourth floor apartment she shared with Howie Liemen. Fumbling in her purse, she pushed aside a ball of tissue and assorted cosmetics before finding her key ring. Their mailbox surrendered a catalog of exclusive women's apparel, desirable things she could no longer afford, plus several windowed envelopes. She winced at the return addresses. She knew what they contained. Late notices for overdue payments she should have made months before. The weathered door, thirsty for a touch of paint, opened grudgingly, the squeal of dry hinges lost in the noise of traffic. She started up the four flights of steps.

Since she had met Howie six months ago, she had been having trouble making her money go as far as it had in the past. She didn't blame Howie. How could she, when she loved him so much? As soon as he found work, everything would be fine. It was difficult for someone who had served five years in prison to find a job.

She paused at the second floor landing to catch her breath. The steep steps exhausted anyone who tried going to the top floor without resting. The smells of kerosene, garbage and stale cigarette smoke mixed with beer interlaced with an almost tangible atmosphere of defeat. Tory missed the apartment she had lived in before meeting Howie. It had been a newer building and people close to her own age made up the majority of tenants. She had never minded the forty minute ride into the city, but Howie thought they would be able to make her money stretch farther if they lived closer to the Loop. Then, she could walk to work. He insisted they live in a more economical apartment as an additional attempt at thrift. The money they saved had gone for marijuana and "candy" for Howie. She had dabbled in drugs before but never to the extent that her lover did. In the recent past, she found herself using more than she had ever planned. What did she want? Escape for her frustrations since she could not leave her meager surroundings?

A smile crossed her full lips. She wondered what Sam Dayton would think of her home. He'd probably hate it. That would suit her fine. When she had first gone to work for the psychiatrist, she had fallen in love with him. She couldn't wait to get to the office, thinking up excuses to stay after her normal quitting time, just to be near him, to see him, to talk with him. Somehow she knew instinctively that he felt as attracted to her as she was to him.

Most of her income went for new additions to her wardrobe, things she could wear to work, hoping he would be impressed. Hundreds of ideas were designed to lure the doctor to her apartment; all cultivated, then cast aside. It seemed as though every time a plan appeared workable and destined for success, some unknown factor or obstacle would interfere. At first, she found the thwarted schemes and her reactions to their failure humorous. Undaunted, she always renewed her efforts.

Then a bitter irony slowly replaced her flippant mood. By the end of her first year-and-a-half of employment, Tory discovered her feelings for Sam Dayton were no longer loving. Her unfulfilled ardor quietly turned to disappointment, then to an aggravating annoyance. Peculiarly, in either extreme, she had never once demonstrated how she thought or felt about him.

He merely looked on her as an employee, someone to do his typing and care for the drudgery of running an office. Did he even know she existed as a living, breathing person? Feeling as functional as his tape recorder or the diplomas hanging on his office wall, she slavishly ensconced herself in the outer office. When her attitude had completed its full circle, she wallowed in a state of calm bewilderment.

Then she met Howie Lieman. She had been struck by the fact he had listened to her that first night in a singles bar. When she realized he was interested in her as a person, she opened up, and by midnight he knew practically every detail of her life. And it had been Howie who had helped her sort out her emotions concerning Samuel Dayton.

Tory stopped to rest at the third landing. Howie should be home by now if he had gone out to look for work. Her hopeful thoughts that he had found something, or would soon if he hadn't today, were interrupted by a baby shrieking at the top of its voice from an apartment whose door stood wide open. She detested this building but would have lived in the gutter if Howie asked her.

Step by step she mounted each riser until the last one fell behind her. Walking along the dark hall, she made her way to the last door on the right, at the rear of the building. The delicate fragrance of her own perfume and cosmetics filtering from the one room apartment into the squalid corridor, evaporated within a foot of the entrance. She slipped her key into the shiny, out of place Yale lock, quietly turning it.

Closing the door behind her without a sound, she looked around the dingy room. Howie, soundly sleeping in the nude, lay on the Murphy bed. Stirring when she kicked off her shoes, he rolled over. The noise of the springs when he moved made her glide about the room like a phantom. From past experience, she had learned two things about Howie. She knew it was not wise to wake him abruptly or disagree with him about anything upon which he had decided. Slipping out of her blouse, she used it to wipe the perspiration from her large breasts. It had been warm walking the thirty-two blocks from Doctor Dayton's office. Her discomfort brought a thought to her tired mind. How hot would this apartment be once Chicago's infamous summer began? Her skirt, hose and panties followed the blouse into a laundry bag. A gentle breeze reluctantly entered the one room apartment through the single, dirty window she had left open that morning.

"When did you get home?" he asked sleepily from the bed, stretching.

"Just a few minutes ago. Did you have any luck today?"

"Fuck, no! I didn't go anyplace. I smoked up around eleven and got all screwed up timewise. Christ, the day went fast," he mumbled, vigorously rubbing his thinning brown hair in an attempt to wake up.

"We've got to do something soon, honey," Tory said. She held the mail up for him to see. "Look! Dunning notices again. They're going to haul me off to jail soon if I don't pay up. Please try to find something tomorrow?" She threw the envelopes, unopened, on the sideboard which served as their dining, dressing and lamp tables combined.

"Okay, okay, okay! Just don't nag me, goddamnit! You don't have any idea what it's like to be turned away time after time. I wish to hell I was back home. At least I got some friends—lifelong friends—there. I think I'll try to score big and retire," he said, motioning for her to join him on the bed. "You'd like Santa Fe. Besides, it's close to the border and easier 'n shit to get Mexican grass."

Crossing the room she sat next to the beefy man. "Would I be able to find work there in a psychiatrist's office? I suppose Doctor Dayton would give me a good reference."

"Probably as good as he would for his telephone or filing cabinet," he snorted. Running both hands over his fleshy face, he rubbed his eyes before stretching again.

"I—I don't understand, honey," she said softly. "Don't you like Doctor Dayton?" When he turned, glaring at her, she slid off the bed, retreating to the far side of the room.

"You'd never catch me talking to one of those goddamn mental sawbones again," he snapped. "I had enough of 'em in 'Nam when they tried to get me to stop smokin' *shit*. They're all the same. And that one in stir was really off the wall."

Tory visibly recoiled. She knew how he had been grounded when it was discovered he not only was smoking marijuana, but dealing in it and pills as well. She had concluded that it had been unfair of the military to make such a big thing of it. But he had not minded spending the last eight months of his tour of duty in a stateside stockade since it was far removed from the day to day encounters with death. Being a helicopter pilot had had its advantages, but the big drawback was the stray bullet from some gook's rifle. She was glad he had gotten in trouble. Glad he had been sent to a stockade. Glad he had survived so they could be together now.

"Did I ever tell you," he asked, "about the woman shrink in stir?"

Tory shook her head even though she knew the story well. How many times had he told her? Still, experience had taught her to let him have his own way. It was easier than being beaten, or worse—rejected.

"She tried to get me to admit I was trying to self destruct. She even said I'd never straighten out unless I admitted it to myself. Christamighty! Just because I had a chance to fly five tons of *shit* into this country from Mexico, I want to destroy myself? Goddamn establishment screwed up my life with a war nobody wanted, ruined any chance of me becoming a football coach, and then pays some bitch to convince me I want to destroy myself. Fucking idiots! Money! Bread! That's the name of the game—the only game!" Grinning, he ran a hand through his hair again, smoothing the mussed strands into place.

"I know, honey," she said, moving closer to him. She didn't like it when he raved about his time in prison. He would get worked up, then start smoking pot or popping pills or drinking and be weird for several days. Her job—her only job, she was convinced—was to straighten him out so he would be able to find work. Then, they could get married and he could take care of her.

"Five goddamn years in stir. For what? For flying a goddamn, fucking airplane. No justice in the world." Standing quickly, he grabbed Tory by the arms.

She screamed as his fingers dug into her flesh.

The sound of her cry brought him out of his crazed state. "I—I'm sorry, Tory. Really, I am. It's just that I get so crazy pissed off when I think of the last ten years, that I gotta yell a little about it. Come here," he said tenderly, gentle in his embrace.

Encircling his neck with her arms, her naked breasts flattening against his lower chest, she buried her face in his shoulder.

She pushed him back toward the bed until he fell onto the mattress. Collapsing in a tangle of arms and legs, Tory kissed his face, mouth, eyes before running her tongue down his chin toward his throat. Howie lay on his back, allowing her to kiss and lick his nakedness, his aroused manhood. Kneeling, she threw one leg across him, receiving his rigid member into her body. When he reached his climax in seconds, she attempted to satisfy her own need but found it a useless effort. He quickly shriveled inside her. Satisfied, he pushed her off. She began masturbating desperately while he watched, a contemptuous smirk clouding his naturally swarthy face.

Finishing, she rolled next to him, exhausted. He could be a satisfying lover if he took his time but that happened only on rare occasions. More and more she found herself having to resort to other tactics.

"Get me a joint," he ordered.

She rose slowly, obediently going to the bureau. Opening the bottom drawer, she folded back her panties and hose to reveal a small pile of cigarettes. After selecting one from the pile, she rehid the others with her underwear. Lighting the *stick*, she returned to the bed, handing it to him. Slowly exhaling the sweet, heavy smoke, she delighted in the quick wave of giddy relaxation washing over her body.

Howie dragged, held the smoke in his lungs, gulping air to push the pleasantness deeper before slowly exhaling. A euphoric expression crossed his face.

"Want to hear about the tape I transcribed today, honey?" she asked, a lilt to her voice.

"No," he snapped, sucking again on the cigarette.

"This woman has a hangup because she's fucking her husband's younger business associate," she said, oblivious of his answer. "Christ, she's all bent out of shape because of it. She feels guilty as hell but wants to continue screwing the shit out of him."

"How many ropes we got left?" he asked, disregarding the indiscreet revelations. He rolled the cigarette back and forth in his fingers, studying it.

"Huh? Oh, two or three. Anyway, I'm not a psychiatrist or anything, but if she wants to stop feeling so goddamn guilty, why doesn't she just stop fucking the guy?" She propped herself up on one elbow, giggling uncontrollably when she realized she had uncovered the solution to the woman's problem. Reaching out, she took the cigarette from Howie, dragging hungrily.

"I gotta come up with some caper that'll make a lot of bread."

Chortling, she continued snickering and handed the joint back.

"What's so funny?"

"Nothing." She laughed again but he tried to ignore it.

Her infectious good humor finally reached him. His shoulders shook and his flabby belly started quaking as her mirth infected him. He suddenly guffawed.

"But that—that woman's a—real flake." Tory fell sideways on the bed, tears rolling down her cheeks.

"What woman?"

"The one—the one—I just told you about."

"I don't remember anything about—about a woman." Howie heehawed a laugh, snorting as he spoke.

Tory repeated the story, confusing different aspects until it made no sense. When she finished, he sobered and sat up on the edge of the bed. Hunching over, he held his head in both hands. She watched him for several minutes before moving to his side.

"What's the matter?" she asked, slipping an arm around his shoulder. Taking the spent cigarette, she butted it in a full ashtray on the floor next to the bed.

Howie straightened up to stare out the open window at the gray, smoke encrusted wall across the alley. It would be dark soon. "How much money you got?" he demanded.

"I don't know. Twenty, thirty bucks until payday Monday."

"Give it to me. I've got to do some thinking tonight."

"About what?"

"I've gotta come up with something."

"What?"

"Us getting some bread. Making a big score."

Tory looked at him completely puzzled. "What do you want for supper?"

"Fuck supper! Get me the money. I'll be back in an hour or two."

She reached for her purse on the table. Withdrawing two tens and a five, she shoved the remaining five dollar bill to the bottom of her bag before handing the money to her lover.

He roughly grabbed it, clenching the crumpled paper in his teeth while he pulled his pants on and slipped a tee shirt over his head.

Stepping into a pair of sneakers, he said, "If you want to make something for supper, go ahead. But have it ready when I get back. I gotta have lotsa thought time tonight. I'll get some *ganja* with this two bits and we'll talk about it."

She stared, not comprehending anything he said.

After Howie had left the darkening room, Tory shivered, uncomfortable in her solitude. She pulled the chain hanging from the bare bulb in the middle of the ceiling, blinking at the sudden brightness before realizing she was not dressed. Donning a cotton robe and humming a tuneless melody, she took a can of soup from the almost empty cupboard.

Trina and Jon sat propped up in bed, reading and listening to an early Beethoven String Trio as it softly complemented the bedroom's tranquil atmosphere. She found it impossible to concentrate on the novel leaning against her knee. Their love making had not been as satisfying as she had hoped it would be. She wondered if Jon's first meeting with Doctor Dayton earlier in the day could be at fault. Or had she overreacted to his momentary personality change while pouring the wine? She knew he didn't drink heavily at all. In fact, she considered him more of a marginal abstainer, at best. Still, she couldn't help feeling as though she had encountered a stranger when her husband began vehemently raving about the Beaujolais. *"I don't drink wine! I never have!"* She shuddered at the recollection.

"You cold?" Jon asked when she shivered.

"What? Oh, no. I'm all right," she said, realizing she had been too responsive to her own thoughts.

"In a way, I'm looking forward to my next appointment with Dayton." When she didn't respond, he looked at her. "And where are your thoughts?"

"I'm sorry, darling," she apologized. "I guess my mind is wandering all over the place."

He recounted his feelings, returning his attention to the book he held when it became obvious she didn't want to talk.

Trina lapsed into her reverie again, recalling the strange expression he had displayed when he had said something about wine affecting his decisions and his ability as a leader. Had he actually finished the word? He had corrected himself so quickly she wasn't certain. Maybe her imagination had played tricks on her. She would have to be more on guard against making wild interpretations of things that might easily be normal.

"Let's go on vacation," he said suddenly.

"What?"

"Let's go on vacation."

"All right. Where do you want to go this summer?"

"Not this summer. Right now. Tomorrow!"

"Tomor—? I can't. How could I? School isn't out for another five or six weeks."

"Quit."

"I can't. You know that. What brought this on?"

He shrugged.

"It can wait until next month," she said patronizingly.

"Don't do that!" Jon snapped. "Don't humor me. I want to go now."

"Why?"

"I don't know. I just feel I have to go someplace."

"Where?"

"It doesn't matter."

"You must have some idea."

"West. To California. Yeah. Come on, Trina. We've never gone west. Let's do what Horace Greeley advised."

"That leaves me out, then."

"Why?"

"I'm not a young man," she giggled.

"That's not funny." His voice harbored an unfamiliar air of authority along with a tone of injury.

Trina only caught the hurt in his voice. "I'm sorry, darling."

"I just feel an overwhelming desire to go to California."

"You're certain?"

"Positive."

"You aren't trying to avoid seeing Doctor Dayton, are you?"

"I just said a few minutes ago that I'm looking forward to seeing him again. But you know, somehow, it doesn't seem to be California, now that I've said it out loud."

"What do you mean?"

"You know, like when you're trying to think

61

of someone's name and you can't quite get it. Then you try saying it aloud and suddenly you spit it out. It's like that—only now that I've said California, I know that's not the place I want to go."

"Well, why not sleep on it?" she asked. "You've had a different type of day. You might be thinking about everything you and Doctor Dayton talked about more than you realize."

"I don't think so," Jon said irately. Dropping his book on the floor, he fluffed his pillow. "I'm going to sleep."

"When school's out, we'll go wherever you decide."

He grunted and turned his back to her. After several minutes of silence, he said, "I wish you'd quit teaching tomorrow, regardless of any trip."

"I can't—not this close to the end of the school year. I wouldn't mind, though. It would be kind of nice to lead a lazy life for a change," she said, leaning over to kiss his ear. She ran her tongue over the top, jabbing him with it once above the lobe. "G'night, sweetheart."

"G'night," he mumbled, slipping off to sleep.

Trina often wished she could go to sleep as quickly as Jon. Tonight, in addition to her normal rolling and turning until she fell asleep, she would rehash the unusual event that had taken place earlier. His wanting to have her quit teaching so suddenly, too, was out of the ordinary. Really extraordinary. She recalled how they had planned their budget for one year to allow him to take his leave of absence. At first, he refused, saying it wasn't right to use part of her inheritance to support them while he tried to write. But in the end, she had had her way.

Maybe he really needed a vacation trip to someplace. They had always gone to Florida during Christmas vacation and to the Wisconsin woods during any summer trips they had taken. She had never been to California and something different might be just the thing the doctor ordered. The doctor. She made a mental note to think about calling Doctor Dayton on Monday morning to tell him of the change in Jon's personality and his peculiar limp. After a while, she dropped off to sleep, an unnatural scowl on her oval face.

CHAPTER THREE

Trina clung to Jon, their lips pressed together in a lingering kiss. Holding her away from him at arm's length, he studied her. "What's the matter? Don't you want to go to work?"

"In a way, no," she said, fluffing her hair into place. "I thought about it all weekend. Maybe I should take some time off."

"When I agreed to your idea of taking a year off to write, the deal was I would have the peace and quiet of the daytime hours to myself, to write. Just how much to you think I'd accomplish with you underfoot all the time?"

"I wouldn't bother you."

"You would. That's why I suggested that I don't write during weekends, although I might have to, to make up for the time I lost last week in the hospital."

"Funny," she said. "You'd better think about having me around this summer when I'm finished with school."

"I'll figure something out," he said, looking at the clock on the fireplace mantel. "You'd better get going."

"Will you be all right?"

"Of course."

"I can call in sick. They can get a sub for me."

"Hey, come on. I'm not an invalid."

"I know, darling. See you at three-thirty." She kissed him on the mouth and was gone.

Jon straightened up the kitchen, putting their few breakfast dishes into the dishwasher before going to the living room. Slowly sitting down at his desk, he stared at the typewriter.

Trina gathered up her briefcase and purse, throwing her raincoat over one arm. The day had been cloudy when she arrived at school but by noon the sun was shining brightly, enhancing Spring's rebirth in all its glory.

She hurried out of the parking lot and unlocked the Mustang. In seconds, the late afternoon traffic absorbed the red car. Guiding it by automatic reflex, she replayed her conversation with Doctor Dayton. She had called the psychiatrist during her break at ten, after mentally wrestling with the idea most of the weekend. He had seemed interested in her observation of Jon's limp, remarking that he, too, had noticed a degree of lameness at the end of their appointment Friday afternoon. Jon's sudden change in personality caught his attention and he asked several questions. Then, the doctor thanked her and when she hung up, she felt relieved. His closing words remained fresh in her memory. "Don't look for things. There's nothing drastically wrong with your husband. In time, the idea of his visiting a psychiatrist will be quite commonplace for both of you."

Don't look for things. She resolved to treat Jon in a normal manner. Why should she act differently? The dream would soon be understood. When it ceased to occur, they would have nothing bothering them.

Still, she hated to admit, since she felt one of them should be strong at this point, that her own confidence might be wavering. She had been the one to suggest she stay at home before she left for work. What would she do if his visits to the psychiatrist brought about further changes in Jon? Alter him in such a way that he wouldn't love her anymore? Maybe she wouldn't love him. No! She would never allow that to happen.

That damned nightmare!

"A dream is a dream is a dream," Jon had said on their wedding night when the nightmare had struck.

She remembered trying to quiet him but apparently someone had heard his screams and called the motel manager. Only seconds, at least it had seemed like seconds, passed when the pounding on their door began along with loud demands to open up.

After slipping into a negligee, Trina had crossed to the door. Cracking it, she found the pasty-faced manager with his fist poised, ready to hammer on the hollow core door again.

"What in the name of God is going on in there?" he demanded shakily, his slack jaw trembling. "I had five calls within a minute or two reporting someone was being murdered."

Despite being upset to the point of feeling weak because of Jon's experience, she fought to keep from laughing at the mousy man. "I'm afraid my husband had a terrible nightmare."

"Nightmare? Come on, lady. Don't give me that. The people who called said they never heard such a blood-curdling scream before in their lives."

"I assure you, he—" she stopped when Jon came up behind her.

"I—I did have a bad dream, I'm afraid," he croaked, his voice barely a whisper, "but I'm perfectly all right, as you can see." He managed a fragile smile for the frightened man.

"Nobody else in there?" he demanded. "You know if you sneak someone extra into your room without paying for him, you're breaking the law. You'd be defrauding an inn-keeper." He raised himself up with more assurance, almost certain no one had been hurt or killed in the room. Straining to look taller than his five-foot five-inch frame would allow, he tried to look directly into Trina's eyes.

"Would you take someone along on your honeymoon?" Jon demanded, stepping around his wife to openly confront the intruder.

The manager faced him, relaxing his exaggerated height when he realized he could never match Jon's stature, even on his tiptoes. "I've been in this business twelve years and I've seen it all. Nothing would surprise me anymore.

I guess I'll take your word for the fact nothing out of the ordinary has happened." Glancing slyly at Trina, he suggested, "Try to hold it down, will you? People are trying to sleep, you know. Goodnight."

While closing the door, Jon heard the man mutter under his breath, "Goddamn perverts with their weird fucking sex."

Despite his aching head, Jon turned to face Trina who also heard the comment, and burst into laughter. "Would you like to rejoin me in bed, *ya goddamn pervert?*" he had asked, imitating the manager's voice.

"Sure, why not?" Trina had answered.

Slowing to a stop for a traffic light, she beamed when she finished reliving the episode. They laughed every time they thought of the incident. She looked at her watch. Three-sixteen. A few more blocks and she would be home.

Jon would be all right, she told herself. He had to be. "Dear God," she whispered softly as she drove, "let everything be fine with Jon."

A sudden gloom clouded her face. Neither she nor Jon went to church anymore. At best, she had been a lukewarm Catholic when they met. Jon had allowed his faith to be destroyed when his mother died. "How could a loving God allow my mother to die?" he had asked bitterly the night they discussed religion. As far as Trina was concerned, she would go to church if Jon wanted to but as long as he felt the way he did, she wouldn't push the subject. After all, she enjoyed those lazy Sunday mornings in bed with coffee, the *Tribune*, and Jon.

She suddenly caught herself praying again. "Please let everything be fine with Jon and I'll start going to church again." A small tear formed, swelling in size until it dropped down her cheek. Was it all right to bargain with God?

Jon hurled his eraser across the room. "Sonofabitch," he cried. "Who the hell said I could write, much less type? That has to be the millionth mistake today."

He had lost track of time during several daydreaming episodes since Trina left that morning. The same sheet of paper he had inserted at seven forty-five remained in the typewriter, a dozen smudged lines gracing it. He looked at the clock on the mantel. Three-fifteen? It couldn't be. In a few minutes Trina would be home and he had all of a half page finished. What the hell could be wrong with him? He couldn't write! Why waste his time? Why waste Trina's money? She had such faith in him. Could he disappoint her without at least trying?

Standing, he stormed around the room in a circle again—the same path he traversed whenever his mind got cramped, as he put it. After making two rounds, he sat down heavily to stare at the paper.

"By God, I'll finish this page before Trina gets home—or else." He began again, immediately making a mistake. "Aw, shit!" he screamed. Without looking, he groped for the eraser but couldn't find it. Then he recalled throwing it across the room. Pivoting on the chair, he abruptly froze in position, his eyes open but blind to his surroundings, as the minute hand on the clock moved toward the six.

Trina turned into the alley behind the mansion, pressing the electric eye button to open the garage door. Carefully driving ahead, she parked the Mustang and turned off the ignition. Her hands shook and she was vaguely aware of a drop of sweat trickling between her breasts. Feeling light-headed, she suddenly thought of Jon. He had to be all right. He *would* be all right.

The car door seemed to resist opening and with a quiet grunt, she pushed until it swung clear of the frame. Stepping out, she locked it, and stood swaying for a moment. Her knees trembling, she leaned against the side of the auto to regain her equilibrium. Dizziness gave way to an overwhelming fright and she felt ill, fighting the gagging urge to vomit. She had to be strong now when Jon needed her most.

The minute hand moved slowly, inexorably past three twenty-eight while Jon remained rooted in his rigid position. Droplets of sweat drenched his face, his soaked shirt clinging to his body. *In the distance he could hear the cheering.*

Shaking her shoulders, Trina valiantly tried to throw off the heavy-hearted depression that had gripped her since entering the garage. She took a tentative step toward the door, which led

71

outside, happily discovering she felt better.

The screams of adulation faded away and Jon could hear the pounding of his own running feet.

Her heels clicking on the concrete floor, Trina crossed the dim garage, gray with subdued sunlight fighting its way in through grimy windows.

Plunging headlong through the familiar dream forest, Jon could feel his wildly beating heart. His body and seared lungs ached.

Forgetting the locked garage door, Trina came to an abrupt stop, opening her handbag for her keys. She found the ring with the tiny yarn ball attached, pulling them out only to drop them. Quickly retrieving the ring, she inserted the key.

Jon shrank back from the people grabbing at him with emaciated fingers, their sallow faces deformed with loathing.

Turning the lock, Trina opened the door wide. The wash of fresh air made her immediately feel more comfortable. Closing the garage, she inhaled the glorious day's clean, fresh air. Leaves on the trees in the back yard were almost full size and the rich, green foliage hid chirping birds. She made her way toward the walk leading past the side of the house. In minutes she would be with Jon.

The fog parted and Jon saw the figure of the blond woman motioning for him to join her. Knowing the people pressing about him would not impede his course, he began approaching the indistinct form.

Trina loved this time of year—the reawakening of nature, the comforting thoughts of school being dismissed soon, a new routine for her and Jon during the next three months. Both enjoyed summer since they could be together that much more. Feeling impulsively satisfied with her love for him, she broke into an ecstatic smile.

The blond woman now lay at his feet. He tried vainly to repel the cajoling pantomime of the pressing crowd. He shook his head furiously but knew he could not resist. He would obey.

Trina turned the corner and bounced up the eight steps to the portico.

Slowly he raised the dream gun to his temple, at the same time squeezing the trigger.

The tumblers quietly flipped over in the outer door.

Jon felt the burning headache begin . . .

Trina inserted the key in the lock of their apartment. She turned the knob as Jon screamed.

Throwing the door open, she saw him fall from his chair at the desk. The sight of blood flowing from his eyes, nose, ears and mouth transfixed her in the entryway, unable to move.

Her breath came in short gasps as her own cry of terror built. "Oh, my God!" she screamed, running to the still form of her husband. Lifting his head, she cradled it as she sat on the floor. "Oh, my good God," she wailed, tears dropping from her face to mix with the blood covering her husband's face. "What happened? What happened? Oh, God! Oh, God! What happened?"

An almost audible moan snapped her back to reality and she stared at her husband. Alive? Could he be alive? She fumbled for his pulse, finding a strong, steady beat. Relief intermingled wildly with her terror.

Gently laying his head back on the floor, she stood. What should she do? Had he shot himself? They didn't own a gun of any sort. What had happened? She should call someone, but who? Paramedics? A hospital? A doctor? But which one? Who could be of the most help? Then, like a blazing neon sign, Samuel Dayton's number flashed in her mind, the same number she had dialed that morning. Dashing to the phone, she juggled it for a long second before getting a firm grip on the instrument. She spun the dial three times and then slowed, to avoid a mistake. Somehow, her composure reluctantly inched its way back into place. She wanted to scream. But she couldn't. She had to help Jon.

The buzz sounded only once before the receiver was lifted on the other end. "Doctor Dayton's office," Tory Worthington announced.

"Please, I *must* speak with Doctor Dayton. Now! Immediately!" she managed.

"I'm sorry," Tory said. "Doctor Dayton is with a patient. Who's calling?"

"Trina Ward. Jon Ward's wife."

"Are you a patient of Doctor Dayton's?"

"No. I'm not, but my husband is."

"Would you like to make an appointment, Mrs. Ward?"

"Listen to me. This is an emergency. My husband is in deep trouble. I must speak with the doctor this instant. If my husband dies, it will be your fault!"

"Just a moment, Mrs. Ward."

The line went dead. Trina suddenly found herself questioning the wisdom of calling the psychiatrist. If anything, Jon needed someone who could tend his wound. What had happened? Why was he bleeding? If he hadn't shot himself, and she wasn't positive he hadn't, what had caused so much blood? Perhaps she should hang up, break the connection, call the emergency number. But what was that number? There were only three digits to remember and she couldn't recall a single one. How had she remembered the psychiatrist's number?

She reached for the bar to cancel the call when Tory broke into her wild thoughts. "One moment, Mrs. Ward. Doctor Dayton will speak with you."

Again, the line went dead. She waited.

"Mrs. Ward? What seems to be the problem?" Sam asked.

"It's my husband," she choked, feeling immediate relief at the sound of his voice. She quickly related everything that had happened since she opened the door to their apartment.

When she finished he didn't speak immediately, but cleared his throat instead.

"I'll call an ambulance and we'll get him to Presbyterian Medical Center. I'll contact the emergency room there. Are you all right, Mrs. Ward?"

Tears of relief gushed down Trina's cheeks. Nodding her head, she managed, "I'm fine, Doctor. Tell them to hurry."

"Do whatever you can to help him until they get there." The doctor's voice was gone with the click.

Trina looked dumbly at the receiver in her hand before slowly replacing it in its cradle. Wiping her eyes, she turned when her husband moaned again.

Sitting up, close to the spot where she found him, Jon rubbed his head. She screamed, her bewildered expression distorting into one of confusion.

She could not see a trace of blood—anywhere.

His legs trembling, Jon moved to the mirror in the living room's short hallway. He could not recall when the dream had left him so exhausted, so weak. Then, too, he could not remember having the dream at any time other than when he was in bed, asleep. He ran one hand over his face before pressing gently on his eyes with his finger tips. Other than the headache and severe nausea, he felt weakened but unharmed. Turning, he found his wife sitting in the antique rocker, her face drained of color, her eyes red from crying.

"I still don't believe it," he said shakily. "There isn't a trace of blood anywhere—not on my face, or neck, or on my shirt. There's no sign of any stains on you. I simply don't believe it, hon!''

"I—I know—what—I—saw," she sobbed. Could she be losing her mind? She tugged on the handkerchief Jon had given her. She felt devastated. Blood! She had seen blood gushing from every opening in his head. It had covered his face and neck. His shirt had been soaked with it. After talking with the doctor, she turned to confront the gory scene and Jon had been sitting up, holding his head. The blood had vanished.

Crossing the room, Jon breathed deeply and crouched next to her. "I'll admit this much," he began, "that's the first time I've ever had the dream during the daytime. And, for what it's worth, this is the worst I can ever recall my head hurting. But I just can't believe this stuff about blood."

"It was there," she timidly insisted. Standing, she left Jon, hunched next to the empty chair, which bobbed gently back and forth. "It was there! I saw it! You were unconscious, how would you know?"

"I don't see any signs of blood anywhere. Do you?" He stood, recrossing the room to be closer to her. The sick feeling was passing, but his head continued to throb.

"Do you want anything before the ambulance gets here?" she asked. "Some aspirin might—"

"Ambulance? What ambulance?"

"I called Doctor Dayton and when I told him how you were bleeding, he wanted to get you to the hospital immediately."

Jon moaned. "Oh, for chrissakes! Do you realize how foolish we're going to look? Now I wish to hell I hadn't let you talk me into going to see any doctors in the first place. None of this would be happening now. I'm not going back to the hospital."

Trina put her hands firmly on her husband's shoulders, anger sparking in her eyes. "Now, listen to me, Jon Ward! I don't know about you, but I've had enough of your dream, nightmare, hallucination, whatever you want to call it. I want you to be healthy and normal. Not—"

"Normal?" Jon broke in. "You mean to tell me you think I'm abnormal or something?"

"You know what I mean. There must be something wrong someplace."

He shook his head for a second, felt dizzy from the sudden motion. Cradling his head in both hands for a moment to allow the pain to subside, he said softly, "All right, darling. You're probably right. I'll go." He didn't want to argue. That wasn't his nature. His recalcitrance usually acted as an asset but now the dream seemed ready to drive a wedge between Trina and himself. He knew that neither of them wanted that. Aside from the nightmare, his health was good—even robust. Get rid of his nightmare phantasms, then everything would be perfect. He gently rubbed his right temple.

"Your head's really bothering you, isn't it?"

"More than ever."

"We're doing the right thing."

"I know," he agreed.

The doorbell rang.

Opening the front entrance, Trina admitted two white uniformed men who jockeyed a stretcher into the living room. The taller of the two stopped short when he saw Jon standing next to the couch.

"Where's the patient?" he asked.

"My husband is the patient," she said, motioning toward Jon.

"What's the problem?"

"The crisis is past," Jon said. "But we decided I should go to the hospital anyway."

"We were told there was a man bleeding to death in this apartment. You playing a game or something?" the attendant gruffly asked, eyeing the couple.

"There must be some mistake about that," Trina said quickly before Jon could answer. "My husband passed out just as I got home and his head is hurting him terribly."

"What about the blood?" the man persisted.

"Well," Jon said, taking Trina's cue, "there isn't any I can see."

The spokesman for the ambulance team glanced cautiously at his partner before redirecting his attention to Jon. "Do you think you can walk to the ambulance?"

"Yeah, no problem," he said, before turning to his wife. "What about a bag? I'll need some things in the hospital."

"I'll bring whatever you need later, hon."

"Okay, then," Jon said, sounding relaxed and calm, "let's go." He followed the attendants, Trina walking at his side.

Within minutes they were out of the quiet

neighborhood and in heavy traffic. Smiling ruefully, Jon said. "You know, I'm disappointed. No siren! No drama!"

Trina nodded but said nothing.

The attendant who rode with them remained silent, continuing his observation of Jon.

Looking out the side window, Jon watched the blurring traffic move against the maze of store fronts slipping past without being identified. Suddenly, pain hammered again at his skull, stretching to a frenzied threshold he had never before experienced, not even while regaining his sensibilities on the floor of their living room. Opening his mouth to speak, he slipped into unconsciousness, slumping forward.

"Jon!" Trina gasped.

"Better hit the horn, Jake," the attendant snapped through the intercom.

"Okay, Tim." The raspy answer punctuated the rising scream of the siren.

With Trina's help, Tim eased Jon onto the empty stretcher. After checking the heart with a stethoscope, he rolled one of Jon's shirt sleeves up to record his blood pressure.

Trina sat close to her husband, holding one limp hand while the attendant held the other arm.

Several long minutes later, the ambulance's siren ended its wailing when the vehicle pulled into the emergency entrance at the medical center. Throwing the back door open, Tim helped the two male nurses waiting at the entrance. Strong hands grasped the stretcher bearing Jon, withdrawing it hurriedly but gently, and rushed him into the hospital.

The window blinds remained drawn, as they had been since he was placed in bed shortly after his arrival at Presbyterian Medical Center. The soft night light, barely illuminating the room, managed only to create heavy shadows everywhere except on the wall behind Jon's head.

Trina, sitting near her husband, studied the visible contours of Jon's face. He looked peaceful, appearing to be sound asleep. Reaching out, she delicately caressed his hand. She had no idea what she would do if the doctor discovered something drastically wrong with him. She would survive, but she felt it would be an empty existence without Jon. Their life together had been more than the love story for which she had hoped. It had been an adventure in living, loving and learning about each other—and about life. In time, in the near future she had hoped, they would begin thinking about having a child— another person to share their life odyssey. An irrepressible sob shook a tear loose from her wet lashes. The future. Did they have a future? Would they have all the tomorrows they had planned together?

"What's wrong with you, Jon?" she asked quietly. "Why is this happening to us? Why? Why us? You've got to be all right! You just have to be."

She stood, tiptoeing to the window. Pulling back one side of the shade, she gazed out at the glow of the traffic streaming by many stories below. The horizon glimmered mockingly with its halo created from street lights, signs, marquees and the endless flow of cars. She dropped the shade, returning to stand at the foot of the bed. Jon moved his legs. Reaching out, she patted his feet. Could something be wrong with his legs as well? Or was it part of this schismatical nightmare?

She recalled Friday, when she had first noticed Jon's limp. During the next two days, she had observed him favoring one of his legs several times. It was slight but nevertheless a distinct, halting gait. He hadn't mentioned anything about his legs when she first perceived it and she wondered if he might not be aware of it. The lame pace seemed to be replacing his normal walk.

Sunday afternoon, she had finally mentioned it.

"Now, I ask you, Mrs. Ward, am I a cripple?" he had asked, decisively striding about the living room.

She shook her head slowly. "Maybe I'm imagining things," she said weakly. "I could have sworn—"

"Lay off the swearing," he said, grinning. Sobering, his mood changed. "God, sweetheart! There's nothing wrong with me. The doctors found nothing. Besides, I wouldn't let anything go wrong. You know that."

Allowing herself to be embraced, she had impulsively thrown her arms around his neck. "I'm sorry, darling," she had said, but decided to call Doctor Dayton Monday morning.

Her gaze, traveling up his quiet form lying in the hospital bed, stopped to study his handsome features. The half light created an illusion of puffiness and lines in his face. The feeble glow shone on his right eye and forehead while darkness covered the left side of his upper face. Directly above his mouth the shadow of his nose gave him the appearance of wearing a small moustache. Despite her concern, she managed a fragile smile. Then the door opened and the light from the hallway spilled in.

Trina turned to find a heavyset nurse framed in the doorway.

"Mrs. Ward?" the woman asked.

Trina walked toward her and into the hall when the woman motioned for her to follow.

"I'm Selma Overton. Doctor Lehigh asked me to visit with you for a moment. He was on his way here but was called to an emergency operation. Doctor has looked at the results of the tests your husband underwent when he was admitted this afternoon. Everything seems to be within normal ranges. However, he has suggested Mr. Ward undergo another angiogram."

Trina cringed inwardly at the thought. She remembered Jon's trepidation about the angiogram he had had administered the previous week. Although the possibilities of a reaction or blood clot existed, nothing adverse had happened. Now, he would apparently have to have another of the tests.

"Is it necessary?" she asked.

"Doctor seems to feel that since it is so close timewise to his having experienced the dream, something might show up on this test that didn't before."

Trina nodded, understanding the logic, but fearing Jon's attitude.

"Doctor also suggested that you go home and get a good night's rest. Your presence here will not help your husband at this time."

"When will the angiogram be administered?" she asked.

"Very early, tomorrow morning. I believe he's scheduled for seven."

"I'll have to call in early so the school can get a sub for me but I'll be here. Probably earlier than that."

"Don't worry, Mrs. Ward. Your husband should sleep the whole night through with no effort. We have orders to check on him every fifteen minutes. If he should wake up, we're to notify the doctor on duty immediately. As a result, he'll be under observation all night."

Trina studied the older woman. An air of professional conduct prevented her from smiling even though laugh lines were in evidence at the corners of her eyes. Her ruddy complexion contrasted sharply with her white uniform while dark eyes peered steadily at Trina.

"His vital signs are all normal, Mrs. Ward," she continued. "Right now, he's sleeping. Everything should be fine for tonight."

"If you're certain it's all right," she said.

"You won't be worth anything to him when

he's awake in the morning if you stay up all night, Mrs. Ward. Please. A good night's sleep will work wonders for you, as well as for your husband."

"Very well. I'll get my purse and be on my way," she said, moving to the door.

It took a second for her eyes to adjust to the half light of the room before she walked to the side of the bed. Jon still lay on his back, asleep. Bending down, she tenderly kissed him. "I'll see you in the morning, darling," she whispered.

Leaving his side to retrieve her handbag from the bureau, Trina moved silently to the door. Before she left, she turned to look at her husband once more. The shadows still painted his face in a surrealistic manner. Quietly opening the door, she stepped into the hall.

Only Jon's steady breathing disrupted the silence in the room. Then his eyes opened and an evil smile curled his lips.

CHAPTER FOUR

Trina hoped Jon had not noticed her haggard
appearance. She vaguely remembered the clock
in the living room striking four before dropping
off to sleep, and then, in what seemed like
seconds, the alarm clock had rung. Her
thoughts, filled with concern for him, had
managed to keep her awake most of the night.
Suddenly, the closeness of the elevator seemed
to press in on her. She wanted to speak to Jon
but felt she could not in the presence of the two
strangers who stood with them.

Studying Jon lying on the gurney convinced
her that he was still confused about the experience he had suffered yesterday. The thought of
blood pouring from his head had dominated her
nighttime reflections. Had she imagined the
whole thing? Was his dream beginning to affect
her in some strange way? He had screamed just
like he did whenever he had suffered the nightmare. She remembered throwing the door open

to see him fall from his chair. She remembered the blood. No one could ever convince her that she had not seen it. She didn't care if it had disappeared, leaving no trace or stain of any kind. She had seen it.

Taking her eyes from him, she looked covertly at the two orderlies who were taking Jon to the radiology department. She found the young man and woman lost in whispered conversation.

When she felt Jon pull on her arm, she looked down at him.

He mouthed the words, "I'm doing this for you," and smiled.

She nodded and lovingly touched his hand.

The car gently settled to a stop, its doors sliding open without a discernable sound. Trina followed her husband's cart into the hall. Several turns through the labyrinthian corridors brought them to a double door and the woman turned to face her.

"We'll let you know when you can come in for a few minutes, Mrs. Ward." Without waiting for a reply, she left her standing alone in the hall.

Trina leaned against the cool, tile wall. For some inane reason, she felt guilty about all of Jon's problems. But, why now, of all times? Her own sense of responsibility and concern had vacillated from deepest worry to full acceptance of anything the doctors might find. At least if the cause of the dream were known, it could be countered intelligently. She smiled ruefully. Why should she feel as though she were committing some abominable crime for having her husband's welfare foremost in her mind? Would the doctors discharge Jon with a clean bill of health, only to insist that she seek help either for her eyes or her imagination? Doctor Lehigh, the resident internist, had irked her when she told him of the blood shortly after they had arrived at the hospital.

"Really, Mrs. Ward, what you're telling me is something completely out of the range of normal medicine. I wasn't prepared for something like *disappearing blood* while I was in school," he had said curtly.

When he appeared to have dismissed it as the product of an overwrought imagination. Trina decided not to mention the incident again.

The double doors opened and the woman who had accompanied her and Jon in the elevator appeared, motioning for her to enter.

Jon blinked at the brightness of the room. Lights placed every foot-and-one-half around the room's perimeter were enhanced by more ceiling lights. The orderlies transferred him to a table and before settling down on the hard surface, he stretched lazily. A male nurse deftly shaved, then scrubbed a small area next to the previous test site, on the inside of his right thigh. Suddenly aware of another person standing behind him, Jon turned his head and saw Dr. Orval Rodgers.

Rodgers, a huge man, had appeared portly in his suit and tie the first time they met, but now had taken on an ungainly mien in his green surgical scrubs, just as he had during the first angiogram.

"Good morning, Mr. Ward," he said softly. "We'll be ready to start as soon as we make our incision."

Rodgers turned, passing out of his range of sight, but Jon could see the young man and girl who had accompanied him on the elevator going through the door by which he had entered. Then Trina came in.

In seconds she stood at his side. "Everything will be all right, darling," she said quietly.

"I know it will." He took her hand, squeezing it is his. "Don't be upset with me. Don't worry about me."

"I will worry. It's my prerogative." She flashed her best *I love you* smile.

He grinned, pointing to his head. "I don't think they'll find anything new except more jumbled up plot lines and some pretty wild characters I haven't put down on paper yet. That and a lot of thoughts about you."

She bent, lightly kissing him on the mouth.

"You'll have to leave, Mrs. Ward," the male nurse said. "You can wait down the hall or return to your husband's room. We shouldn't be too long." He smiled confidently, dispelling any last minute fears for either patient or spouse.

She calmly returned the young man's look and waved to Jon. " 'Bye, honey, see you soon."

He watched Trina crossing the room and relaxed with the thought that tonight, tomorrow at the latest, he would be able to go home.

The male nurse stepped aside when the other

nurse came forward to cover Jon's lower extremities with a green cloth. He could see a small hole when the woman flared it out to settle in an open position. Moving it around, she placed the opening over the area that had been prepared.

Dr. Rodgers came into view again and the two nurses stepped back. He examined the opening and grunted, "Xylocaine." In seconds, one of the nurses appeared, handing him a vial.

The doctor shot a stream of anesthesia away from the table, expelling any remaining air from the syringe. Jon felt a prick as the needle entered his leg, a comforting sensation of numbness spreading quickly.

"Feel this?" Rodgers asked after several minutes, pinching the flesh through the cloth close to the exposed spot.

Jon shook his head.

"Get me an Amplatz needle, Joanie," the doctor ordered. The young nurse turned to an instrument tray, quickly handing the device to him.

Jon spotted a monitoring TV set and could see the incision being made. He turned his head away just as Rodgers inserted the large needle.

Rodgers positioned the X-ray tube over Jon's head. Satisfied it was set properly, he went to the machine which would record the journey of the dye about to course through the patient's head.

"First, a test dose," he said from across the room. The woman tending Jon's incision, responded to the order.

Jon tried not to pay attention to the terse dialogue. He had blotted the room out of sight by closing his eyes tightly. Now, he would only have to concentrate on shutting out the voices of the doctor and nurses.

"Inject the first dosage, Joanie." Rodger's voice seemed distant, remote.

Jon felt queasy, a wave of nausea firmly entrenching itself when he heard the voice of the radiologist say, "Inject the IRS again and—" When the voices faded, he tentatively opened his eyes. He remembered when he had had the same test last week that there had been several injections. The sensation of heat emanating from his face and head would feel highly concentrated as the iodinated radiopaque substance passed through the blood vessels in his skull. Maybe there would be complications this time. He should have rebelled at the idea of a second test. Hadn't he been warned the last time that something could go wrong? But he hadn't really been consulted about this test. He had slept the whole night and awakened to find Trina at his bedside. She had told him of the impending test and in his bewildered state, merely nodded. Hadn't the doctor said last week the possibility existed that—what was it he had said? He couldn't concentrate.

He had to stop thinking about the scalding effect. But, how could he? Searing fire seemed to singe his face and head. His throat burned as though he were exposed to a blast furnace. He knew it would pass but would he be able to stand the pain this time?

Closing his eyes again, he tried to block the white room from sight. The cold, sterile walls should have helped him fix his thoughts on something other than those of discomfort and burning fever. But they hadn't. He didn't think he could stand it. He opened his mouth to scream.

"But I still live!"

Jon's eyes flew open, searching. Who had said that? He hadn't. Had he thought it? No. It was more of a voice within him that had uttered the words. But how? Who? His eyes darted from the ceiling to the X-ray machine above his head. To the nurse standing near his lower extremities who cared for the incision in his leg. To the flickering screen that displayed his groin area. There were no indications that the woman standing near him had said or heard anything. The monotonous hum of the machine was the only sound in the room. Every once in a while, the radiologist spoke, giving an order to one or the other of his assistants, but Jon could not understand the words.

The warmth of the baking heat that filled his head suddenly felt comforting. The room blended into a swirl of shadows and whiteness before an opaque curtain settled before his eyes. Was he dying? If this were death, it felt good. He welcomed it as relief from the misery to which he had been subjected. Now the heat flared again and he decided his face and shoulders were actually smoldering. Opening his eyes, he saw below him the trees turned into people burning, mouthing their silent screams of agony and death. For an instant, he savored the experience of hovering near the ceiling, dangling in mid air.

His head felt fragmented, the ache pounding more severely than the previous afternoon. There were no feelings of anger or injury or desperation once he acknowledged the pain in his skull. At first he wanted to scream, just as he always did whenever awaking from the nightmare, but a sensibility of peace enveloped him offering warmth, security. A new sensation of freedom washed over his being and a sense of floating startled him. He no longer had the fiery burning in his face and head and when he looked down, he gasped. The dying people had vanished and in their place he saw his own body lying on the X-ray table, the attendant nurse standing next to his right leg where the incision had been made. The doctor continued making notes as the machinery of modern medicine hummed its one note litany.

"There's the body I live in."

Now Jon knew it wasn't his own voice he had heard before. Powerless to question the mystery, he sensed no real panic. Was he actually dying? Could this be death? The scene below him slowly faded when rolling clouds blocked his view.

Eagerly awaiting the fog to clear, he found his curiosity aroused to the fullest. Death would not be so bad if he could continue functioning in some mental capacity.

A memory-filled wave of emotion tore him from the arms of complacency and happiness.

Trina! Where was Trina? He suddenly wanted to see her—just once more. To be able to touch her. To kiss her. To hold her. Just one more time. Stifling a sob, he pushed the thoughts of his wife from his consciousness.

Then concussions battered him. Barely noticeable at first, they grew in intensity until wave after wave buffeted him. What was happening? Death, destruction seemed to surround him. The initial mood of comfort slipped away, forgotten, as did the melancholy of Trina's absence and loss. Feeling he would not die, he wanted to scream, "I AM ALIVE!" A joyful exuberance he had never known before washed over him, penetrating the depths of his soul.

The smashing impacts continued their assault but he no longer cared. Somehow he knew they couldn't harm him. Elated, he soared high above the zone where the strange blows first struck him. For a moment, he felt responsible for the chaos and ruination. Nonchalantly pushing aside any sense of guilt, he laughed forcefully when more comfortable impressions forced their way back into his consciousness, driving everything aside, even the thoughts of Trina, releasing him at last from the fiery torture. Happier than he had ever been, he simply wanted to scream, "I'M ALIVE! I STILL LIVE!" But was he alive? Or dead? Perhaps he was insane and would remain in a world of shadows and unrealities for the rest of his days. The thought terrified him. Recognizing this fear, he became aware of a change in his surroundings.

The brightness left, only to be replaced with a damp darkness, as though he were in a lightless cellar, blindfolded. *He had to be dead!* Condemned to the netherworld for eternal punishment.

Then he perceived someone else's presence. Not one but two—two beings whose emotions he recognized and understood—fear from one, insatiable lust from the other. Panic, bordering on hysteria, more than equalled the maniacal sexual drive. The frightened thoughts remained constant but the second intellect grew more erratic in its observations, memories, desires. An overpowering wish for violent sex suddenly dominated the muddle of emotions.

Helpless, unable to resist, he drifted toward the fitful thoughts, feeling them grow. Suffocating as though inundated, he vividly recalled a childhood memory of being drawn under the surface of a swimming pool, sucking water into his mouth and nostrils. His sinus cavities had been swamped with fluid and he could feel the same choking strangulation now as the invisible attraction drew him closer.

Still, ecstacy filled him, commanding him to scream, *"I STILL LIVE!"* When he surrendered to the urge, the very words, hammering at him since he floated away from the X-ray table, clearly rang out. Opening his eyes, he found himself in a cavern or tunnel of some sort. At his feet, the nude body of a sobbing woman—a young, beautiful woman—trembled, cowering in fear. Her milky white breasts, her smooth stomach, her flared hips centered with a patch of yellow hair, sent his senses reeling as he hungrily desired her. Somehow she looked familiar but he could not place her. Her face flickered into sharp lines for an instant before hazing into an unfocused blur. Who was she?

Obliquely aware of frenzied activity taking place somewhere around him, he looked down to see long, thin hands, unlike his own square shaped ones, unbuckling a belt which held torn pants around someone's waist. Whose? His? He didn't know. The momumental sexual drive pushed every other conscious thought from him while a vague awareness of kneeling, then lying upon the body of the woman, indifferently ricocheted through his mind. Roughly spreading the woman's legs, he pushed his blood gorged erection into the golden pubic triangle, a thrust with his hips, and another and another, until the sensual rhythm was established.

Tears streaking her cheeks, she relaxed, strangely reposed, at peace. Appearing to be asleep, she accepted her cruel fate. Her beautiful, sad face evaporated from his sight when a constant pressure began squeezing in on him until he knew he would be squashed into nothingness. The continuing strain crushed him until he felt like the size of a sand grain. Then more weight bore down until the compression stopped in a sudden wave of release.

Tumbling about, he instinctively began swimming—he had to swim to survive. He would fight the tumultuous current of odds that would not allow him to live beyond the next forty-eight hours. Darkness closed in. He continued swimming.

A gentle hand shook him by the shoulder until Jon looked into the eyes of the nurse who had been monitoring the incision, injecting the substance into his arteries. A feeling of relief jabbed at him when he realized he had been dreaming.

Tory pulled the sheet of paper from the typewriter, adding it to the stack centered on her deck. At least she had finished Mrs. Nelumbo's last session with Doctor Dayton. With thirty-five minutes left before the office closed, she would not have enough time to begin another tape. Inserting the transcribed conversation into a folder, she moved to the bank of cabinets and filed it in the appropriate drawer. When she had removed the tape from the machine, she sat down behind her desk.

How had she managed to get so much work accomplished today? When she had left home that morning, her thoughts had been focused on Howie. He looked awful. He wasn't sleeping properly. He wasn't eating enough. He was smoking too much marijuana and drinking too much beer. What would she do if something were to happen to him? She loved him more than anything or anyone else in her life. Considering herself lucky to have found him and to have fallen in love with him, she stared at her desk top.

Tomorrow, when Doctor Dayton did not come into the office, she would concentrate on different plans to help Howie. First, he would have to find a job. Once that was accomplished, their happiness would virtually be secured. She loved to fantasize about the two of them living in a small cottage in some woods, without a care in the world.

Snapping out of her reverie, she knew there must be a way for him to find a job. There just had to be. Everyone found work of some sort. Why couldn't he? Most employers didn't want to hire former convicts but that shouldn't stop the two of them from realizing their own goals and happiness. There had to be a way they could get enough money to be happy and be together forever.

Opening the bottom drawer of her desk, she withdrew her purse and spread it apart. She checked her billfold. Three hundred fifty dollars to last until the middle of the month? And the rent still had to be paid. What had happened to all the money she had gotten at the bank yesterday when she cashed her check? She had given Howie money to buy some grass. But how much had she given him? They had smoked a lot last night and he had been more tender in his lovemaking than usual. When had she given him the money? Before they smoked? Yes, shortly after she arrived home. He had taken her purse and counted the money, withholding four hundred dollars which he said would be enough for marijuana and other necessities until she was paid again. Then, too, she had stopped at the delicatessen and bought enough food to last them a week.

She smiled when she thought of Howie tonguing her breasts and nipples. When he took his time, he was a great lover. But most of the time, he just jammed it in and finished in a moment or two. Still, she loved him almost more than life itself. On her way home, she would stop and get him a twelve pack of beer. He'd enjoy that and if she could get him into a good mood, he might want to take his time making love tonight.

Closing her purse, she watched the clock. In five minutes, she could leave for home and Howie.

Jon watched Trina disappear through the door of his hospital room. The doctor had said he could go home in the morning and she jumped at the chance to get a good night's rest. When she had told him about her sleepless night, he had insisted that she go home. It would do no good to have her become ill because of him. Besides, he knew he had been preoccupied when she had been sitting at his bedside, trying to get him to carry on a conversation. The test results had again been negative and since there was no cause to talk about them, he had concentrated his thoughts on his experience during the angiogram.

Dreaming. He had dreamt while the test had been administered. The nightmare—his nightmare—had, after all these years, continued beyond the normal waking point. Or was it a new fantasy? Regardless of what it was, Jon swore to himself, he would never reveal the contents of it to anyone—not even Trina. Anger over the consequences of telling one too many persons about his dream filled his mind. This dream, this nightmarish episode would be divulged to no one—ever.

PART TWO

THE VOICE SPEAKS

May 11, 1979
to
May 29, 1979

CHAPTER FIVE

Preoccupied with the transcript on her desk,
Tory traced a route with a well manicured nail
from her throat to the exposed cleavage of her
breasts. She laid the paper aside, satisfied it
held no mistakes in typing and quickly inserted
another sheet into the typewriter. Smoothing
imaginary wrinkles in her vermillion polyester
dress, she opened the bottom desk drawer and
pulled out her purse. She checked her hair in a
compact mirror, stopping to study her full,
natural lashes. A smile curved her lips and she
winked at herself before returning the mirror to
the handbag. Once the drawer was closed, she
stared into space.

The one thing she liked about her job as secretary to Dr. Samuel Dayton, was the fact that
she didn't have to work with anyone else. It
would have been difficult for her to cope with
another woman on this job. She found it an
effort to make friends with women. With men

she had no problem at all. Ever since Howie had come into her life, she had used her time on the job as an opportunity to physically and mentally regenerate herself for him. Her love for Howie seemed to know no bounds and many times in the last six months, she had found herself fantasizing a conversation with her mother.

"He loves *me*, Mother. He really does."

"You're not worth the love of a good man. Is he *good*, Victoria?"

Tory blanched at the imaginary question posed by her mother. Howie had all the makings of a good man, a good husband. It wasn't his fault that the government had made him join the army and go to Viet Nam. Tory knew that her mother and father probably would have liked him. In some ways, he reminded her of her brother, Tony. For some inexplicable reason, they had focused their attention on him, ignoring her while she and Tony had grown up. He was a first class member of the family while at best, she could claim a secondary status. She had assumed there were people who did not treat their offspring equally and when she had removed herself from her parents' presence, she realized that her father treated her mother as a piece of property. Shortly after she met Howie, she understood that her mother had been trying to tell her to find a man who would take care of her, although her method of relaying that information had been abstract.

When Tony, the family's pride and joy, drank

himself into a stupor one night and drove off a bluff overlooking the Mississippi River, her parents' reason for existence seemed to end. Discovering they were inconsolable to the loss of their only son, and that she would never be able to fill the gap created by his death, Tory left their home in Dubuque and moved to Chicago. She had not been in touch with them since.

Still, Tory was happy. Happy with her love for Howie, happy with her job, and happy just to be happy. Realizing it was almost quitting time and that the weekend was before her, she began putting the files together. On her way home, she'd think about ways to please Howie. She formulated little plans which made her feel good and warm inside, even though most were impractical.

Since Doctor Dayton had already left, she'd lock up and leave a few minutes early. When her desk top was cleared, she quickly perused the outer office and turned off the lights. Stepping into the hall, she locked the door and walked to the elevator.

The weekend passed too quickly for Tory and by Sunday evening, she concluded that the two days had gained nothing. Howie had moped around the one room apartment, barely speaking, either staring out the single window into the alley or pacing about like a caged animal.

"What's bothering you, hon?" she asked quietly.

Howie continued walking back and forth, lost

in thought. "Huh? Did you say something?"

Grateful to have gained his attention, she said, "What's bothering you? Let's talk about it. Maybe I can help."

"That'd be the day."

"Seriously, I mean it. Talk about it and maybe it'll go away. The problem, that is."

"It's not a problem. I've been trying to think of something. That's all."

"Think of something?"

"Yeah. Of where I heard something."

"Like what?"

"Like a woman's name. I'm not sure if I know it or even heard it. But for some reason, this broad's been in my mind. She fucks around. She—"

"Howie," Tory gasped. "You're not thinking of—of—of fooling around with her, are you?"

"What? Oh, for chrissake! No. I'm just trying to get a handle on what I heard."

"Tell me what you know." Tory moved to the bed and sat on its edge, motioning for Howie to join her.

"Well," he said, flopping next to her, "there's this broad who's having an affair with her husband's business partner. At least, I think it's his partner. She's afraid of her old man finding out about it but won't quit fucking her lover. That's all I can remember. If I could think of her name or where I heard about her, I'd get all the details and be able to make some easy money."

Tory stood, the color draining from her face. How could Howie have found out about Carol Nelumbo? Carol Nelumbo was a patient of

Doctor Dayton's who was having a difficult time handling her guilt because of an affair with one of her husband's junior partners.

"What's the matter, Tory?" Howie asked when he looked up to find her face ashen.

"Huh. Oh, nothing—nothing."

What had she told him? She could get in all kinds of trouble with her employer if he found out that she was telling people about his patients. Had she told Howie when they were high or drunk? Oh, God, she *was* in trouble. She turned away, moving toward the window but not before Howie caught her expression.

"Hey, what gives with you? Wait a minute. Did you tell me about this dame?"

She could feel tears welling in her eyes. What would happen to them if she lost her job because of something as stupid as telling Howie about a patient?

Howie leaped from the bed, crossing the room in three steps. Grabbing Tory's arm he whirled her around. "Tell me, goddamnit! Were you the one who told me about this woman?" He squeezed tightly until she whimpered.

"It—it sounds—sounds like Mrs.—Mrs. Nelumbo," she managed as tears streamed down her cheeks.

"Who the fuck is that?"

"A patient of Doctor Dayton's."

Howie released his grip. "No shit?" He turned away and began pacing again but this time, a nasty smile twisted his normally dark good looks.

Tory rubbed her bruised arm, mentally going

through her wardrobe, deciding which dress would cover her upper arms and still be cool enough to wear to work the next day. When she looked at Howie, she sighed. At least he was smiling. That was more than he had done all weekend.

Suddenly, he bolted for the door. "I'm going out for a while. When I get back, we've got some serious talking to do." He opened it and stopped.

"What about, Howie, honey?"

"It'll wait."

"Give me a hint. Please?" She crossed the room, throwing her arms around his neck.

"You've given me an idea. An idea that'll get us out of this rat's nest and give us some real important bread." He pulled her arms from around him and stepped into the hall. "I'll be back in a few minutes."

Dumbfounded, she stood watching him run down the steps. She had given him an idea? What had she said?

Forty minutes later, when Howie returned, carrying a small bundle, Tory still had not figured out what she had told Howie to animate him in such a way. Elated that she had inspired her lover to take action, she watched mesmerized as he entered the apartment and went directly to the closet. Fumbling around on the shelf, he searched for something until an expression of relief crossed his face when his hand apparently closed on the object.

When he turned, she saw the cigaret roller in

his hand. "There's paper in the top drawer of the chest," she offered softly. Was that all she had managed to do? Get him out of the apartment to buy some marijuana? How could rolling joints and getting high get them out of this apartment and into good money? "I thought you said I'd given you an idea. I didn't even mention marijuana."

"Geezus!" Howie growled. "Don't be your usual dumb self. I need this shit to get my act together while I make plans. Then, once they're made, I'm off crap and beer until I'm finished with the job."

Her head whirled. First at the insult and then at the fact he was going to quit grass. She tried to understand him and his bitterness against the world, wishing he would be more considerate of her feelings. Her concern for him usually was met with complete indifference and, if he was high, derisive laughter, causing her to feel unloved, unwanted by him. Still, rather than run the risk of losing him, she was willing to accept him as he was.

But why would he consider quitting smoking up? What had she said? She turned to face him. Everything had been pushed off the table and he sat cross-legged on a wooden chair whose back had been lost long before they had moved into the apartment. Sliding the other chair into position, she sat next to Howie who neatly placed the papers next to the crumpled brown leaves.

"When this shit is gone," Howie said slowly,

"we're going straight. No more candy or booze or shit or nothing 'til I get what I want. Understand?"

A sense of relief swept over Tory. Maybe he would be able to find work if he stopped the pills and drinking and smoking. But she had to find out for herself. All of this was too good to be true. She wanted him to tell her he would find work. Spell out every detail. Then soon they could get married. "Why, honey?"

"Because I want my brain working full time. I told you before I left, you've given me one helluvan idea." He held up the first cigarette for inspection.

"I did?" She could scarcely believe what he had said. He had actually repeated it. But what had she said to make him want to abstain? "Tell me about it."

"When you told me about the woman I was trying to remember, all the pieces fell into place. Remember I said, if I could find out all the details, I'd get some easy money. I'm sure she wouldn't want her husband to find out about her playing around. So, ol' Howie's going to give her a chance to buy his silence on the subject. Ain't that beautiful?"

Tory's mind reeled under the impact of Howie's idea. When he first mentioned it, she thought he had been joking. What would happen to her if Doctor Dayton found out? She'd be fired. Then what would she and Howie do? What would they live on? Oh, God. Why hadn't she kept her mouth shut? She turned, looking at him, fear of the consequences contorting her face. She stood, her knees shaking, and moved to the window.

"You're speechless," he gloated. "See, all you gotta do is make copies of everything she says about her fucking around. Then, I go visit her and tell her I've been meaning to stop in and see her old man and tell him what I know. But for a consideration, a considerable consideration, I can forget his address. And we're in the money."

"You can't, Howie," Tory squeaked.

"Who says I can't?"

"I won't help you. It's against the law. We'll get in trouble."

"Against the law?" he shouted. "What about all the fat cats who cheat on their income tax walking around free as birds? What about them? What about this bitch who's fucking somebody other than her husband? That's against the law! Sort of! How about all the illegal things so-called honest people do? Nobody gives a fuck if they do or don't. Finally, I come up with the perfect plan to get us off and running with some real bread for a change and what are you going to do? You're going to queer the whole goddamn thing by fucking it up before we even get started! I thought you loved me."

"I do, honey. I do. But it's wrong." She turned to face him.

"Smoking shit's wrong, but you do it. Popping pills is wrong, but you do it. How come you're getting so—so fuckin' sanctimonious all of a sudden?"

"It's my job, honey," Tory whined. "We need my job to exist. Don't you understand?"

"Christ! You're the one who doesn't understand, you stupid bitch! You get enough people to come across like this dame will, and we can retire. Simple numbers, that's all. We get five, no, make it ten thousand from her. If the shrink has fifty patients like her, that's—that's, holy shit! That's half a million skins. We'd be on easy street." Howie rubbed his hands together before returning to the job of rolling cigarettes.

Tory's eyes widened at the amount he thought possible to obtain through blackmail. She couldn't do it. It was too risky. They'd be caught and put in jail. For years. They'd be separated and grow old alone. She wanted them to be together. Forever. She didn't know what she would do if something were to happen to Howie. She'd die, probably.

No! Definitely no! She would not do it! She would not take the chance of being taken away from him. She watched him roll another cigarette and said, "I won't do it, Howie."

He looked up, his brows knitting in the way they did whenever he was angry. Then just as quickly, they smoothed out. "Okay. Okay, Tory. Fuck you. I don't need you. I'll get another girl who *will* help me. One who won't be so unappreciative.

"Howie!" she cried, running the few steps separating them and dropped to her knees in front of him. She threw her arms around his legs, nuzzling his crotch. "Don't say that. Don't ever say you'd get another girl to take my place.

I'd kill myself if you ever left me. I couldn't live without you. Do you hear me? I'll do it. I'll do it."

He smiled thinly. "That's better."

Tory thought for several minutes before regaining her feet. When she realized he was aroused, she moved away. Maybe a blackmail plan could work. Maybe this was what they needed. She cleared her throat. "What will I have to do?"

"You said you type everything these sickies tell the shrink. Right?"

She nodded.

"Then, all you have to do is make an extra copy. Bring it home an ol' Howie will take over from there."

"That's all? That's all I have to do?" she squealed. She didn't know what she had anticipated but if this was all she had to do, it would be easy. Doctor Dayton seldom if ever bothered her while she typed and she had the office all to herself every Wednesday, his day off. A quick trip to the copy machine and she would be safe from detection. It *would* work.

"That's it." He stretched, staring at the ceiling.

"Like what kind of people do you want?" she asked, her enthusiasm growing. If this plan would benefit Howie's future and hers, she wanted to do as much as she could to make it successful.

"I think most everybody who goes to somebody like this asshole, Dayton, has something they'd just as soon not have spread around. Like this broad, people with guilt complexes. Anything that could ruin them if the right word got out. I'll guarantee the word won't be spread—for a consideration." He laughed.

"Are you happy, honey?" she asked when he had quieted.

"Right now? You bet I am. Finally, I've got a foolproof scheme going for me and it's all mine —er, ours."

"Would you be just as happy if you were teaching school? You know, like nothing ever happened and you never went to prison or whatever?"

His face clouded thoughtfully. All he had ever wanted to do at one time in his life, was be a good teacher and do some coaching. Howie's ambitions had been normal, planning to pattern his career after Mr. Flynn, who taught history at the high school he had attended in Santa Fe. How long ago had that been? But now it was totally impossible. He shook his head, clearing the memory and shrugged his shoulders. "I don't know," he said slowly in a voice Tory seldom heard. It was soft, well modulated, not harsh and grating the way he usually spoke.

"You would have been a good teacher," she said, rumpling his hair.

"Me? Yeah, I could have taught them how to roll their own joints." He scowled before returning his attention to the cigarette roller.

"Seriously," she insisted. "I never went to college but I would have loved to have had a teacher like you. What was your favorite subject?"

"History," he answered without lifting his eyes from the bits of leaves.

"Why? Why history? I always found it dull and boring in high school." She had studied enough of Doctor Dayton's sessions while typing them to understand the intricacies of getting people to talk about themselves. Usually, Howie resisted but because of their impending venture, his expansive mood might allow her to probe. She liked him even better this way.

"That's where I found it all at in school."

"I don't understand," she pressed.

"I liked all the rats in history."

"You don't mean that, do you?"

"Sure I do. I found them interesting. Only good thing about stir was the prison library. Spent most of my free time there, reading a lot." He stacked the cigarettes to one side.

"What did you read?" she asked, helping him clean the table.

"World War II mostly. No good, analytical works were available on Korea or 'Nam. Besides, there weren't any nasty heavies in those two like there were in World War II. You know, Mussolini, Hitler, Tojo. And don't forget the traitors and all those characters. Lord Haw Haw, Axis Sally, Tokyo Rose. Real neat people!"

He stood and returned the small machine to the closet. Laying four cigarettes on the table, he put the rest in the bottom drawer where the others were hidden. "Just remember, when this shit is gone, that's it. We're straight."

Tory lit two joints, handing one to him.

Taking a drag, Howie held the smoke in his lungs for several seconds before allowing it to flow from his nostrils. "Good shit," he muttered, motioning Tory to take his hand. He gripped it tightly, pulling her to the bed. "Let's smoke up and then fuck."

The next day, Tory began making photostats of every page she typed, placing them in a large manila envelope on which she had written an address and affixed postage, to allay any suspicion on the doctor's part, should he become curious. If he said anything, she would simply tell him it was something of hers she had to mail on the way home. If he ever did ask, she would have to devise another method of concealing the stolen information.

By Thursday night, Howie was angry since the last four days had offered no one who could be considered blackmail subjects. Tory's efforts revealed patients well on their way to conquering their neuroses, past the stage of exposing hidden facts that could be used by Howie.

When Friday's work was finished, Tory realized the day had not been different from the rest of the week. Before leaving, she opened the appointment book, running her scarlet nail down the list of names. Monday, May 18, Jon Ward, 3 PM. A new patient. Maybe he would be different from the others. On Tuesday, Mrs. Nelumbo was scheduled to come in. And later in the week, Sterling Tilden had an appointment. If she recalled correctly, Sterling Tilden had the type of problem that would appeal to Howie.

She closed the book. Next week would have to be better or Howie would become more than angry. And that she did not want to happen. Not when the possibility of a fortune seemed to be within their grasp.

When she reached the apartment, she found Howie half drunk. "Next week had better be more productive or you've had it," he said bitterly thumbing through the pages she had brought him. "It's your fault, Tory. This was your lousy idea and so far it hasn't worked for doodly crap." He stormed out of the room, returning after a while with two twelve-packs of beer.

The rest of the weekend, they alternately drank and slept. When awake, Howie refused to speak to her. Sunday evening, after sleeping all day, he awoke hung over but unyielding in his resolve to make their efforts pay.

"This week had better be a good one, Tory," he mumbled, holding his head in both hands.

Studying him, she commiserated with Howie and his rotten hangover. But hadn't he broken his own rule about keeping a clear head? Maybe it *was* her fault nothing worthwhile had come across her desk. She wasn't certain of anything anymore. The beer had taken its toll on her as well. When they had money, they wouldn't have to drink beer or smoke pot for good times. The joints they had made the week before had been gone since Wednesday and Howie's dejection over the apparent failure of their scheme continued growing. She would simply have to try harder, become more selective in her choice of possible victims. They would have to be in the early stages of analysis, or middle at best, when they told everything.

Bits and pieces of different patient histories zig-zagged through her head. One man didn't work. His wife supported him. She had inherited a lot of money or something. Who was he? Suddenly the name blasted in her mind. Jon Ward. Wasn't he coming in for his second appointment the next day? She remembered seeing his name in the appointment book along with Carol Nelumbo and Sterling Tilden. She would bypass the other appointments holding no promise of success where she and Howie were concerned.

Howie fell back on the bed. "You'd better come home with something excellent this week —or else," he growled, his voice muffled by the pillow half covering his face.

Tory smiled confidently. This week would be good. She just knew it.

CHAPTER SIX

"If you'll be seated, the doctor will only be a moment," Tory said, smiling broadly to herself after Jon had entered the office.

Easing himself into the only comfortable appearing chair in the waiting room, Jon picked up an old *Time*. Absently thumbing through it, he wondered what would happen when and if the doctor hypnotized him. The whole of the situation suddenly marched before his mind's eye. He had passed the point of being agitated and seemed to contemplate only the end of his dream, the end of his appointments with doctors, and the beginning of an existence with Trina without the nightmare. For years he'd distrusted the medical profession and everyone in it, hating every doctor, nurse and hospital. But, because of Trina, he had been hobnobbing with them, telling medical people who wanted to listen, everything about his medical history. More than once since his first appointment with

Doctor Dayton, he had thought of his visits with the psychiatrist as going to confession. A good parallel. He had agreed to tell everything he'd ever done that might trigger a stupid nightmare. In the confessional, one was supposed to tell the priest everything that had been done that might be construed as a sin or wrongdoing.

Confess. He recalled the last time he had gone to confession right before leaving for Christmas vacation his second year at Morris College. He had felt if his sins were confessed before the break began, he would not have to worry about doing it once he reached his home and could devote his full attention to his bedridden mother.

Squirming in the chair, Jon remembered the incident as having been awkward. He had made love with one of the girls from Clearmont, a college for women, a few miles from Morris. For several days he had wrestled with the problem of confessing the "sin" and still had no idea how to say it to a priest in the confines of a confessional.

"Bless me, Father. I fucked a girl who is not my wife. No, I'm not married."

"Bless me, Father. I screwed a girl—"

"Bless me, Father. I was intimate with a young lady."

He had decided on the last choice and promptly wondered about the priest's intentions when he asked Jon to go into a detailed account of the incident. What difference? It had been the last time he had gone to confession.

But now, he would be going to confession again. Except this time it would not be to a priest but to a doctor—while he was hypnotized—without control over what he would say in an open room. Could he go through with it? He would for Trina, if for no other reason.

"Doctor Dayton will see you now, Mr. Ward," Tory said, breaking into his thoughts.

He stood, limping across the room toward the door that led to Dayton's office. Despite his ruminations, he felt no apprehension about meeting with the psychiatrist.

Standing to meet his patient, Sam approached Jon, extending his hand. After exchanging greetings, each took the same chair they had occupied during their initial appointment.

"What did you do to your leg?" Sam asked, once they were seated.

"My leg? Why, nothing," Jon said, surprised by the irrelevant question. "Why?"

The doctor's face skewed into a puzzled frown for a moment. "I thought I detected a limp."

"A limp? Me? I don't think so, Doctor," Jon said, frowning when he saw him make a note on his pad. How could the doctor's mistake, the same one Trina had made the weekend before Jon entered the hospital for the second angiogram, be pertinent to his analysis?

Sam looked up. "As you know, the results of the second test revealed nothing. Consequently, I feel we can safely rule out anything mechanically wrong at this point. There is one thing that does bother me, though."

Jon waited.

"The blood your wife claims to have seen. Do you have any ideas about that?"

He shrugged. He had not really thought much about Trina's raving that blood had been gushing from his head when she opened the door. There had been no stains or evidence to support her seemingly impossible story. Still, Jon had felt she would have sworn to the fact, had anyone suggested she take a vow as to the veracity of her statement.

"I guess I more or less just dismissed it. Maybe I shouldn't have. Is it, what Trina says she saw, possible?"

"Physically, I don't think so. But, in Trina's mind, I'm certain it was as real as anything she's ever seen in her life. Perhaps, during your analysis, evidence will surface that can explain or at least substantiate the reason for such a phenomenon as she claims to have witnessed."

Jon nodded slowly. Could his dream, his nightmare be contagious? No, that was ridiculous. "You don't think Trina's flipping out, do you Doctor?"

"Of course not. It's not uncommon for someone to overreact to a situation wherein a loved one is placed in peril. I'm sure you've heard of people performing super herculean feats of strength in moments of emotional stress. I feel that Trina's situation would more than likely fall into that category. Let's not worry about it for the time being. I met and spoke with her at the hospital and I believe she's perfectly normal."

Jon relaxed, first realizing that he had tensed greatly while discussing Trina and what she had seen that Monday.

"Since I last saw you, have you had problems of any kind? Has the dream recurred? Sam asked.

None whatsoever," Jon said confidently, "and no it hasn't."

"Are you and Trina getting along all right?"

"Absolutely." He wondered why the doctor had asked that question. What did that relationship have to do with understanding his twenty-eight year old dream?

"No small differences of any type?" Sam persisted.

"Well, just one little flap, but that was of no consequence."

"Will you tell me about it?" Sam asked, sitting forward. "Let me turn on the recorder first." He pressed a button on his desk, activating the machine hidden behind louvered doors. Nodding, he indicated Jon should begin.

"I don't think you'll like this, Doctor," he began, smiling impishly.

"Why?"

"It concerns you in a way."

"Go ahead. I have a remarkably strong constitution."

"It happened only a couple of days ago—ah, last Friday, when she returned home from school. I told her I felt like cancelling today's appointment." He hoped he wouldn't embarrass the doctor or himself.

"Why?"

"I felt, and I still feel to a certain extent, I'm wasting my time and Trina's money. I've had the dream off and on for a long time and so far nothing adverse has happened to me. I haven't had the nightmare since April 30th, when I went into the hospital."

He stopped, recalling the continuation of the dream he had had while the angiogram was being administered. Trina knew nothing of it and he was damned certain Doctor Dayton was not going to be told. Now he found it odd that he hadn't given more thought to that strange experience. Mentally promising himself to dwell on it when he had time alone, he suddenly sensed the psychiatrist staring at him.

"Jon?" Sam asked. "Did anything else cause you to think like this?"

"That wasn't the cause of the disagreement, if that's what you want to call it. Trina suggested I should cooperate, that maybe I need a rest of sorts. All right. I'm here cooperating and if you think I should slow down and rest or take it easy for a while, I'm willing to go along with the idea. But the evening after my first appointment with you, she suggested a vacation."

"What's so unusual about that?"

"Well, I asked her where she'd like to go and she said California. But then, she intimated that it was my idea."

"Was it?"

"I remember talking about it but I think she suggested it."

"What happened next?" Sam asked calmly.

"We played ping pong with the idea over the weekend—you did . . . I didn't . . . until she suddenly stopped. I thought I had won. But when I asked if she was angry about it she said, 'I don't want to talk about it anymore. Let's just drop it.' "

"Well," Sam said when he had finished jotting a note, "I don't think we should spend too much time on it now. I thought we would talk a little about dreams before attempting to hypnotize you."

Jon slowly nodded. In a way, he was looking forward to being put in a trance but he still held one or two slight reservations.

"The state of sleep is most intriguing and is currently being studied more than it ever has been in the past," Sam began. "Sort of surprising when you consider man has been going to sleep every day or night since he's been on earth. When we sleep, we actually awaken to another form of existence. We dream. Sometimes as the hero, sometimes as the villain, we create stories against backgrounds of beauty or horror. Regardless of the role we elect to play, we're the authors of our dreams. We call up from our memory banks persons and events we haven't thought of for years. Still, despite all the odd facets of dreams, they are completely real to us while they are being experienced.

"A poet once posed the ambiguity of dreams when he said: 'I dreamt last night I was a butterfly and now I don't know whether I am a man who dreamt he was a butterfly, or perhaps a butterfly who dreams now that he is a man.'"

His expression reflecting the enigmatic puzzle, Jon remained silent.

"Dreams can be either a reflection of past events or a sounding board of things to come," the doctor continued, "but in either case, they will usually be disguised as some meaningless, yet puzzling symbol. One job of a psychiatrist is to help unmask the symbols and reveal their meaning. In dreams, we tend to make ourselves more or less than we actually are in waking life.

"I want you to understand, Jon, simply because your dream is a recurrent one, that it is not particularly unusual."

"It's not?" he asked, surprised. "I thought I was unique. At least I gathered as much from your attitude."

"Let me say this—the fact that you're my patient makes the situation unique. You see, I've never had a patient who's had this problem. Nevertheless, there are many similar cases recorded. Such a dream is usually centered around the main theme in a person's life. More often than not, this theme is the key to understanding the dreamer's neurosis or his personality's most important aspect."

"Which am I?" Jon asked. "A neurotic or a fascinating personality?"

Dayton failed to suppress a smile, sobering immediately. "We don't know yet. And don't let the word neurosis throw you. It simply means a functional nervous disorder. Let me give you an example. A teenage boy with a record of three suicide attempts because of alcoholic parents who fought constantly and beat him a lot; extra-marital affairs by both parents; no food; inappropriate clothing; filthy living conditions and so forth, had the following frequent dream from as early an age as he could recall:

"He dreamed he was on a down escalator but trying to walk up to the next floor. He tried valiantly to make progress and found the only way he could, was to run up faster than the steps moved down. Just as he neared the top and success seemed imminent, someone, he was never certain who, would kick him in the chest and the boy would fall. Before he could regain his balance, he'd find himself at the bottom once more and the process would be repeated over and over."

"Hell," Jon said, "I'm no psychiatrist but I can figure that one out."

"It's painfully obvious when you know the boy's background. His dream remained constant until his problem was solved. Sometimes, in cases like this, there will be subtle changes, making the solution more difficult to attain. Your dream however, seems to be unchanging. I admit I find the symbolic content more than just a bit intriguing. Admittedly, there are complexities and the symbols themselves appear at this time to be highly sophisticated."

"Well," Jon quipped, "if you're going to have

one, it may as well be the best available." He felt the doctor was laying the groundwork for a long period of sessions and wondered how much time and money would ultimately be involved. As long as he did not feel emotionally dependent on the psychiatrist, he'd be able to call a stop to the meetings any time he wanted. For now, he would go along with the idea since he suddenly found his repetitious dream as fascinating as did the doctor.

"I'll add at this point, Jon, that if you can live with the dream, fine. Apparently you've not had any serious complications in your life because of it, and it certainly hasn't prevented you from functioning in a normal manner."

"How long do you think it'll take to uncover the cause of the dream?" Jon asked, rubbing his elbow. His face contorted momentarily from pain before he stopped the impromptu massage.

"Something the matter with your elbow?" Sam asked, his eyes fixed on his patient.

"My elbow?" Jon snorted. First the doctor had been curious about his leg; now, his elbow. "There's nothing the matter with it, Doctor," he said tranquilly. "Why?"

"You were rubbing it quite vigorously just then. You seemed to be in pain," Sam offered in a disconcerting manner, leaning forward in his chair once more.

"My elbow doesn't hurt and I didn't injure my leg," Jon said, his voice tinged with anger. Checking his irritation, he forced a smile wondering what the doctor hoped to accomplish with this type of question.

The psychiatrist studied his note pad momentarily before looking up at Jon again. "You asked about the duration of time we'll spend together. There's no way of telling but I feel by using hypnosis, we'll get to the solution much quicker."

Jon sighed inaudibly.

Standing, Sam walked to the windows, closing the heavy drapes. The room, with its artificial nightlike mood, took on an ominous atmosphere. Shadows lurked in the far corners of the office, hugging the furniture and walls. He turned on a small desk lamp, filling the area with subdued half-light. The psychiatrist adjusted Jon's chair to a forty-five degree angle.

"Just relax, Jon, and listen to my voice," he said unhurriedly. "I'm going to turn on a strobe light and I want you to fix your eyes on some object you can see without turning your head." He flicked a switch and the blinking white light of a strobe rhythmically mixed with the unobtrusive glow of the desk lamp.

Without turning his head, Jon mentally placed the strobe to his right and slightly behind him. He had noticed the fixture when he entered the room, recalling it appeared to be nothing more than a floor lamp with three lights extending from it. His eyes flitted about, seeking an object to concentrate on, as he had been instructed to do. A small statue on a table caught his attention. He studied the delicately

131

formed alabaster figure of a ballerina, pirouetting on one leg, her arms held gracefully to either side.

"I want you to relax," Sam continued in his quiet, steady voice, "and think of yourself as being on a comfortable bed. You're exhausted from a day's hard work and the bed feels very good, very soothing to your tired muscles. You realize how exhausted you actually are and welcome the ease with which you find yourself dropping off to sleep. You may clasp your hands together if you wish."

Jon's hands slowly came together, his fingers interlacing while he continued focusing his attention on the ballerina. As the doctor's voice droned on, he felt his muscles sag until they felt like jelly. Sensing his body's relaxation, he stared at the small statuette intently. Had it moved? Was the figure actually waving her arms up and down? He thought he detected a slight smile on her face and then—she winked. The statue evaporated from his sight.

"Your hands are together, Jon," Sam continued, "but you cannot pull them apart. Would you like to try?"

Jon knotted his flaccid muscles attempting to separate his hands, but found the simple task impossible. He tried several times before stopping.

"How do you feel?"

"Foolish," Jon answered in a flat, monotone voice.

"Explain that," Sam ordered gently. "Why do you feel foolish?"

"I think I'm just humoring you, but I don't want to hurt your feelings." His eyes, although wide open, could not see the ballerina on which they were fixed, or anything else in the room.

Sam stood, moving to his side. He placed a hand over Jon's open eyes, closing them, and returned to his chair. "You can separate your hands now."

Jon effortlessly pulled his hands apart, letting them drop to his lap.

"I want you to remember the words *blue trees*," Sam said softly. "From now on, whenever you hear the words, *blue trees*, you will automatically go into a deep trance. *Blue trees*. Now, Jon, my finger is extremely hot. It is as hot as a poker. My finger *is* a red hot poker."

Reaching across the distance separating him from Jon, he moved his fingertip to within a fraction of an inch of his patient's hand. Wincing at the suggested heat, Jon quickly drew his hand back, rubbing it with the untouched one.

Convinced Jon was in a deep state of hypnosis, the doctor said, "I want you to tell me about your dream, Jon. From the beginning to the point where you normally wake up. Do you understand?"

Nodding stiffly, Jon described the wild, tumultuous cheering, the screams of acclaim, how they grew in volume.

"Where are you, Jon?"

"At a big meeting of some sort—out of doors. There are thousands of people, wild with adulation."

"Do you understand what is being shouted?"

Jon screwed up his face, listening intently. "No! It sounds like *Dee-hah! Dee-hah! Dee-hah!*"

"For whom are they cheering, Jon?"

He didn't answer immediately until a smug grin crossed his mouth. "Me!"

"Why?"

"I'm running now—all alone—alone—by myself."

"Why are you alone all of a sudden?" Dayton asked, making a note of the unanswered question.

"Deserted. My friends have deserted me," Jon said in the same dull tones he had used since entering the somnifacient state. But now his voice cracked emotionally, tears welling beneath his eyelids. "Trust nobody—all alone. Blackness all around me."

"Where are you running, Jon?"

"In a forest. I'll hide in this forest."

"What forest is it? Does it have a name?"

"I don't know. Ohhhh—"

"What's the matter?"

"It's foggy and I fell."

"Are you hurt?"

"No."

"How did you fall?" Sam asked, carefully extracting each detail.

"I fell."

"Did you trip?"

"No, I *was* tripped."

"By whom? There's no one around, is there?"

"No one."

"Then who tripped you?"

"A tree tripped me."

"Don't you mean you tripped over a tree's root?"

"No. The tree *tripped* me."

"How?"

"A root jumped out of the ground and tripped me!"

"That's not possible, is it?"

"I *didn't* fall. The tree tripped me, on purpose," Jon said, marked agitation creeping into each word.

"What's happening now, Jon?"

"Oh, my God!" Jon's voice whispered hoarsely. "The trees!"

"What about the trees?"

"They're turning, changing, into—into people!"

"Trees can't do that, can they, Jon?"

"I know! But these are," he said, his voice trembling. "These are."

"Who are they?"

"Don't know—I don't know! They hate me—they want to kill me!"

"Why? Why do they want to harm you, Jon?"

"I don't know," he moaned.

"Are you certain you don't know?" Dayton asked.

Jon didn't answer but the psychiatrist noted the expression on his patient's face changing slightly from one of fearful concern to one of guilt. Apparently, Jon knew why the people wanted to harm him but was not about to reveal the reason.

"How are they dressed?" Sam asked.

"Dirty clothes—filthy. White and black—maybe gray—with black stripes."

"Tell me about their faces, Jon. Can you describe them?"

"Horrible! Horrible! They're filled with hatred! Loathing! Disgust!" he cried. His own face held firmly in an unmoving mask until white lines formed, cracking deeply into his countenance.

"Where—" Dayton began, but was cut off by Jon.

"What's that?" he asked, his face brightening momentarily as he strained to hear something inaudible to the psychiatrist.

"What is it, Jon?"

"A call."

"From whom?"

"The woman."

"Who is she?"

"I don't know," he said, the same guilty expression crossing his face.

Despite the deep hypnotic state, Jon was somehow managing to evade certain questions.

"Have you ever seen her before?" Sam asked, making a note of the subterfuge.

"Only here—in this place." His expression remained constant.

"Are you certain?" he persisted.

Jon didn't respond, striving instead to place the face of the mysterious woman. After several minutes, he said, "I know her but I can't say her name."

"Try."

"No."

"Why?"

"I DON'T WANT TO," he said loudly. Convulsive sobs suddenly racked his body.

"Leave it, Jon. Relax for a moment. You're very comfortable and happy. Nothing is bothering you now. Are you at ease?"

"Y—yes." His face softening, the lines disappeared.

"When the woman called you, what name did she use? Does she call you by your name?"

His mouth set in a straight line again, Jon remained quiet.

Waiting for several minutes to see if his patient would speak, Sam watched Jon's face with renewed interest during the silence imposed by his refusal to answer. Now his features alternately contorted and relaxed as though Jon were struggling with the decision to answer. When the muscles slackened, Sam felt he was about to answer only to have the grimace heave the facial structure into vivid motion again.

"Can you tell me why the people want her dead?" the doctor asked after consulting his notes. He was moving the dream further along without waiting for Jon to relate the incident.

"They hate her, too."

"Too?"

"They hate me."

"Why do they hate both of you?"

Jon paused as if searching for the reason. When he continued, he spoke tentatively. "She is associated with me."

"What have you done?"

Again, the facial contortions told the doctor of his struggle to answer.

Jon brought his right hand up in front of him, clenching an imaginary pistol that he pointed toward the ballerina. He contracted the index finger against the non-existent trigger several times. He began weeping. "She's dead."

"Did you kill her, Jon?"

He sobbed. "No. I don't think so."

"Why did she die if you didn't shoot her?"

"Something else killed her."

"What killed her?"

No answer. Instead, he brought his right hand up toward his own temple.

"Why do you want to kill yourself?"

"I must. I cannot be taken prisoner."

"Prisoner of whom—?"

"They're burning up," Jon said hollowly, lowering his hand. "Burning all up!"

"Do you know why they're burning, Jon?"

Jon's face agonizingly twisted in an attempt to answer, his mouth remaining a clamped, slash of white lips. The struggle within him subsiding, he again brought his hand, formed as though holding a pistol, up to his temple and pulled the dream weapon's trigger.

Jon screamed long and loud.

"I'm going to bring you out of the hypnotic state now, Jon," Dayton said firmly. "Remember, when you hear *blue trees* the next time, you will quickly go into a state of hypnosis. When I touch your shoulder with my hand, you will awaken, refreshed and relaxed. You will have no memory of what we talked about." He stood, approaching Jon, his hand outstretched to touch him lightly on the shoulder.

Before the psychiatrist made contact, Jon continued speaking. "I'm floating up—up. I feel concussions. Explosions—"

Sam could not stop his hand when Jon continued speaking, and unable to check his motion, came in contact with his patient, breaking the hypnosis.

Jon opened his eyes, smiling up at the psychiatrist. "I don't think it'll work, Doctor."

"You're a very good subject, Jon," Sam said, going to the window where he drew the curtains back. Both blinked at the sudden brightness.

"You mean—?" Jon asked and stopped.

"You went into a hypnotic state very easily. Look at your watch if you don't believe me. What time was your appointment?" Sam asked, crossing the room to the tape recorder.

"Three," Jon said, looking at his watch with disbelief. "It's—it's almost four-fifteen." Bewildered, he shook his head.

Moving to his desk, Sam jotted down several items in his notebook.

"What did I say, Doctor? What's causing the nightmare? What—"

"Wait a minute, Jon," he said, holding his hand up to silence his patient. "Granted, I said hypnosis would help shorten the span of time needed to analyze your dream, but don't expect a one-shot miracle. I'll need time to go over the tape we made while you were under and get some direction as to how to conduct our next session. At this point, I know very little in addition to what we both knew before you were hypnotized."

"But you do know something?" Jon asked excitedly.

"As I said, very little. One or two minor points came out but didn't necessarily clear up anything. They'll give us a little more material to work with, that's all."

"Such as?"

"I'm afraid our time is up, Jon. However, I'll visit with you, if necessary, about today's trance the next time you're in."

Jon stood, discovering he felt rested.

"How do you feel?" Sam asked.

"Surprisingly," he answered, moving his shoulders, "very good. I feel as though I've had a long nap. Is that normal?"

"Absolutely. That should be your reaction each time."

"Fantastic! I think I'm going to look forward to these sessions if this is any indication as to how I'll feel," Jon said walking toward the door.

"Make an appointment with Tory for next week. I'll see you then, Jon."

After making an appointment for the same time on Tuesday of the following week because of the Memorial Day observance, Jon light-heartedly rode the elevator to the ground level. Tomorrow, he'd be able to write without any trouble.

After Jon left his office, Sam went to the tape recorder to replay the last few minutes of the session. The high pitched babble of voices filled the room momentarily before stopping the machine. He restarted it.

They're burning up, Jon's voice said. *Burning all up!*

Do you know why they're burning, Jon? he asked. The silence following the question seemed interminable until it was punctuated by Jon's high pitched shriek.

Sam listened to himself giving the instructions to bring Jon out of hypnosis. The psychiatrist recalled approaching him to touch his shoulder and then: *I'm floating up—up,* Jon's voice said clearly, strongly. *I feel concussions. Explosions—*

Sam shut off the machine, a concerned look crossing his face. Jon's dream apparently continued and by awakening him, he had inadvertently stopped his patient from revealing this new aspect. The next session would have to begin where this one had stopped. Maybe then, the thread leading to an answer would be found. He wondered if Jon knew of any additional details which belonged to the dream. Would his patient hold back information for some reason?

He turned on the recorder once more to rewind the tape and then moved to his desk, retrieving his notebook. His reminders were not too plentiful. He had found the answers to his questions fascinating and had written only terse remarks about incidents that had bothered him at the time. Why hadn't Jon answered the question concerning the reason for his being cheered? He wondered if his patient knew the answer.

Sam frowned deeply at the next written passages: *Patient is able to resist answering questions. Not all, just some. Thirty-one minutes into hypnotic state: Again refuses to answer. Thirty-five minutes into hypnotic state: Third time he refused. Thirty-nine minutes: Is he lying? How can he refuse to obey simple commands? Fourth time: forty-four minutes, appears as if he wants to tell me the answer but for some reason he cannot obey.*

After Tory transcribed the session, he would play back the tape, focusing on the questions at the different times he had noted. Perhaps Jon had merely misunderstood the questions.

When the tape was rewound, he removed it from the recorder, placing a new reel on the machine. Since Jon had been the last patient for the day, he was looking forward to a martini and a quiet evening at home. Maybe he'd give Marie a call. Turning out the lights he went to the outer office.

Tory looked up without smiling. "Calling it a day, Doctor?"

"Yes, I am," he said, handing her the tape. "After you transcribe this one, I don't want you to erase it. Label it and put it on the shelf in my office. Good night, Tory."

She wondered if she should ask Doctor Dayton for the rest of the afternoon off. The last thing Howie had done before she left for work that morning, was to order her home immediately. Knowing he was anxious to read any files purloined that day, she thought it would be a pleasant surprise to arrive home half-an-hour early. Tory opened her mouth to speak, suddenly deciding against it. Why ask for something that might possibly arouse Dayton's suspicions? What if she inadvertently revealed something of their plan? Howie would be furious.

She turned the reel over in her hand. Was there something special about this tape? Only cases out of the ordinary were not erased. Once transcribed on paper those tapes were kept intact in the doctor's office.

"Good night, Doctor," Tory said softly as the door closed. She stared at the reel he had given her. She'd have to pay particular attention to it. The digital clock on her desk showed four-thirty-five. Deciding not to waste time, she removed the tape she had been transcribing. She threaded Jon's onto the machine, pressed a button, and sat back.

CHAPTER 7

"It was absolutely fantastic, Trina," Jon said, describing the sensation of being hypnotized. "I felt like a million bucks when I came to. At first I thought only a few seconds had passed but I knew differently when I looked at my watch."

"I'm glad to hear you like the treatment," Trina said, smiling to herself. Ever since Jon had arrived home he had raved about his appointment. She looked at the remaining tests to be graded.

"You know, I think for the first time in my life, I'm going to find out what the hell this goddamn dream is all about."

"I'm happy for you, darling." She closed the folder. If they weren't ready tonight, she'd finish them in the morning at school before class.

Locking his fingers behind his head, he leaned back. "I can't help talking about it. I feel positively exhilarated."

"When's your next appointment?"

"Week from tomorrow. Next Monday is an off-day for you, my dear. Memorial Day."

"I forgot," she squealed. "Let's do something."

"Like?"

"Anything." She left the couch, moving to sit on the arm of his chair.

"Okay. Let's go someplace."

She looked askance at her husband. Would this be another instance of forgetfulness when and if the idea were mentioned later?

He caught the mistrustful expression. "Hey, come on," he reprimanded. "It'll give us an opportunity to practice for that vacation."

"You're serious?"

"Absolutely. This time, I promise, I'll remember. Where do you want to go?"

Her lips puckered in thought for several moments before a wide grin dazzled her face. "Galena!" she cried.

"Galena? You've got to be kidding."

"Seriously. Marilyn Frazer, one of the teacher assistants at school, told me about it. It sounds like heaven."

"Or a step back in time," he added.

He knew Galena well. Since it was less than thirty miles from Morris College, he had passed through the old town on every trip between home and school. "What's there that's such a turn-on?'"

"Antique shops by the score and a delightful old mansion where we could stay. It has a great restaurant, too. Ahhh, I think Mumman's Manor is the name of it. I'll ask Marilyn tomorrow, to be certain." She smiled gleefully, clapping her hands in anticipation. Then she sobered. "You do feel up to a trip, don't you, darling?"

"Oh, for—of course I do. There's nothing wrong with me. I'm fine." He sat forward in his chair, a touch of disgust flashing for a second across his face.

She instantly regretted her question but saw him brighten, which told her everything was normal, or as near normal as she could hope for. "I'll check the name of the place tomorrow and we can call ahead for reservations."

Jon leisurely settled back in his chair again. Anticipating an enjoyable long weekend out of the city matched his buoyant mood. Nothing could possibly interfere with his life now. He had everything under control.

While thoughts of Howie's fury over an accidental disclosure of their plans persistently bothered her, Tory forced herself to concentrate on Sam Dayton's explanation of dreams. Would this Jon Ward be a suitable candidate for their scheme? Would he disclose something to the psychiatrist that might be right for Howie's plan? Some embarrassing incident for which the patient's wife would be willing to pay a large amount of money to Howie for his silence on the subject?

When the psychiatrist began hypnotizing Jon, she listened closely, no longer thinking of any possible mistake on her part or the resulting retaliation from her lover. Once Jon began

147

answering the doctor's questions, she recalled the dream sequence she had typed following his initial visit. Each question and answer issuing from the machine refreshed her recollection of the previous session.

Unaware of the time, she listened to the entire tape, shaking her head in disbelief at the peculiar descriptions. When it finished, she went to the bank of file cabinets, quickly finding Jon's folder. She withdrew the several sheets of paper it contained, crossing the room to the copy machine. She'd need everything she could get since last week's patients had given them nothing. If only the transcriptions she made were not put on microfilm, she would be able to copy anything she wanted. But, since she could not devise a system to make such records for Howie and herself without arousing suspicions, she would have to be content with Jon's file. There had been nothing else of consequence today, other than the new patient. Tomorrow, Mrs. Nelumbo would be in for her appointment.

Turning off the copier, she stuffed the papers into the brown manilla envelope before returning the originals to the file. After locking the drawers, she straightened the top of her desk and left.

Once out of the office building, she hurried along the streets clutching the precious envelope to her breasts. Gradually, she felt pangs of fear eating at her like a cancer. Howie would be furious—she just knew he would. She was late. It would be well past six-thirty by the time she arrived home. Would she be able to calm him if he were upset? All he wanted was the chance to leave the Midwest for Santa Fe or someplace in the Southwest. There, they could be happy. She knew if they failed, it would be her fault. Reaching the old building where he waited, she sniffled, tears welling in her eyes. It would be awful.

She ran up the stairs two at a time. In seconds she stood on the fourth floor heaving for air. Her legs trembling, she slowly made her way down the darkened hallway toward her apartment where she could see light seeping from beneath the door. Hesitantly turning the knob, she had it ripped out of her hand when Howie roughly pulled the door open.

"Where the hell you been?" he demanded. "Did you get anything today?"

"Howie?" she said in a tiny voice.

Glaring, he leaped foward, punching her in the stomach as hard as he could. She tried desperately to breathe, managing only to inhale spasmodic gasps of air. The glaring light bulb hanging from the ceiling spun around in a circle, changing color as she sank to the floor in a heap.

Sam Dayton absently swished the olive around in his half-finished martini. Normally, he had no problem leaving his work at the office but for some reason he found it impossible to dismiss Jon Ward's dream from his mind. Jon had continued referring to impressions he witnessed after the scream, something he apparently had never done before, to the best of Sam's knowledge.

Emptying the glass, he filled it again, raising it in a toasting gesture to the lavishly decorated apartment. Tasting his drink, he nodded his satisfaction and walked slowly across the room toward sliding glass doors which opened onto a small balcony. A little night air would be a good chaser for the martinis he'd already drunk, and the one he'd finished now before eating. He closed the doors behind him, inhaling deeply. He took several deep breaths of the cleaner than usual air.

If the dream did not finish at the scream, what else followed? Had it ever occurred before? And if it had, why had Jon neglected to mention it? Did he even know of it?

"I think," Sam said loud, "I shall call Marie and confer with her. I also should not talk aloud to myself." He grinned foolishly, looking about. Even though several other tenants were enjoying the balmy spring evening on nearby terraces none were within earshot. Reentering the living room, he turned on the stereo, adjusting the volume to gently flood the apartment with soft music.

Marie crossed his mind again. Marie Von Keltzer. An eminent associate in his field, he had called on her as a confidante on more than one occasion. The fact that she was a brilliant psychiatrist had reassured him when he found himself falling in love with her. At thirty-eight, he had decided he'd never find the perfect woman—one who could share his profession, his lifestyle, and still be able to fill the role of wife and lover. He found Marie capable of fulfilling the requirements of the perfect mate he had set down as a young, ambitious psychiatrist. As thorough as his perusal had been, he had been totally unprepared when she subjected him to much the same scutiny.

His frustrated emotions reacting, he realized his desire to consult her on a professional basis outweighed the prospects of a social evening. They seldom mixed business with pleasure, but tonight he felt he should talk with her about his new patient.

Picking up the telephone, he dialed her unlisted number, listening to the buzzing ring six times before she answered. "Marie? Sam."

"Hi," she said, her throaty contralto dangerously titillating his senses beyond his three martini level of resistance.

"What took you so long to answer? With a patient?" his liquor-softened voice teased gently.

"Naturally. In the shower, no less."

"Sounds like interesting therapy. Busy tonight?" He didn't really have to ask. They had reached the point of advising each other of any activities that did not include them as a couple.

"You know I'm not. What do you have in mind, Sam?"

"I've already had three martinis and dinner's just about ready—for one, unfortunately. However, I'd like to get together to discuss a patient I'm just starting into therapy. Want to visit? Maybe have a few drinks?"

"I thought maybe you had some ulterior motive in mind. Would you care if I came dressed for work? You never know, we might exhaust your patient's case in record time and have nothing left to talk about."

"Bring a bag. In fact, why not move in tonight? You know—"

"I will, when I'm ready, Sam. See you in an hour. *Ciao!*"

Staring at the quiet receiver in his hand, he smiled before returning it to its cradle.

Tory's period, due the next day, had been precipitated by the vicious fist Howie had unleashed to her lower abdomen. Now, she lay on the open Murphy bed clutching her stomach, still aching several hours after the blow had been delivered. God, it hurt. She hoped nothing was injured. Having slept fitfully after wiping the bloody discharge from the threadbare rug, she was horrified to find the pain still present. She opened her eyes and could see Howie sitting on the backless chair hunched over, holding his head.

"Ho-Howie?" she managed through clenched teeth, the pain increasing when she attempted to sit up.

"Are you all right?" he asked, hurrying to her side.

"Fi-fine. You shouldn't have done that," she said, sitting up with his help.

"I know. I feel like—like—I don't know what.

You're going to screw this whole operation up if you do something to yourself and can't work," he said, passing over the opportunity to apologize.

"I'll be all right, I guess. What time is it?"

He turned, looking at her watch on the all-purpose table. "Eight-thirty."

She got to her feet, finding the pain, which tore at her midsection, not as great when she stood upright. Perhaps her muscles had become cramped from inactivity for the hour and a half she had slept. "S'funny," she said, "I feel fine now that I'm standing."

"Why were you so late?"

"I stayed and listened to the last patient's tape."

"Oh. Was it a good one? Anything we can use?"

"I don't know yet," she said approaching him. "They've got money, but the first two tapes didn't really offer anything. I—I love you, Howie."

He accepted her embrace before pushing her away.

"Mrs. Nelumbo has an appointment tomorrow," she said softly, tantalizing him with a seductive smile.

"That one should be money in the bank." His mood suddenly changed. "Can you get into the office anytime you want?"

"Hey, yeah! I've got my key. Why couldn't we just go down at night and help ourselves, Howie?"

"Because, you dumb bitch, that's running the

risk of getting arrested for unlawful entry," he snarled. "I was just curious in the event Dayton ever caught on, or was told by one of his patients about being blackmailed. It might not look so good for you if it appears to be an inside job." He flashed his teeth in a cruel smile.

"I never thought of that. Maybe we shouldn't go through with it, Howie."

"Don't worry, babe," he said smoothly. "Lots of people got keys to those offices; cleaning ladies, janitors, watchmen."

Tory thoughtfully nodded. Why hadn't she thought of that?

Sam and Marie lay side by side, their naked bodies barely touching. His eyes unblinkingly stared at the ceiling while Marie had hers closed, her long lashes resting against the lower lid. Their lovemaking always satisfied them and tonight had been no exception. Shortly after her arrival, he had told her everything he knew about Jon Ward and his peculiar dream. She found it interesting but hadn't given it her full attention until after they'd made love. Now, with her afterglow diminishing, she mentally reviewed the strange case he had outlined.

"You know, Sam," she began after several long minutes of silence, "the fact that his dream never varies is one interesting aspect of his case. But, and I find this the most intriguing part, the symbols are almost movielike in the way you described them."

"Not my way," he said without taking his eyes from the ceiling. "Jon's way. He's so absolutely precise in his descriptions that it makes one wonder."

"Wonder about what? The fact that he's a writer and might be embellishing the actual scenes to make them fit his conscious interpretation of the dream?"

He thought about her statement. The idea had passed through his mind several different times while pondering the dream since he had first heard it described by Jon three weeks earlier. But the Vienna-trained psychiatrist lying next to him voiced the question after hearing the dream content only once. "The same thought occurred to me but after today's session, I don't think that's the case. He answered just about every question I put to him. While in the hypnotic state, his statements told me the dream was exactly the same as he had described to me before."

"What do you mean—just about every question?" she asked, sitting up on the bed.

"It was really peculiar. There were several questions he absolutely refused to answer."

"Under hypnosis? Impossible!" she said intently.

"Really, Marie. I'm not fooling. He absolutely refused—didn't speak. I think—I *know* he was going through a mental struggle. One part of him wanted to answer but something prevented him from doing so."

Marie bemusedly stroked her left breast, studying him. "Do you think he might have two personalities?" she asked slowly.

He quickly sat up next to her. "I—I never

once thought of that. Not at this point, at least. It's too early in the analysis to even consider that. Still—"

"What? What is it, Sam?" Her voice showed real interest.

"His wife told me about a total change of personality Jon went through one evening because of a bottle of wine."

"What happened?"

"I don't recall all of the details but, and this is the important part, she was very upset by it. She said he was totally different; his views, opinions and things he said, were completely out of character for him. Even his voice sounded different, according to her. Another intriguing thing she mentioned was his occasional limp. I noticed it the first time I met him but didn't think anything of it."

"Do you have in your notes what he said when he changed?"

"Not word for word but the subject matter is there."

"I should like to see it," she said, her words no longer reflecting interest in her personal, physical satisfaction. A cool, professional tone had replaced the throaty, beckoning voice of Marie, the woman.

"Multiple personalities?" he pondered aloud. "Could that be possible?"

"Why do you say multiple? It's bad enough having a patient display two. What makes you think there might be more?"

"Nothing. Still, every case history I've read

where there were two strong personalities fighting for possessing of one body, there usually were more, minor personalities looking for release." He got off the bed slipping into his robe.

"And usually the subjects are women," she reminded him.

"It's not impossible for a man."

"Of course not," she said, standing. "Still, men are definitely in the minority when it comes to evidence of dual or multiple personalities."

"I know. Want to shower?"

"If we can continue talking about this Jon Ward. I find him and his dream fascinating," she said, following him toward the bathroom.

"Want to stay the night?" he asked, adjusting the temperature of water in the shower.

"Naturally," she purred, casting aside her professional aplomb. She stepped into the shower, focusing her thoughts on Jon's dream once more. Something vaguely familiar about the hightlights persistently eluded her probing. She'd want to read Sam's file and listen to the tape of the hypnotic session. Maybe then, it would come to her.

Trina and Jon sat across from each other at a small table in the basement restaurant of Mumman Manor. They had spent a relaxing Saturday and Sunday browsing through the antique shops lining both sides of Galena's Main Street. Other, more elaborate shops, set up in nineteenth century mansions, had been scoured for relics which would appeal to both of them. Tired but happy, the couple finished their meal.

"The prime rib was delicious, darling," Trina murmured contentedly.

Jon raised his glass of Beaujolais. "I propose a toast. To us; may we always be as happy with each other as we are right now."

She lifted her glass, sipping to the proposed pledge of never-ending love. Lifting the bottle, he attempted to pour more but she stayed his hand.

"Let's take it up to our room and toast each other there," she whispered, a tiny smile playing at the corners of her mouth.

Nodding, he winked. He motioned for their waitress, and stood as the string group playing melodies in lush, rich tones, began the familiar strains of Strauss' *Voices of Spring*. After signing the bill, he caught up to his wife.

"This is so unique," she said as they left the vaultlike room. "I could do this every night. It's so—so—"

"Continental?" he offered.

"Yes, continental."

"Well, let's go upstairs and do it the continental way," he quipped.

"The continental way? How do—?" She paused, turning to face her husband.

"You have a cup of coffee with your roll," he explained lightly.

She laughed, continuing up the narrow stairs with Jon following closely. Once on the main floor, they made their way side by side to the wide staircase leading to the second story where they had spent the last two nights. It had been her idea to leave Chicago Friday afternoon when she got home from school, which enabled them to have all day Saturday as well as Sunday to roam through the quaint old town. Jon suggested an early departure Monday morning to avoid the holiday traffic they knew would begin building shortly after noon. If they were lucky, they would arrive home by midday.

When they stood outside their room, Jon scooped Trina in his arms. Once inside, he laid her on the antique bed and began unbuttoning his shirt.

"Don't I get a chance to undress?" she asked.

"Of course. Be my guest," he said gallantly, bowing deeply.

When Trina stood nude, Jon enveloped her in his embrace. Their tongues gently probed each other's mouth, hands tenderly massaging muscles tensed in anticipation. Lowering his wife to the bed, he covered her full lips with his mouth, tracing a route of kisses down her chin, throat and shoulders. Her nipples stood erect, aroused to their fullest by his love making. His lips slid to the center of her chest, touching first one mound of flesh and then the other before exploring the brown aureoles of her breasts. He bit teasingly while running his free hand down her stomach, gently kneading her lower body, until his fingers intertwined with her pubic hair.

She arched her back, feeling the tingling burn of passion rising within her loins. Groping for his hardened manhood, she gripped it carefully yet savagely, sending a wave of pleasure through her husband's body. Grasping his head, she brought it back to her shoulder and then, their faces touching in another deep kiss, he penetrated her. She moaned softly while the tenderness of his rhythm built to a gentle frenzy.

They climaxed simultaneously and clung to each other until their passion ebbed.

Later, several hours after falling asleep, the nightmare happened for the first time since Jon's discharge from the hospital. Vividly, each detail presented itself in sequence. Raising the gun to his head, Jon opened his mouth but his face was pushed into the pillow, muffling his suicidal scream.

Trina breathed deeply, lying on her back, completely oblivious of his cry.

He dreamed of floating, of being buffeted, of being drawn to the personality exuding lust and violent sex. Slowly, he rose to a kneeling position on the bed, straddling his wife's naked body. His hands groped at his bare waist, seeking the belt that held torn, tattered pants. Satisfied that he had dropped the trousers, his frame suddenly grew rigid, every muscle contracting, knots of hard flesh flexing over his body. Clenching both fists, he raised his blank eyes to the ceiling of the Victorian bed chamber and screamed, "*ICH LEBE NOCH!*"

Trina immediately awoke, stifling the urge to

scream when she saw her husband kneeling over her, his massive erection throbbing, thrust out in front of him, a maniacal look incising his handsome features.

CHAPTER 8

While the relays clicked into place and before
hearing Sam Dayton's office phone ringing,
Trina glanced about the teachers' lounge to be
certain she was alone. She needed isolation to
speak freely. The episode at Mumman Manor
hammered at her mind. All the way from
Galena to Chicago, Jon remained tacit about
the incident. It had given her the opportunity to
review it, to prepare her for the trauma of
telling the psychiatrist. Monday evening had
been equally quiet and they had lain awake for
hours before finally dropping off to sleep. Now,
away from Jon and the suffocating atmosphere
of tragedy and doom that had effectively
engulfed them, she felt the strength and determination to tell everything to Doctor Dayton.
Jon had to be helped—cured, rid of this nightmare once and for all.

"Doctor Dayton's office," the voice broke into
her jumbled thoughts.

"This is Mrs. Jon Ward. May I speak with Doctor Dayton?"

"One moment, Mrs. Ward," Tory mewed.

"Yes, Mrs. Ward." Sam's voice sent a wave of reassurance coursing through Trina. Suddenly, she felt foolish. Should she tell him of the peculiar thing that had happened in Galena? Of course she should tell him. She wanted Jon free of this—this thing.

"Doctor?" she said, "Do you have time to speak with me now?" She looked at her watch. Not quite nine-thirty.

"Yes, I believe I have time. What can I do for you?"

Quickly relating the bare facts of how she and Jon had gone to Galena and Mumman Manor, Trina reached the moment in her narrative she dreaded.

"Everything had been perfect," she said quietly with marked determination, "until Sunday evening. We finished eating and went to our room." She hesitated. Did she dare tell him about their lovemaking? Why not? He dealt with this sort of thing all the time and she feared the consequences if she left a single detail out. "We made love and after a while went to sleep."

"Just a moment, Mrs. Ward," Sam interrupted. "I'd like to record the rest of our conversation if you have no objections."

Her mind raced. "Would you ever play it for my husband?" she asked, summing up her apprehension.

"Of course not. It's merely to assure me that I have an accurate account of whatever it is you're going to tell me."

"I see," she said, slowly regaining her composure. With an evenly spaced "ping" sounding every few seconds, she continued at his request. "About four o'clock Monday morning I awoke, or rather, I should say was awakened by Jon screaming at the top of his voice. When I opened my eyes, he was kneeling over me, a—a—aroused to the fullest. His erection, his penis, seemed larger than I've ever seen it. And he had the most frightening expression on his face."

Sam waited to see if she would continue. When it became apparent she was soliciting a question with her silence, he asked, "Can you describe his face, the expression he was displaying?"

She closed her eyes, the awful scene smashing into clear perspective once more. She related how in the gloom, Jon's tumid face had appeared to be creased with countless worry lines, his breath pumping in short gasps. Once wide awake, she had screamed, realizing he had been trying to rape her while both were sound asleep. His trancelike manner frightened her more than the appearance of his exceptionally swollen penis or his dominant position over her.

When her cry did not awaken him, she tried rolling away but found normal escape impossible with his legs straddling her body. Wiggling, she worked her way into an upright position. Face to face with the man she adored, she slapped him hard on the left cheek. His head popped to the right from the force of her blow. The slap brought no response, his facial expression remaining set when he turned to stare at her again with unseeing eyes. When he lowered himself to enter Trina, who had moved without his awareness, she jumped up on the bed, then lightly bounded to the floor.

She listened intently for a moment to see if their cries had been heard by anyone. There had been only two other couples staying at the Manor and, if she recalled correctly, both were on the third floor. Hearing nothing in the hall, she turned her attention back to her husband. Writhing on the bed, his buttocks pumped up and down in a sexual frenzy.

Gasping, she rushed to the bedside. How could she awaken him? She had struck him harder than she had intended but it had had no effect. Jon stopped his movement, lying motionless for a moment. Then, slowly at first, he began throwing one arm after the other toward the headboard, scissoring his feet up and down in swimming motions. Gradually, his efforts intensified, the movement increasing rapidly until the whole bed shook.

Transfixed, Trina could not tear her eyes away. She watched him draw his legs up until his knees touched his chin, a pleasant smile crossing his mouth when he tightly wrapped his arms about his legs. Low groans rumbling deeply within his chest, he lay motionless on the disheveled bed. Her immobility snapped when she heard the moans.

Hurling herself across him, she pounded on him, calling his name over and over. Jon suddenly grew rigid, freezing in position. Then his body slumped, the dream sequence ended.

Trina completed her narration. "It was simply awful, Doctor. And when I specifically questioned him about it, he didn't remember a thing. He plainly said 'Remember? Remember what?'

"Then, I made the mistake of telling him what had happened from the time I had been awakened," Trina said softly into the mouthpiece. Her eyes moist, she fought a sob persistently rising in her throat.

"I find it very interesting to say the least." Sam spoke slowly, deliberately. "Did he seem to recall any of the dream he was apparently experiencing as you described his actions?"

"I think he did. The more I told him, the more troubled his face became, the more quiet he grew. By the time we left for Chicago yesterday morning, he ignored my questions and statements as though I weren't even there."

"Do you know if he dreamt *his* dream, the one he's told us about, prior to this incident?"

"I think he must have," she said after several seconds. "I noticed him rubbing his head shortly after he awoke. He must have had the nightmare and was suffering from a headache."

"You did exactly right by calling me, Mrs. Ward," Sam said.

Breathing a sigh of relief, she dabbed at her eyes. She had been unsure about interfering with Jon's therapy since she had received no such assurance after talking with Sam about the wine incident. But now she felt relieved because she had told the doctor. Mental anguish would have gone hand in hand with her decision if she had chosen to keep the information to herself. "You won't tell Jon, will you, Doctor?" she said, suddenly concerned her husband would in some way find out.

"Rest easy about that, Mrs. Ward. Jon'll have to tell me about this episode himself. Were I to tell him about this conversation, he'd lose all confidence in me as his analyst. It's absolutely confidential."

"Do you want me to report anything out of the ordinary?"

He paused for a moment. "I'd like to ask you if you felt your argument with Jon about vacation plans was out of the ordinary?"

She thought back to the week before they went to Galena. "I didn't think too much about it. Why? Did Jon tell you?"

"Yes, he did. At any rate, thank you for the information, Mrs. Ward. Do feel free to call me anytime regarding Jon."

"Thank you, Doctor. Will he be all right?"

"We'll be finding the right track to run on soon," he said. "Goodbye, Mrs. Ward."

She placed the phone in its cradle just as several teachers, entering the lounge for their coffee break, interrupted her train of thought.

Sam broke the connection placing his finger on the cradle bar and immediately releasing it.

Dialing Marie's private office number, he waited only seconds before he heard her say, "Doctor Von Keltzer speaking."

"Marie? Sam," he said, wondering why he always indentified himself to her. She knew his voice as well as he knew hers. Could it be he considered her above him in some way because of her educational background? Did he subconsciously feel it necessary to name himself when he was about to speak to her?

"Yes, Sam," she said, her voice changing ever so slightly from its professional timbre to one of something more than friendship.

"I just had the most peculiar call from Jon Ward's wife," he began, quickly relating everything Trina had told him.

"The attempted rape, if that's what it was," she said when he finished, "is interesting to say the least. So far the dream has been pure symbolism. This desire or need to act the dream out is, I believe, more than symbolic. I could be wrong, but you might want to view it in that manner when working with him."

"I was thinking along the same lines," he agreed.

"However, I find the fetal position he assumed after the rape utterly fascinating. Do you have any ideas about it at this point, Sam?"

"It could be a desire to return to the womb or, and this is part of that desire, a unique Oedipus complex."

"I never thought of the Oedipus," she said slowly.

Sam paused. Did she think he might be going

off in the wrong direction? At this point, couldn't anything be possible?

"You're not certain if this experience your patient had is part of the dream you know about. Or are you?"

"I know this much. He was about to experience something after the dream's normal end during our first hypnotic session. I intend to begin his session today at that point."

"Be careful, Sam," Marie admonished.

"Of?"

"Of hypnotizing him. This is more than just an ordinary attempt to gather information or insight into his problem. If he's acting out the dream as he experiences it, you must provide absolute safeguards while he is being allowed to recall it. Have him relax to the ultimate as he speaks. Don't let him become overwrought by anything he may recall during the session."

"I understand, Marie," he said humbly. He knew what had to be done, appreciating the cautious advice she offered. However, if he did understand the significance, why did he feel so damned self-conscious about accepting her counsel?

"Call me tonight and tell me what happened?"

"Why not come over for dinner?"

"What time?"

"Seven?"

"Sounds fine. *Ciao.*"

Sam replaced the phone. Crossing the room to the shelves, he found the tape he had requested his secretary to place in the tape file after transcribing it. Quickly threading it to the console, he turned the machine on. Listening to the dream sequence unfold, he picked up the phone to check his schedule of patients with Tory. Jon was the last one at three o'clock. If he needed more time, he would be able to take it.

Tory's fingers flew over the electric typewriter keys as she typed one of the earlier patients' sessions. Every once in a while she would stop, peering about the room. Although no one was waiting to see Doctor Dayton, she reveled in the knowledge that his patients would prove to be her ticket to happiness with Howie. Carole Nelumbo had been in for her weekly visit and soon their plan would be in full operation.

Looking up when the door opened, she saw Jon enter the waiting room. She looked again to make certain it was the same man who had been there in the past. His ashen complexion accentuated the puffed circles below his eyes.

"Good afternoon, Mr. Ward," she said cheerily, and blanched. She had moved too quickly, sending a familiar though diminished pain through her abdomen. The aftereffects of Howie's rashness only bothered her if she remained in one position too long or moved too quickly.

Picking up the phone to announce Jon, she again noted his tired expression, his worn out attitude. "You can go in, Mr. Ward," she said returning to her work. She'd be interested in hearing his recording later.

Jon opened the door, entering the inner office where he found the psychiatrist closing the louvered doors to the recorder.

"Sit down, Jon. I'll be with you in a moment," he said. Crossing the room, the doctor took his position opposite his patient. "How have you been since we visited last?"

"Question, Doctor," Jon began. "Is confession good for the soul, as they say?"

"In certain cases, where a third party won't be injured, I'm certain it is. Why?" He ignored Jon's haggard appearance, thankful that Trina had called him that morning.

"Well, I'm about ready to confess something to you," he said. Jon slowly told of his experience in the hospital while on the table during the angiogram, and then about the repetition of it at Mumman Manor.

Sam could fully understand Trina's fright as Jon related the different aspects of the dream's continuation. Now he felt almost certain the two parts were related, not separate as he had thought they might be. He could confirm his suspicions once Jon entered hypnosis.

"How did your wife react to this new aspect?"

"Scared the crap out of her, I guess. We didn't talk on the way home from Galena and we were just as out of touch last evening. I just didn't want to talk about it. My God! Trying to rape my own wife in my sleep! Trina must have been scared beyond belief. I'm glad she didn't push for talk 'cause I sure didn't want any."

"What was your reason for keeping the second part of the dream to yourself?"

Jon stared at the alabaster ballerina, ignoring Sam's look of compassion.

"Do you know, Jon?" he asked.

"At the time it seemed like a good reason. Selfish for the most part, I guess."

"What was the reason?" the psychiatrist persisted.

"Remember, at the time, I was still pretty much against doctors in general and having to be in the hospital again. I don't know if I've changed that much where the two of them are concerned. But I felt then that I was being inconvenienced too damned much. If I told anyone about it, I might have to go through the same thing for a third time. So I made up my mind I'd explore it myself and try to get to know it as well as the other part."

"How do you feel about your reason now?"

"It was stupid."

"How do you feel about your experience in Galena?"

Jon didn't answer immediately, looking away from him to stare at the ceiling. "I'm afraid."

"Afraid? Of what?"

"Of hurting Trina. My God! Suppose instead of rape, my dream concerned murder and I had tried to kill her. Worse yet, what if I succeeded?"

"Do you know the woman you saw lying on the floor of the cave?"

"I—I'm not sure. I think she looks familiar in a weird sort of way as though I should know her. But I can't place her."

"I see. Please sit back and relax now, Jon. Close your eyes and think of yourself resting on a very comfortable bed. You're surrounded by *blue trees*!"

Closing his eyes, Jon slipped into the somnific reverie immediately, sinking back in the chair. Sam stood, quietly crossing the room to close the drapes.

"Jon, I want you to begin by telling me about floating upward after you have raised the gun to your head," the psychiatrist said, taking his seat after turning on the dim desk lamp. Picking up his note pad, he waited for Jon to adjust to the induced state, to find the place where the dream continued.

Jon's face twisted momentarily before relaxing to form a slack mask.

"What is happening, Jon?"

"I'm floating—up—up. I feel so light, weightless."

"What do you see?"

"Nothing. It's completely black, pitch black. I'm all alone again."

"Are you frightened? As frightened as you were when you found yourself running?"

"No. I'm happy. Ecstatic. Free. I'm actually free. But I still live." His voice held the same monotonous tone he had employed in the first session, reflecting none of the emotion his words indicated.

"Do you see anything now?"

"No, nothing. Still blackness all around."

"When you had your dream in the hospital,

what did you see?"

"Floating up, toward the ceiling in the room above the table, I looked down and could see my body. A voice said, 'There's the body I live in.' "

"A voice? What voice?" Sam sat forward, fascinated by the new twist.

His face heaving, Jon attempted to answer.

"Tell me, Jon, what voice you're speaking of. Was it your voice?"

"No."

"Then whose voice was it? Someone in the room? Was it the doctor or one of the assistants?"

"No. It came from within me."

Sam jotted down a note concerning the voice before he continued. "Why were you able to see at that time?"

"I had full control of my faculties then."

"You don't now?"

"No."

"Who does?"

"You do."

Sam paused for a moment, a smile briefly crossing his lips. Having placed himself so securely in the psychiatrist's care, Jon felt an obligation to wait for the order to open his eyes and actually witness the second part of the dream. Perhaps it was nothing more than the power of suggestion but the doctor felt more than satisfied with the degree of control he found himself exercising over his patient. "You may open your eyes now, Jon," he ordered softly.

His lids slowly lifted, his glazed eyes riveting

on the alabaster figurine.

"Now what do you see?"

"I'm moving upward—toward the ceiling—going through the ceiling."

"This ceiling? Are you in this room?"

"No."

"Where are you?"

"I don't know—it's all black again."

"Are you still moving?"

"Yes. Upward."

"I want you to relax even more than you are, Jon. Do you feel comfortable?"

"Yes."

"Are you still moving upward?"

"Yes. It feels wonderful. So free. So absolutely free."

"Is it still black?"

"Yes."

Sam paused. He had a question he wanted to ask but feared the consequences in the event it triggered a negative reaction. If the statements preceding his query were worded to relax the patient, he felt there would be no dire results. "I'm going to ask you a question, Jon, which may sound strange. It will not upset you. You will answer it directly and then forget both the question and the answer. Do you understand?"

Jon nodded.

"Are you dead?" He held his breath, waiting for the answer.

"My body is—but," he began laughing softly, "I still live!" His voice choked with malevolent humor. "I STILL LIVE!" he shouted. When the sound of Jon's voice died down, breathless silence filled the room.

Feeling a chill sweep through his body, Sam tried to swallow. Before the psychiatrist could pose another question, Jon's eyes widened. "What do you see now, Jon?" he asked quickly.

"It's no longer black—I'm floating in space. I'm above a city."

"Tell me what you see. Do you recognize the city? Is it Chicago?"

"I don't know. I don't think so. Ruins all around. No people—just ruins. I—" He stopped, falling to the right side of the chair. Then, as though being pummelled by someone or something, his body hit the opposite side, forcefully striking the armrest.

"Relax, Jon. It's not necessary for you to move about. Relax even more. That's better," Sam said gently. Jon settled back into position in the center of the chair. "Can you tell me what happened?"

"Something struck me. Something invisible. Like a shock wave."

Sam scribbled hurriedly on his notepad. "Going back to before you were hit, if your body is dead, how could you see the city? Can you still see it?"

"My body is not dead. *His* body is dead. I see with my eyes."

"Who's dead?" Sam asked, furiously writing another reminder.

"He is—*the other one*. Rather, his body is dead."

"Does he have a name?"

"I don't know. I don't—know—*him.*"

"Leave it for now, Jon. Don't be disturbed by anyone else's presence. Relax. Let your muscles loosen. Let your entire body go limp. Now, can you describe the shock wave you felt?" The words *other one* were scribbled hurriedly with his notes.

"I sense them more than I feel them."

"Can you describe the sensation?"

"They're like—concussions. Explosions. I see buildings destroyed by explosives . . . or bombs . . . or shells."

"I understand. Can you tell me what's happening now?"

His face began puffing to assume an inflated expression, slowly changing the handsome features until they no longer resembled Jon Ward.

Sam made a note of the time and question he had just asked, enabling him to pinpoint the change in facial expression when replaying the session. "What is it, Jon?"

"I—I don't know. Strange—weird feelings. Very frightened feelings."

"Are *you* frightened?"

"No. Someone else. But I can sense anxiety—fear."

"Like telepathy?"

"I don't know," he said chokingly and jerked forward in the chair.

"Relax, Jon. Don't be upset. You're merely relating something to me and not experiencing it first hand. Do you understand?"

178

"Yes." He eased back in the chair once more.

"What made you sit up like that?"

"I sense another being with the first."

"What do you sense? What do you feel now?"

"Sex drive. Lust. Arousal."

"Yours?"

"No."

"Do you know to whom these feelings belong?"

"I don't know." Jon cringed in the chair, vigorously rubbing his crotch with both hands.

"Relax, Jon, relax. It isn't necessary to relive this particular experience."

His features twitched spasmodically, moving for the first time since his face had swollen.

"What is it Jon? What's happening to you?"

"I'm going to them. I must. I'm being drawn to both of them. Irresistible— Emotions too powerful."

"Just sit back. Ease off. Be calm and tell me what happens."

"I'm going down. It's like being pulled down. I—I'm surrounded by blackness. All around me. I think I'm going to hell. No, wait. Now I can see again."

"Where are you now, Jon?"

"In a big cave. Like a tunnel. Maybe a subway. Those feelings are stronger here."

"What do you see? Do you see anyone?"

"Yes. A man and a woman."

"Who are they? Do you know them?"

"I—I don't know. I—I think the man is in some kind of uniform."

"Do you recognize the uniform?"

"No. It's all torn and shredded. It looks more like rags. The woman is on the floor. I don't believe—I—I recognize her."

"Is she all right? Is she the one who is frightened?"

"She's crying. Her dress is all torn. I can see her flesh."

"Do you recognize her? Do you know her?"

"Her head's turned away. I can't see her face." A puzzled look crossed his enlarged features.

"What is it, Jon? What's the matter?"

"The soldier's personality—too strong. Uncontrollable sex drive. Violent sex. I'm going to him. I'm joining with him."

"Why are you doing that, Jon?" Sam's voice rose sharply.

"I must! I must in order to live!"

"What? Explain that, Jon."

"I MUST IN ORDER TO LIVE!" His voice rasped angrily.

"Take it easy, Jon. You feel very relaxed." Waiting until his patient had settled back, Sam said, "Why do you have to go to them in order to live?"

"I don't know," Jon said weakly as though he had been drained of all strength.

Sam noted the change in voice, wondering if he should continue. "Are you all right?"

"Yes." His voice grew stronger.

"You feel well and relaxed. You are very comfortable. Now, tell me what happens."

A vicious leer swept across Jon's face when he spoke. "Got to fuck her."

The voice no longer sounded like Jon's. Instead of the smooth baritone, the clipped words were spoken in a harsh manner, but not accented. Sam quickly made another note.

Before the doctor could speak again, Jon continued in the strange voice. "Why not fuck her? The war's lost. I'll have fun with this bitch before I'm taken prisoner. I'll take what I can get now. I've suffered enough." Jon stood quickly, unbuckling his pants, and let them drop to the floor around his ankles. Kneeling before the psychiatrist, he slowly lowered himself to the floor.

"Stop, Jon Ward," Sam ordered gently but firmly. "It's not necessary for you to act out the scenes you are witnessing. Do you understand?"

Jon stopped at the mention of his name. "Yes, I understand," he said shakily in his own voice.

"Then, stand up and dress. When you are finished, sit down and lean back. Picture yourself resting beneath a shade tree in the middle of a meadow. You're very comfortable. Birds are singing. A gentle breeze is blowing. Your wife, Trina, is coming toward you. Can you see all of this?" Sam asked once his patient had returned to his chair.

"Yes," Jon whispered when Trina's name was mentioned. Settling back farther into the chair, he smiled while watching the suggested scene unfold, the swelling gradually leaving his face.

"Do you feel well now, Jon?"

"Very well. Trina will be with me in a moment."

"Do you feel well enough to return to the tunnel?"

"Yes," he answered, his voice indifferent again.

"Good. Now just tell me what happens. You don't have to move anymore. Do you understand?"

"I won't move anymore."

"Can you see the woman's face now, Jon?"

"Yes." A hint of anguish overshadowed the neutral tone he had used for the last several exchanges.

"Who is she?" Sam persisted.

"*I want to wake up!*" he cried sharply, sitting up straight.

Sam knew from past experience with patients who had been hypnotized, the sudden desire to wake up, to overcome the control of the hypnotist, indicated the subject did not want to experience an imminent painful recollection. Since Jon had been reexperiencing a dream and not recalling something from his past, the psychiatrist surmised he faced something that would trigger a strong emotional reaction.

"You are *not* going to wake up," he ordered firmly. "You're in a deep sleep and are very comfortable and relaxed. Whatever is going to happen next, will not bother you or cause you unnecessary anxiety. Continue. Everything is very clear and you are willing to describe everything you see."

Jon visibly relaxed, slumping back in the chair.

"Who is she? Who is the woman?"

His head rolled back and forth from side to side, a cry of torment rising in his throat until his plaintive scream filled the office.

"Who is she?" Sam demanded a third time.

"MY MOTHER!" Jon wailed, crying uncontrollably.

Sam, who had been inching forward in his own chair, fell back, staring aghast at his patient. Perhaps he had been on the right track after all with the Oedipus Complex. He quickly readjusted his own thinking, ordering his patient to stop. "Everything's fine Jon, just fine. Rest for a moment."

Looking at his watch, he wondered if he should continue any longer for fear Jon would go into shock. Would he be able to free him from the hypnotic state if that were to occur? Jon had been in hypnosis for sixty-five minutes. How much more of the dream had to be covered? He reflected momentarily on his conversation with Trina earlier in the day. Following the attempted rape, Jon had gone through the swimming motion before he assumed the fetal position. After that, he had been easily awakened by his wife.

Myriad thoughts pounded at Sam. The idea of his patient wishing to be nonexistent crossed his mind. What else could the desire to sexually have his mother represent, but a wish for the warmth and security of her womb as indicated by the fetal position? Could his patient subconsciously not want to exist as a living human? Trina had reported a contented smile on her husband's face once he had assumed the fetal position which might prove that real happiness for him could be had only as an unborn child.

Sam wanted to move ahead now. He anticipated tearing apart today's session with Marie later that evening. Despite his own jumbled thoughts, he decided to cover the last two known aspects of the dream.

"Do you feel rested enough to continue, Jon?" he asked calmly.

"Yes."

"How do you feel?"

"Very well."

"Fine. Let's continue with your descriptions. These events cannot hurt you or trouble you. Do you understand?"

"Yes."

"Tell me what is happening now."

"Wet! I'm all wet." He squirmed uncomfortably in his chair, shaking his fingers to drip nonexistant water from them.

"Go on, Jon!"

"Swimming. I'm swimming!"

"Where are you swimming?"

"Don't know.it's very dark! Pitch black!"

"Are you a good swimmer? Are you afraid of drowning?"

"I'm not afraid of drowning, but of dying. I can swim as good as any of the others."

"What others?" Sam asked, wondering if the dream had changed radically or perhaps a part had been omitted in their pause.

"Thousands—maybe millions of others all around me."

"Are they swimming, too?" *He must be refer-*

ring to other spermatozoa, Sam thought. It would be consistent, considering that he expected Jon to assume the fetal position or at least describe his existence in his mother's womb.

"Yes."

"Why are you swimming?"

"I must swim to survive. *I* must be the one to live. No one else." His voice assumed arrogant overtones.

Sam marvelled at the complete reversal of testimony when considering his own premature conclusion drawn only moments before. Were thoughts from one spermatozoon the answer to this segment of the dream? "Who are the other swimmers, Jon?"

"They're like me—only—not like me!"

"I don't understand."

"I have a will—a powerful desire—to survive! I have a reason to succeed while they are only acting out of instinct."

"What is your reason?"

"I must live," he said softly, his voice fading on each word.

Sam leaned forward to hear better and said, "Why must you live?"

Jon mumbled incoherently.

"I can't understand you, Jon. Speak louder and more distinctly," he ordered gently.

Jon's eyes blazed brightly, the corpulent countenance reappearing. When he spoke, the words rang out totally unlike his normal voice or the guttural one he had used earlier. And they were in clear, crisp German.

*"Endlich kann ich sprechen und gehört
werden. Ich wollte mir nicht das Leben nehmen
—ich hatte keine Wahl—jeder hat das erwartet
—ich konnte mich nicht gerfangen nehmen
lassen. Aber, wie Sie sehen, ich lebe noch, Herr
Doktor!*

*"Ich bin sehr schwach gewesen—jeden Tag
werde ich langsam stärker. Mein Gastgeber ist
schwer überwältingen—bald werde ich ihn
beherrschen—dann kann ich das beanspruchen,
was rechtmässig meins ist!*

*"Bis diese Zeit kommt—muss behalten:
hundertneun Grad West — siebenunddreissig
Grad Nord—sechzig Kilometer Sud—sechzig
Kilometer Ost—Mitte von einem—Warzeichen
in der figur eines Hakenkreuzes.*

*"Zozobra hat die Leute entfernt—niemand
war da wegen Zozobra—niemand weiss—nur
ich!"*

Falling back in the chair, his face draining of
color, Sam stared at his patient.

PART THREE

BLUE TREES

May 29, 1979
to
June 6, 1979

CHAPTER 9

Several seconds passed before Sam recovered from the shock. Jon had spoken German. Sam was positive of that. But why? What did it mean? Another facet which fascinated him was the animated manner in which his patient had delivered the foreign words.

Regaining his composure, the psychiatrist noted his patient's turgid mask subsiding and he appeared to be resting easily. "When I touch your shoulder, Jon," he said softly, "you will awaken and feel refreshed as though you've had a good night's sleep. You will not remember anything you have told me and will only react to the command *blue trees* the next time you hear it. Is that clear?"

"Yes," Jon answered, his voice no longer vibrant. When he had spoken German, the sharp clipped inflection had expressed a high degree of excitement not previously displayed by the hypnotized man.

Reaching out, Sam touched his shoulder. Jon sat up interlacing his fingers and stretched.

"How do you feel?"

"Fantastic! Utterly fantastic. I would think you'd make a fortune doing this for people who don't sleep well or suffer from insomnia."

Sam smiled wanly. "Before you leave today, I'd like to ask you a few questions."

Jon looked at his wrist watch. "Ten of five?" he exclaimed. "Trina will be concerned if I'm too late but go ahead if it won't take long."

"If I recall correctly, the form you filled out when you first came here indicated you were born in Germany. Is that correct?"

"Yes. I was born in Bonn, where my mother went after marrying my father. She was to—"

"How old were you when you came to this country?"

"About nine months old."

"I see. Did you ever learn German?"

"No."

"Did your mother ever speak German around you?"

Jon's forehead wrinkled thoughtfully before he spoke. "No, I don't think so. My father didn't speak German and my mother became very Americanized. When I was old enough to understand, she told me she never once spoke her native language after arriving in the United States. She felt if she were going to be an American, she should not speak any language other than English."

Sam jotted the information in his notepad before continuing. "She might have before you were old enough to recall the fact—say four or *five* years of age?"

Missing the emphasis the psychiatrist had put on the word *five*, Jon replied, "Naturally, I can't swear to it. But you would have had to know my mother to understand that she never went back on her word. It was almost an obsession with her to be completely honest."

Mulling over his patient's answers in his mind, he met his perplexity head-on. If Jon had never been exposed to German, where would he have picked up sufficient vocabulary to speak at such great length? Sam didn't understand what had been said and felt more than thankful for the tape recorder which had dutifully captured each word of their conversation. If he didn't have the close relationship with Marie, who would be able to translate it, he would not have found the situation impossible. Someone would be available to translate the foreign words into English, but Sam disliked working with a stranger. An eagerness to find the meaning of whatever Jon had said in German swept over him.

"What point are you trying to make, Doctor?" he asked when he saw Sam lost in thought. He checked his watch again. Five o'clock. *Five?* "It just now dawned on me, Doctor, how you emphasized the word 'five' a few minutes ago. Have you found something?"

"I thought perhaps I had. But I have no reason not to believe you where your mother is concerned. Apparently I misinterpreted one phase of today's session. However, now you understand the validity of taping. I'll replay it before your next appointment and be able to better understand what was said today."

Jon nodded. Questions he wished the doctor would answer began swirling about, showing themselves clearly in his mind while his face assumed a puzzled look. What did the number five have to do with anything? Why did he ask if he spoke German? How could his birthplace be involved? Where did his mother fit in? Would it be right to push for answers now if the psychiatrist wanted more time with the recording of his session? He doubted it. "Is there anything else before I leave?" he asked, pushing down this new concern to a level with other unanswered questions—questions he knew they would explore in the future.

"No. I believe that'll do it for today, Jon. Thank you," Sam said, standing. He reached with one hand to turn off the recorder while extending the other to his patient who grasped it firmly. "Be certain to make an appointment with Tory before you leave."

"See you next week Doctor," he said, closing the door.

Sam hurried to the louvered doors across the room, quickly rewinding the tape which had almost been completely used. Since Marie was coming to dinner, he would have to hurry. Instead of background music to woo and win a fellow psychiatrist as his life's mate, he would play Jon Ward's hypnotic session. Instead of soft words, they would attempt fathoming this new aspect of the dream, trying to unravel what was becoming to him more than a puzzling mystery. Placing the reel in its plastic box after he fixed another in place on the machine, he crossed to the door.

Tory looked up, smiling at her employer when he entered the outer office. "Is that one ready for transcribing, Doctor?" she asked soberly, indifferently, concealing her own interest in the tape.

"No. This one isn't ready yet. I'll give it to you when it's to be processed." He reached for the large envelope lying on her desk.

Quickly grabbing it, Tory said sharply, "That one has some stuff in it that has to be mailed."

"Stuff?" Sam asked.

"It's mine," she offered shakily, opening a drawer and handing him an empty envelope.

Sam dropped the tape box in, folding the flap in place. "See you Thursday, Tory."

"Very well, Doctor."

Sam left his office, hurrying to the elevator. He had less than two hours to get ready for Marie's arrival at seven. Knowing she would be prompt, he wanted their meal's preparation completed before she made her appearance. While the elevator descended, he wondered about the ultimate outcome of Jon's treatment. What did his dream mean? Did it have significance, a message? The fact that the identity of the woman in the tunnel had been proven to be his patient's mother brought him back to the Oedipus complex. Since Jon apparently engaged in sex with his mother in the dream, he would have to give it more exploration. Or could he really have another personality locked up inside, one that had been trying to manifest through the medium of the dream and had momentarily emerged, which would explain the German he spoke. Sam knew cases such as these usually resulted in the merging of the divergent personalities into a completely new entity. What would happen to Jon Ward, the teacher? The aspiring author? Would he be able to continue writing? Would he still love his wife? Would she love him? What would the new Jon Ward be like if the two identities melded?

Opening the street doors, Sam joined the crowd of people who hurried toward their homes. Thankful he didn't have to contend with the commuter rush and would only have to walk six blocks to his apartment, he quickened his step, clutching the envelope containing the reel of tape under his arm. Tonight, with Marie's help, he might gain additional insight.

While Sam made his way toward his apartment building, Marie Von Keltzer luxuriated in a steaming shower, relishing the hot water cascading over her well-proportioned body. Stress and tension collected during the day's appointments washed away. Feeling reborn with the exuberance of a twenty year old, she turned the water off, and left the glass cubicle. She toweled her skin dry, then wrapped herself in a terry cloth robe before vigorously brushing her strawberry blond hair.

Thoughts of Sam ran through her mind while she prepared for their dinner engagement. She loved Sam and felt more than confident he loved her. Feelings of guilt gnawed at her whenever he proposed marriage or suggested they live together. She always refused. She had to because of Helmut Rosenspahn. For some reason unknown to her, she had elected to keep Helmut a secret from Sam. Why, she had never been able to comprehend. She and Helmut had been lovers while attending the University of Vienna. When they decided to marry, both families objected strenuously because of the differences in their respective religious and cultural backgrounds. Without marital blessings from their parents, the couple broke up.

Many times, Marie saw an ironic humor in the situation. Since she, in her profession, helped people solve problems, why did she find herself incapable of accepting her own situation? Why couldn't she adjust accordingly?

Dressing, she recalled her first meeting with Sam, shortly after her arrival at the University of Chicago for a series of lectures. He had been a member of the audience and approached her when she finished her talk.

"Doctor Von Keltzer? I'm Sam Dayton," he had said in his boyishly charming manner.

"Yes?" she replied aloofly.

"Could I buy you a cup of coffee, or a drink perhaps? I have a few questions I should like to have you answer—pertaining to the psychology of mass hypnosis."

"I'm sorry, Mr. Dayton, I do not conduct private seminars." Her attitude grew haughty.

"It's *Doctor* Dayton. I'm a psychiatrist, too," he had said, smiling.

They laughed about the misunderstanding many times, whenever the incident came up in conversations. Their friendship grew after establishing a professional relationship. And the thing Marie had feared most happened when Sam told her of his love. She could not deny her feelings for the handsome American but the specter of her affair with Helmut and their thwarted plans hovered menacingly between them. Sooner or later she would have to come to grips with the problem. But she had found it easier to keep Sam's proposals in perspective by not telling him about Helmut.

"You're a fool, Marie Von Keltzer," she chastized her mirrored image, applying a touch of eye liner. "You're thirty-five years old and will not be attractive all your life. Accept Sam's proposal. Forget the past. It would be much easier."

Maybe her brother, Rudy, an ordained priest, had been right. She would be able to enjoy happiness if she allowed herself to recognize it. Happy whenever she was with Sam, she found him occupying her thoughts more and more. The next time he proposed she would give it more serious consideration than she ever had in the past.

Walking into the bedroom, she stopped, checking her reflected appearance in the full length mirror. The rosy earth tones of her soft flowing blouse complemented the mushroom colored Quiana trousers. Dissatisfied with the neckline, she loosened one more button. Adjusting the gold braid sash, she turned to gather her handbag and light coat in the event she did not stay all night.

Would it do any good to be so attractive for Sam tonight if Jon Ward and his dream dominated their conversation? That dream! In her seven years of practice she had not heard of such a detailed, highly sophisticated, symbolic dream. The five years she had spent in the United States had been a combination of lecturing and practicing psychiatry when time permitted. She readily admitted that her exposure to such phenomena had not been extensive; in fact, it was nonexistent. She had studied classic examples but had never witnessed nor treated someone with such a problem. Perhaps she found the dream intriguing because of its nagging familiarity. The dream made her feel she had been privy to something similar sometime, someplace in her past but could not quite recall it.

Leaving the apartment, she threw her coat over one arm. It would be easier to catch a cab than take her own car and worry about finding a parking place. Once in front of the building, she hailed a taxi that whisked her away from the curb toward Sam's apartment building.

Surreptitiously studying Jon across the top of her magazine, Trina squirmed in her chair. He had not mentioned much about his session that day with the doctor. She wondered about his attitude toward giving up his Monday afternoons. At least it had been changed to Tuesday this week. "Does losing half of each Monday bother you during the rest of the week, darling?" she asked, jumping at the sound of her own voice.

He looked up from his newspaper. He, too, had not realized how quiet the living room had become. Laying the *Tribune* aside, he stood, crossing the room to the stereo. Fumbling with the dial until the hauntingly romantic opening of Chausson's *Poeme* filled the room, he adjusted the volume. Satisfied they would be able to converse normally, he returned to his easy chair.

"Not really. Being hypnotized is relaxing. Actually, I feel I'll do better work the balance of the week because of it. Once Dayton figures out the dream and how to get rid of it, I may continue with the sessions just for the after affects."

Unable to determine if he had been completely honest she forced a smile. She recalled how he had talked of possibly cancelling last week's appointment but after being hypnotized, was enthusiastic about the sessions. Now, he appeared at ease. Despite his apparent tranquil mood, she sensed a resentment to his involvement with doctors and hospitals in the last few weeks. She assumed total responsibility for that, which in turn made her suffer guilt pangs, an unfamiliar sensation for her.

She had apprehensively anticipated his return this evening since their weekend had ended so disastrously. They had barely spoken to each other since. When he came home later than usual, she had thought horrible things might have been discovered in the doctor's office.

He had entered their apartment smiling, kissing her deeply, but said nothing about the appointment or what he and the doctor had discussed, nothing about their apparent indifference to each other until that moment. Her curiosity stirred to the fullest, she wanted to know. She felt she had a right to know. "Did everything go all right today?" she finally ventured.

"Yeah. Yeah, I guess so."

"Well, didn't the doctor say *anything*?"

"You mean about the weekend?"

"Yes." She tingled impatiently.

"Not really. Oh, we talked about the continuation of the nightmare when I first arrived. I told him about keeping the rest of it secret from everyone, even you. I'll say this, I felt like an ass when I was telling him. But Dayton's a pretty good guy 'cause he didn't get angry with me for not leveling with him. I did get the impression when I suggested I might hurt you in my sleep, that he felt the dream's content would be confined to the dream itself."

"But you were acting it out, darling." Shuddering, she recalled him kneeling over her, the enlarged proportions of his penis.

"Well," he said shortly, "he didn't prescribe anything and he didn't seem too upset because of it."

"He said nothing? Nothing at all about what you said under hypnosis?"

"He never does. I don't know if I'll ever hear the tapes. All we did was talk a few minutes after he brought me out of it."

"Talked? About what?"

" 'Sfunny," he said, getting to his feet. He crossed the room readjusting the volume when the music rose loudly in an impassioned crescendo. "He asked me about Mom. Did she speak German around the house? Did she ever teach me the language? Dumb things like that. I sure don't get the connection."

He turned, facing his wife. "Want some coffee while I'm up?"

"Yes. Yes, I would," she said absentmindedly. German? Had he spoken German while hypnotized? What would that have to do with his stupid dream?

Turning, Jon limped toward the kitchen, rubbing his elbow as he went.

Swiveling in her chair, she watched him through the doorway. A cold shiver began as a tiny speck in her stomach, spreading rapidly like an epidemic through her entire body. As normal as he had seemed a scant few seconds before, she knew the dream could probably be the most traumatic thing he would ever have to face.

During dinner, Sam and Marie chatted lightly, aimlessly, not mentioning the reason for their being together. She had long since put the memory of Helmut Rosenspahn from her active mind but nevertheless, felt his presence whenever Sam looked at her. She enjoyed Sam's company. In her own way, she loved him. But could she love him in the same way she had loved Helmut? Somehow, that particular question would have to be resolved, removing the barrier it represented to her, to allow real happiness and love to take place.

"Someday, Sam, you will make a good *wife* for some woman. The dinner was delicious. You know I love tempura," she said smiling graciously at him.

"If you have an application blank with you, I'd like to apply for the position," he said softly, winking. He had almost given up hope she would ever accept him on a permanent basis but until that remaining faith surrendered to despair, he would continue. "Why don't we have our coffee in the living room. I can put Ward's tape on the machine and you can listen to it."

"Did you uncover anything new today, considering what happened to him and his wife over the weekend?"

"I can hardly wait until you hear the tape," he said eagerly, quickly holding her chair. He helped her stand and led the way into the living room. It had been difficult not to mention the German speaking episode while they ate. But he knew Marie. If he had, it would have been all business and no idle talk, talk that he hoped would eventually allow her to tell him why she refused to accept his proposal.

With the tape on the machine, he adjusted the volume. Sitting opposite her, he listened intently, studying her face as the recording began to unfold the day's dramatic session. She was a woman whose natural attributes emphasized her beauty. Shoulder length hair matched in color a spattering of pale freckles that complemented her fair complexion. Her brown eyes usually twinkled easily, happily. But he had seen them cloud with hurt on more than one occasion, making him wonder about the core of her apprehension. Could it be him? He had never hurt her, to the best of his knowledge, and would have sooner injured himself than inflict any wound, physical or mental, directly or indirectly, on her.

Totally unaware of his perusal, Marie concentrated on the recorded hypnotic session. With Jon's colorless narration, the events washed over her, coupling to the first part of the dream, which was already registered in her memory. Why did the beginning seem so familiar?

Slowly the hands of the electric clock hanging above the stereo equipment moved toward nine-thirty, the session drawing closer to the explosive moment for which Sam waited. Now he could find out what Jon had said when he spoke German. He watched Marie's face intently for the impact of the words would have on her, if any.

"*I must live,*" Jon's voice said, fading away.

"Why must you live?" Sam's voice seemed too loud compared to his patient's whispering.

Jon mumbled incoherently.

"I can't understand you, Jon. Speak louder and more distinctly."

Then the crisp, clear German rang from the speakers in a completely different voice. Marie's jaw dropped. She listened closely while Sam brought his patient out of the trance to the questions and answers that followed.

Sam stood to turn the machine off. "Well?" he asked, expectantly.

"My God, Sam. That's phenomenal. How do you explain it?"

"I believe there's another personality attempting to dominate Jon. Did you notice the difference in his voice when he spoke German?"

"I certainly did."

"What the hell did he say?"

"I don't know exactly. It took me so off guard. Something about being heard, that he had killed himself against his will. Something about his being weak but getting stronger. Then, something about directions. You're aware, aren't you, that he addressed you directly at one point when he said Herr Doktor?"

"I thought I had heard that but I haven't played back the tape until now. I strongly believe I'm dealing with a dual personality."

Her lips puckered in thought for several moments before she spoke. "I don't know, Sam. At this point in the analysis, it would seem to indicate that that is what you're facing.

However, there's something vaguely familiar about the first part of the dream, something I seem to have heard of before or read someplace —I don't know. It'll come to me. Do you still have the tapes of the first two appointments?"

"Yes, I do. This one is the second hypnotic session. You know, I find it unusual that the voice could manifest itself so readily this soon into analysis and be so strong as well."

"You did say Ward had at least one personality change while he was awake, didn't you? Have there been more?"

"Just one, maybe two in the last few weeks. Prior to those, his wife maintains his only problem was having the dream and waking up with a bad headache."

Her thoughts, now a jumble of bits and pieces of information, spun wildly. She stood, walking to the sliding glass doors, to look at the lights of the city.

After several quiet moments passed, he said, "What is it, Marie? Is something bothering you?"

"He claims he has never spoken German. His mother supposedly did not speak German after coming to his country. Still, under hypnosis, he speaks absolutely perfect German. Austrian German, to be exact."

"How can you be so certain?"

"Remember, I'm from Vienna. There are accents and dialects in the German language just as there are drawls in the southern states; and Brooklyn and Bronx accents in New York; and midwestern twangs here in Chicago. No,

Sam. What you heard was perfect, Austrian German.''

''Doesn't that lend credence then to the theory or possibility of dual personality? What other explanation could there be?''

''You're not Catholic, are you?''

''You know I'm not.''

''Do you know anything about possession?''

''Oh, come on now!''

''I mean it, Sam,'' she persisted.

''Professionally? No. I did read *The Exorcist* and *Garden of the Incubus* when they were on the bestseller lists. They were entertai— Wait a minute! I see what's you're saying. Knowledge of a foreign language when such knowledge is not possible. Is that it?''

''I don't believe Jon is possessed. I'm just trying to point out there could be, and probably are, other explanations that will seem just as correct. I'll grant you this, his German is an interesting turn of events. Play it again, Sam.''

Sam laughed.

''What's the matter? Did I say something funny?''

''You just said one of the most famous non-existent lines ever to come out of a Bogart film,'' he said, rewinding the tape. While they waited, he explained about Bogey and the piano player in the movie, *Casablanca*. He stopped the machine when the tape was ready to play.

''Get me a paper and pen,'' she suggested.

He produced a pen and a small tablet from a table drawer near the stereo equipment.

''Now,'' she said, ''let it run until I say stop.

I'll translate what has been said and then, play a little more when I tell you."

Word by word, phrase by phrase, the German sentences were replayed until the long pause separating Sam's shock and his reawakening of Jon began. He stopped the machine, looking expectantly at her.

"Just wait a minute, Sam," she said, studying the notes she had taken, "I'll put this in better English." She worked for several more minutes before looking up at him. "At this point it doesn't make much sense. It seems to be taken out of context from something else. Perhaps there's more. Here goes:

"At last, I can speak and be heard—I did not want to take my life—I had no choice—everyone expected it—I could not allow myself to be taken prisoner. But, as you see, I still live, Herr Doctor!

I have been very weak—every day I become slowly stronger. My host has been difficult to conquer—soon I will control him—then I can claim what is rightfully mine!

Until this time comes—must remember: 109 degrees West—37 degrees North—60 kilometers South—60 kilometers East—middle of a landmark in the shape of a swastika.

Zozobra took the people away—no one was there because of Zozobra—no one knows—only me!"

Sam stared at Marie when she stopped reading. "What the hell does all that mean?"

"I imagine it might be more symbolism, not unlike the first part of the dream. However, the directions sound authentic. What do you make of it?" She handed the tablet to him.

His eyes flitted across the delicate handwriting before stopping at the bottom. "*Zozobra?* What the hell is that?"

She shrugged. "It's not German. I'm sure of that."

"I thought you said it was all perfect German."

"It is, except for that one word. I have no idea what it means or what language it is. I don't know if it's a he, a she, or an it. It's handled like a noun and not a verb. I wonder—"

"What?" he asked when she didn't continue.

"I wonder if we're dealing with two separate, distinct dreams. The first is so solidly symbolic. Yet, it's as though Ward is experiencing it himself. The second part seems to have more of a fantasy element. More detachment from reality."

"Two separate segments," Sam muttered.

"If, and I say *if,*" Marie continued, "they are of one makeup, it is up to you, Sam, to find the connecting link between the two parts."

"What the hell does any of the German mean?" he persisted. "Directions, swastika, *Zozobra.* Ramblings about being alive. What the hell does it mean?"

"When do you see Mr. Ward again?"

"His regular appointment has been Monday afternoons."

"I'll give you several questions to ask in German. One is, 'Do you speak English?' The other, 'What are you called?' We'll see if he has a name for this German entity. I'd better include, 'I don't speak German.' "

He watched her write the statements first in German, then in a phonetic breakdown. When she finished, he studied the pronunciations for a moment. Convinced he would have no trouble in speaking the German words, he placed the paper on the table. Looking up, he discovered her staring at the stereo equipment, obviously lost in thought. "What are you puzzling over now?"

"The whole of the problem is contradictory. The first segment, I feel, we'll have no trouble solving, in time." She paused when she saw him smiling. "Did I say something amusing?"

"Not really. Just sort of comforting. I like the way you use the word *we* when you referred to the two of us solving the meaning of Ward's dream."

"Oh," she said softly. Maybe she should allow the serious consideration, which she had thought about earlier in the evening, to have its way. Maybe they should forget Jon Ward and his dream for the time being. Still, her training fought her natural instincts for precedence and she knew, for now, they would remain on the subject at hand.

"A penny for your thoughts," he said, wistfully, moving next to her on the couch.

"It—it was nothing. I'm trying to understand how his mother plays a role in his dream. She somehow seems totally out of place." She turned to face him, drawing both legs up on the seat.

"I thought I might have had the whole thing solved today before he started speaking German." Sam reached out lightly touching her shoulder.

"How?"

He told her about his theory of Jon wishing to be nonexistent, considering at first a complicated Oedipus Complex. When he finished, neither spoke for several minutes.

Then she broke the silence. "I always found it difficult to understand why Freud could not come to grips with the idea that dreams could have a basis of truth gleaned from some ancestral or hereditary memory." She lifted her face, her eyes roving about the room.

"What are you saying, Marie? That Ward is experiencing something from his father's or mother's past?"

She shrugged. "Perhaps even more remote. You're not into the analysis far enough to draw any conclusions yet. Still, I believe you should leave the door open to any and all possibilities. The solution could be pitifully simple, or so complex the dream might never be solved."

"I explored at first the idea that it might be caused by certain, current stimuli. But he shot me down at every turn by reminding me that the dream has, at least the first part, remained virtually unchanged since he began experiencing it twenty-eight years ago."

"That's an awfully long time to never

question it."

"His wife became concerned enough to finally convince him to seek help."

"I see. Well, at any rate, you have your work cut out for you."

"That's the second or third time since I mentioned how you were including yourself, that you've *ex*cluded yourself. What is there about me, or us, or our situation, that turns you away from facing what I hope will be inevitable?"

"Not now, Sam. Please," she said huskily, turning to face him.

Her brown eyes stared at him with an air of sincerity he had never seen before and for the first time since they had met, he felt completely at ease with her. The brief sensations of inferiority he had always experienced in the past whenever he thought of their educational backgrounds, each of which had left a tiny scar on his ego, were things of the past. They suddenly evaporated as though they had never existed, allowing a feeling of security to rush in.

"I'll make you a promise," she said after several minutes passed, during which she saw a subtle change come over him. "Next week, I feel I will be able to clear the air once and for all where you and I are concerned. You can believe this or not, but you can thank Jon Ward and his dream."

"What? How do he and his dream figure into this?"

"Until then," she said, ignoring his question, "in addition to thinking about us, I intend to determine why the first part of his dream seems familiar to me. I think I know why, but I don't want to explain it now until I can do some research. If I'm unable to do so, I'll place a call to a friend of mine in Vienna who can possibly help jog my memory. Perhaps I will have more than one answer to both your problems."

"Both my problems?" He decided to accept her elusive attitude concerning the first part of the dream. He knew any speculation at this juncture might influence the manner in which he conducted the next hypnotic sessions. But what did she mean about both of his problems?

Marie nodded, "The solution, or at least the meaning to the first half of the dream—if not both parts. I may also have an explanation as to why I have been so reluctant to make a commitment where you're concerned."

His mind raced. The dream, all but forgotten, seemed insignificant at this moment if she were going to finally explain her own reserved attitude where their future was concerned.

Before he could voice a question, she held up her hand and said, "Don't ask me anything now. You've waited this long, you can wait until next Tuesday." He would have to be patient with her. If Helmut could help solve his patient's dream, she swore she would dispose of her own ghosts at the same time.

"Why Tuesday? Why not Monday night after Ward's appointment?" he asked.

"You've forgotten I leave the day after tomorrow for a five day tour of colleges in Wisconsin and Iowa. If you wish, we can get together Tuesday evening at my apartment and go over everything you have on Ward."

He mentally scolded himself for not remembering the tour she had mentioned several weeks before. He had even marked the dates on his calendar. Noting she had regained her professional aplomb, he paid her the attention he felt she deserved. "I have copies of his initial examination along with the results of the hospital tests. Do you want to see those, too?"

"Yes. Everything you can lay your hands on. Your day off is Wednesday and I had planned to surprise you next week by taking that day off also to recuperate from the tour."

"You're sure you won't be too tired to look at the records?"

She smiled demurely. "I'm expecting you to stay the night. It's up to you if I get tired—or bored."

Sam could not repress the grin crossing his face. "What about the telephone call you mentioned before? The one to Vienna."

"Let's see what luck I have with my own recollections first, Sam. If I can solve the first segment, either in part or completely, my call will be of a different nature. If I can't remember the correlation, then I'll have more questions to be answered." She almost mentioned Helmut's name. But there would be no need to worry Sam about something as spectral as her dead romance with Helmut Rosenspahn.

Rising from the couch, Marie offered her

hand to Sam who stood. They encircled each other's bodies with their arms, kissing deeply. Despite their sudden aroused desires, each was thinking of swastikas, directions and *Zozobra* as they walked into the bedroom.

CHAPTER 10

Tory slowly mounted each step leading to her fourth floor apartment. Howie would be waiting anxiously to see what she had taken from the office files and she didn't want to be out of breath when she faced him. Anticipating few interruptions because of the psychiatrist's day off, she had made good use of the time, concluding that Howie would be more than satisfied with her choices.

After reaching the top floor, she took the time to pat her hair into place. She inhaled deeply before walking the few steps to their apartment door. She felt in control of herself and would not allow him to intimidate her. Just as she turned the knob, the door suddenly swung open.

"Where the fuck you been?" Howie demanded, glaring at her.

"Working. I've got some things for you to read," she said, handing him the large manilla envelope.

Without a word, he grabbed the parcel, tearing it open. Withdrawing three file folders, he pulled his attention away to rivet Tory with a menacing stare. "These better be good, goddamnit! I don't know how long I can stand it without getting some weed or booze to keep me going. I need something to keep me occupied."

"They're good. They're real good," she said, confidence ringing unfamiliarly in each word.

"They'd better be," he snorted, throwing the folder on the bed. He studied the names on the index tabs: Sterling Tilden, Carole Nelumbo, Jon Ward. "Tell me which of these is the hottest item—the most ready for my *service.*"

"Probably Mr. Tilden or Mrs. Nelumbo."

"What's wrong with this Ward?" he asked suspiciously.

"I don't think there's anything there you could blackmail him on—now."

"Then why the hell bring the folder along? Christ, can't you get anything through your stupid head? They've gotta be loaded and they've gotta have something they're ashamed of—something they wouldn't want anybody to know about. Understand?"

Each word struck with a familiar ferocity she knew too well. "I understand that, Howie," she offered lamely. "I only brought it along 'cause I thought you might find his dream interesting. That's all. Besides—"

"Dream? How the hell can I blackmail somebody because he dreams? Christ! You're stupid. Tell me about the others."

"Mrs. Nelumbo is having an affair with her husband's younger partner."

"Okay! I remember her," he snickered, opening the file. "What about the other jerk?" His eyes flew across the page catching key words and phrases but listening intently while she continued.

"Mr. Tilden is a vice president at First Federal Security Bank and—and—he likes boys."

He looked up at her, momentarily forgetting Carole Nelumbo's guilt complex. "He what?"

"Likes boys. He's married, and holds this responsible job and all—"

"And the sonofabitch likes guys," he finished, gleefully whooping the words. "He's a fuckin' faggot and sure as hell doesn't want anybody who's straight, to find out. Oh, Christ, Tory! That's a gem. Beautiful." He threw Carole Nelumbo's file to the foot of the bed replacing it with Sterling Tilden's. Opening it, he paced up and down the small room, stopping every once in a while to shake his head and mumble, "Unbelievable!"

Several minutes passed during which she watched his triumphant expression. Smiling proudly, she knew she had finally pleased him in some way other than when they made love. Even then, she couldn't be certain, since most times he finished in seconds, quickly growing more indifferent toward her than he had been before.

He stopped to look at her. "Listen to this: *If*

you understand the jeopardy you are placing yourself in, not only with your career but with your wife as well, why do you persist in leading a cloaked homosexual life, Sterling? That's the question the shrink asked him. Listen to his answer: *Because I love the feel of their cocks in my mouth. I feel like a real person when I have sex with a man. My wife and I haven't been intimate for quite some time. Years, in fact. I don't even remember the last time we slept together. I don't fear her so much as I do for my position at the bank. No, that isn't true. I fear them equally. After all, her father got me my job and was chairman of the board right up until the time of his death. She still wields a lot of influence with the current chairman and the president. I'd be ruined if either the bank or Millicent found out.* Oh, shit! This is dynamite. And a fuckin' banker yet. Fantastic, Tory! You're incredible."

Grinning broadly, she stepped closer to him. She hoped he'd take her in his arms, demanding to make love to her. Turning his back, he crossed the room to retrieve the other folders. Her look of disappointment escaped his attention while he concentrated on the other folders.

"If these are half as good," he gloated, "we'll really score big and who knows, maybe we're closer to leaving this dump then either one of us thinks." Settling down on the edge of the bed, he studied Jon's first and second session. He found the dream's exploration while Jon was hypnotized interesting, but not material for his scheme. "Why the hell did you bring this one along?" he asked again after finishing.

"Apparently, his wife has money, and it must be a lot if he doesn't have to work. He's trying to be an author or something. At any rate, I thought if a reason to blackmail him came up later, we'd have a full set of records on him."

"Oh," he said, his voice softening a bit when he realized she had had an idea when selecting Jon's records. "We'll save it 'cause it's no goddamn good now." He opened Carole Nelumbo's file, studying it. After several moments he whistled softly and mumbled, "Oh, shit! Do you know what business her husband and lover are in?"

"No," she said, looking at him quizzically. How could he know if she had been the one who copied the transcriptions? What had he seen that she hadn't? She knew of the case and the bare rudiments but had never paid much attention to the tapes' contents, not until she and Howie had thought of extorting money from some of the patients.

"I thought the name Nelumbo sounded familiar. Her husband's a fuckin' *don* in the Mafia, or something. Guido Nelumbo."

"So?"

"Big people! Crooks. But loaded, respectable people on the surface."

"What's a *don*, Howie?"

"The big man. The head honcho. His word's law."

"So why are Carole and her lover important?"

"So the young guy she's screwin' is one of her

husbands *peons*, that's what. Another good one, baby!"

Her mind raced. The Mafia? Hoodlums? Gangsters? Crooks? She didn't want Howie getting involved with people like that. If they didn't like someone, they'd machinegun him and throw his body in the Chicago River or in Lake Michigan. She gave voice to her fears.

"No stupid! They're not gangsters and hoodlums. Not anymore. They're big businessmen, trying to keep a legitimate front to hide all the bread they take in from gambling and hookers and shit that's hustled on the streets. I think Carole-Baby's lover will be more than willing to come across with a hefty bankroll to make certain her old man don't find out about them. They still play dirty when it comes to certain rules of theirs."

"Won't he play dirty with you? Hurt you when you ask him for money?"

"Not the way I intend on running this gig."

"Tell me about it and then I'll decide if I should worry."

"Okay. First I tell you what to write and you prepare two or three copies of the same letter."

"Who do the letters go to? Who are they addressed to?"

"In Tilden's case, to his wife. She must be a bitch to have him so concerned about his job. Probably leads him around by the nose. In Carole-Baby's case, to the big cheese, her husband."

"What happens then, Howie?" Her eyes shone, concealing any genuine doubt she still harbored about the plan. But his detached enthusiasm proved infectious, bringing her to listen eagerly to each detail.

"I approach Tilden, for example. I hand him a copy of the letter to his wife, telling her all about his suckin' cocks. How he likes boys better than her. Then, I top it all off by using a few quotes from his own mouth to convince him I know what I'm talking about. Of course, if he doesn't want to play ball, I just threaten to mail the letter to his wife. That should bring old Sterling around. I'll do pretty much the same thing with—what's Carole's lover's name?" He picked up the folder, scanning it quickly. "Shit! No last name. Only a first, Ed. Well, I'm certain Carole can lay her hands on some bread if it comes to me telling her old man about Eddie-Boy."

"How much are you going to ask for?" she asked, slowly becoming convinced the scheme would actually work.

"In Sterling's case, I'd say about ten thousand for openers. If he comes across fast, I'll go back in a few weeks and hit 'im up again."

Picking up the Tilden folder, she began reading it. She had not taken the time to study each case, except Jon's in complete detail. The confessions of a man who preferred other men as sex partners mystified her. She could understand how they were able to satisfy themselves sexually but could not begin to comprehend the why of Tilden's problem. "Did you see this part?" she asked, handing the page to Howie.

He refused the paper with a shake of his head,

preferring to hold Carole Nelumbo's file open on his lap. "Read it to me."

"He says he'll kill himself if the truth ever comes out. *I could never stand the humiliation I would suffer if the truth about my lovers ever became known by anyone. For years I have served on the Board of Directors at Langley's School for Boys. The institution would be ruined because of me, if the fact I am a homosexual ever came out. The bank would suffer. Everyone would suffer because of me.* Then Doctor Dayton asked him, what he would do if the truth became known. He says, *I'd kill myself.*" She looked up to find him grinning.

"That's a good way to start the letter," he said. Closing the Nelumbo file, he slammed it to the floor. "Get a pen and paper. I'll tell you what to say. Let's see, today's Wednesday, I want to call on Tilden by Friday. Get his home address and type one letter to his wife with two carbon copies; one for the bank president and one I can give him. We're going to open the closet door a crack and threaten to push him out."

Tory fumbled in her purse for a ball point pen and note pad she used for grocery lists whenever she managed to keep enough money from Howie for food. When she found them, she cooed, "Go ahead, honey."

The next day, Tory typed the letter after calling the First Federal Security Bank to learn the name of the president. When she returned home that evening, she found Howie in an expansive mood. They made love in his usual hurried, uncaring way, leaving her unsatisfied. Later, he insisted they go to sleep early. He wanted to be ready for his meeting with Sterling Tilden.

Shortly after she left the next morning, Howie smiled while studying the letter once more. Refolding the single page neatly in thirds, he inserted it into the envelope, laying it with the sealed one addressed to Mrs. Tilden. He would threaten the banker with exposing his homosexuality to his wife first, then to the president of his firm. If that failed, he would contact Langley's. Somehow, he would get money from Sterling Tilden or bring the man to ruination.

At eleven o'clock, he approached the girl's desk to which he had been directed at the information counter. "How do you do, young lady," he said. "My name is Peter Dick Ward. I'd like to see Mr. Sterling Tilden for a moment if I could." He had selected Peter Dick to tantalize his victim if necessary and Jon's last name had just popped into his mind when he entered the bank lobby. He breathed a sigh of relief when he discovered Sterling had a private office and not just a desk in the large room the way some of the other bank officials did.

"Yes, Mr. Ward," the dark-haired secretary said. Margo Kubicinsky's eyes questioningly grew large when he turned his head for a moment. His thinning, long hair and nondescript clothes made her wonder why a man of his type would want to see a high ranking official such as Sterling Tilden. She picked up the telephone, dialing three numbers. "Mr. Tilden, there's a man here, a Mr. Peter Ward, to see you." She paused for several seconds. "What's your business with Mr. Tilden?" she asked, placing her hand over the mouthpiece.

"Tell him it's got to do with Langley's Boys' School," he said, grinning wickedly. *That should make the faggot want to see him.*

Margo relayed the information before placing the phone in its cradle. "He's expected at a meeting in thirty minutes and will see you shortly. Please be seated," she said pleasantly, indicating a row of chairs opposite her desk.

Selecting one, Howie sat down heavily. He didn't like banks or the things they represented. He liked money but had discovered that it could be had without resorting to normal methods which usually involved work or banks. Besides, these white-collared assholes didn't want anything to do with most of the poor slobs who had given up a couple of years from their lives to fight a war nobody wanted. Nobody except the fat cats on Wall Street, the fucking bankers, and the egotistical politicians who wanted to be certain their names would go into the history books. Fuck 'em! Fuck 'em all. Howard Liemen would make money his own way. Hadn't he always? He always tried, but had not always met with success.

When he couldn't find work after he got out of the army, he had hired on to fly a plane load of grass from Mexico into the United States, and that had netted him five years in a Federal pen.

The only good thing about his stay there had been his time spent in the prison library. The thing he hated most had been the sexual assaults perpetrated by the older inmates. Men who had not been with a woman for ten or twenty years, and even longer in some instances, were constantly on the lookout for recent arrivals who would give them some new perverted thrill.

He had been no different than other new prisoners at first and had been raped no less than twenty-eight times during his first year. After his brutal initiation, he didn't care what happened during his confinement. He hated every man serving time with him, including the guards who were just as sadistic as the prisoners. He hated the Drug Enforcement Agency for arresting him and being responsible for his jail sentence. He hated the people who had turned their backs on him when he needed a job. It seemed they always lost interest when they found out he had finished his stay in the service in a stockade instead of fighting a senseless, no-win war. Most of all, he currently hated Sterling Tilden because he had money and prestige. Everything he wanted. And the sonofabitch was queer—a faggot. No goddamn better than the bastards in prison.

"He'll see you now, Mr. Ward," Margo said pleasantly, breaking into his vicious thoughts. She pointed toward a door with open venetian blinds.

Howie slowly rose, forcing the feelings of hatred into the farthest recesses of his mind. He strode toward the door behind which he calculated ten thousand dollars awaited him. Smiling broadly, he threw open the door and said, "Mr. Tilden, I believe I might be the salvation of Langley's Boys' School."

Sterling Tilden stood, taking the proffered hand in a firm grasp. "How—how can that be, Mr. Ward?" he asked, returning to his seat behind the large mahogany desk, his face puzzled by his visitor's statement.

"I believe we'll want total privacy, Mr. Tilden," he said, turning to close the door. When he faced the desk standing opposite his intended victim, he smiled. "I'm not going to beat around the bush, Sterling, you sly devil. I want ten thousand dollars. Preferably in small bills."

"What—what did you say?" he flustered. The well dressed man paled while thoughts of a bank robbery pushed beads of sweat onto his balding head.

"I don't believe I spoke Mandarin Chinese, Sterling. I didn't stutter either. You see, certain information has come my way and I've taken the liberty of writing a couple of letters. One to your wife, and one to the president of this bank. Now if—oh, hell—rather than sit here and bore you with all this information about you, why don't I just give you a copy and let you read it? Here." Sobering, Howie handed a carbon copy of the letter to him and sat back, a smirk furrowing his fleshy jowls.

Taking the paper in his trembling hand, Sterling turned it and began reading.

EVIL DREAMS

Dear Mrs. Tilden,
  Were you aware of the fact that your husband, Sterling, will commit suicide if the knowledge he likes to suck other guy's cocks is spread around to certain individuals such as yourself and the president of the bank where he works? Can you imagine the disgrace you and he will suffer if he's asked to resign from such a high faluting Board of Directors as the esteemed body that governs Langley's School for Boys? And for what? Just because old Sterling likes cocks and assholes instead of pussies—

There was more, but he was unable to read further. His face blanched, reflecting the weary anguish which the information in the letter brought rushing to the surface of his mind. Crumbling the carbon copy up, he threw it on his desk. "Where—? Who—? How—?" He gasped the one word questions, choking before he could form a coherent sentence.

"Don't worry about it, Sterling. Hey, look, I ain't gonna spread the word. Not yet, at least. You show your good faith in me by coming up with ten grand and I'll show you mine by not mailing the letter to your wife. 'Course, if you elect to give me any shit, I'll send it to her. If that doesn't do it, I'll mail the other copy to your boss here at the bank. And don't forget the school."

Sterling, his hands shaking, mopped his sweating brow with a linen handkerchief. Staring at Howie, he suddenly stiffened. "Get out of here, you sonofabitch. Get out or I'll call the

227

police right now," he ordered strongly.

"You don't have to call the fuzz, cocksucker," Howie growled. "Just come up with the bread."

"I won't. If you come near me again, I'll call the police. Now, get out of here," he shrieked loudly.

Howie turned, half expecting the door to burst open any second, framing a curious Margo Kubicinsky, who would want to know if she could help in any way. He quickly recalled the distance between her desk and the office in which he stood. Besides, Sterling hadn't really yelled that loud. Why take chances this first time out? Of course the faggot would be a little hesitant at first. That was to be expected. Give him a little time to get used to the idea of being blackmailed. Then he would come around to the easy way out, paying to keep the information confidential.

Howie started for the door. "Don't be upset, Sterling, old boy. I'll be back and you'd better have the money ready. In fact, just to be certain, I think I'll mail your wife's letter on the way home," he said before leaving.

The banker followed him, locking the door with shaking hands. Pulling the blinds to shut the bustling bank lobby from sight, he crossed the room and sat down. Propping both elbows on the desk, he cradled his head in his hands. A tear ran down his cheek when he reached for a paper and pen. "It's over," were the only words he wrote and unlocked the bottom drawer.

Howie swung past the guard, grinning widely

at him and strutted through the entrance. He didn't hear the muffled explosion from the back of the bank nor did he see some of the employees rush toward Sterling Tilden's office. Satisfied with the way his first attempt at blackmail had gone, and positive neither the banker nor his wife would risk contacting the authorities, he pulled out the stamped envelope bearing Tilden's residence address. Walking up to a mail box, he dropped the letter in. He turned abruptly coming face to face with a tall policeman.

"Good morning, officer," he said smiling, and turned on his heel, disappearing into the crowd of noon shoppers.

CHAPTER 11

Jon plodded along the walk away from the Shedd Aquarium, lost in thought. His normally squared shoulders hunched forward, both hands thrust in the pockets of his slacks, he hugged a small cassette recorder against his body with one arm. What would Doctor Dayton say about his latest episode? Withdrawing his right hand, he patted his breast pocket. The cassette tape seemed to move of its own accord when he checked to make certain he hadn't lost or forgotten it. How many times had he done that since leaving the apartment early that morning? What could be wrong with him? Could he be going crazy, insane? Even his usually excellent memory hinted at letting him down now when it should work. There were certain gaps that needed filling. What did really happen last Friday afternoon?

He found himself wondering if the year off from work had been such a good idea. His writing discipline could not be at fault for his feelings of self recrimination. Most of the first draft he had produced thus far, impressed both Trina and him.

Trina! His tactless answers to her questions over the weekend, his moodiness, this new twist that had occurred Friday—how would she ultimately react to him and his problems? Although he knew he had to trust someone, he found himself harboring doubts about placing his confidence in her. Doubts? About Trina? Ridiculous! How could he have feelings of dubiety where she was concerned? He loved her. Hadn't she unselfishly demonstrated her faith and love by insisting he take the time to write without worry about working? But he loved her, truly loved her, long before he had taken his leave. Perhaps he didn't want to overburden her with this thing that had happened Friday afternoon. Hadn't he kept the continuation of the dream from her? And what had been his motivation at that time?

Who then? Who could he totally and completely trust? Sam Dayton? Jon found himself liking and admiring the man more each time they met. But did that mean he was becoming emotionally dependent on the psychiatrist? If that were the situation, he had no idea what the future might hold for him.

He speculated on what Sam would have to say about the recording in his pocket. Patting his jacket again, he looked at his broad hand. He held up the other one holding the recorder and studied them. Would those strong hands have hurt Trina in Galena? A shudder rippled through his body and he pulled the collar of his turtleneck closer to his jaw.

He rubbed a hand across his eyes. Sometimes he wished he were a turtle or an ostrich. If he were, he could simply hide his head and forget his nightmare. He didn't like what it and its treatment were doing to his world. Would he be all right? How many times had he asked that question during the last five weeks? Yet, he knew he had to face up to the crisis his dream represented. Face up to it. Fight it. Beat it into oblivion. Get rid of it once and for all. Then he and Trina could continue their lives in a more normal fashion. He knew he could do it. In this instance, his stubbornness would serve him in good stead.

Turning to his right, he gazed at the black skyline over Lake Michigan, ignoring Buckingham Fountain spread before him. Perhaps today, he and Sam would solve the puzzle. The cassette might hold the necessary clue to understanding everything. Had he actually spoken German while dozing Friday afternoon? The voice didn't sound like his. It had only been by accident that it had been recorded. Maybe the psychiatrist could explain it. The doctor had asked if he spoke German when he was brought out of the trance last Tuesday. Had he said something in German while under hypnosis to prompt such a question? Jon had tried dozens of times over the weekend to comprehend his sudden ability to speak a foreign language, ignoring his wife while he lost himself in thoughts of this latest twist.

After she had departed for school that morning, he deciced he could not remain alone in the apartment, and left shortly thereafter for downtown Chicago. He had spent the day wandering about the Loop and after having eaten lunch, walked to the aquarium. Glancing at his watch, he saw he had forty minutes to walk to Dayton's office. He picked up his pace from the slow shuffling to his accustomed energetic stride. Shaking off his onerous mood as best he could, he hurried northward, past the Art Institute. He would just make it on time.

Sam sat at his desk holding the reel of tape which held the record of Jon's second hypnotic state. Divergent thoughts of where the sessions might eventually lead him coursed through his mind. What type of solution would be needed? Would he find an answer? Reluctantly admitting the dream still puzzled him, he found little solace reflecting on Marie's attitude. What caused her to be so mysterious about making a call to Vienna? He had tried unsuccessfully to push the subject, hoping she would explain her reason before leaving last Thursday. Why reach out so far for help in what he hoped would be at the climax, an ordinary neurosis helped by ordinary treatment? But Marie had deftly avoided the issue each time he brought it up.

Standing, he crossed the room to put the tape on the machine. He listened intently to each word his patient spoke, feeling the hairs on his neck crawl when Jon faded only to be replaced by the sinister sound of the German speaking voice. When it finished, he rewound the tape, and went to the outer office. He'd have Tory transcribe it. but, along with the recordings of the first two meetings, he would also keep a file of live reproductions as well a the written ones.

Tory looked up from her work when he entered the reception room.

"I don't want this tape erased when you've finished with it, Tory," he said emphatically. "Toward the end of the trance, you will hear the patient speak German. I want you to type in the written translation that's in the box with the reel. Don't try to type the German."

"I'm glad you warned me," she said, accepting the container. "I don't know what I would have done if it had suddenly changed from English. Whose tape is this?"

"Mr. Ward's."

"Isn't that unusual?" she asked curiously, raising her eyebrows.

"Not really," he said hesitantly. Why should she know of the consternation the change in language had caused him and Marie? "You see, his mother was from Germany and Jon was born there. He came to this country while still a baby. Through introjection, he probably was able to speak the language when all his inhibitions were removed by being placed in a hypnotic state."

"Introjection?" A puzzled look crossed her face.

"Introjection is absorbing into your memory bank and personality, certain aspects of your surroundings without being aware of it. Nothing really uncommon."

"I see." She decided to reserve acceptance of her employer's explanation until after she had heard the entire tape. Something about the way he had answered her question made her distrustful. Smiling politely, she masked her suspicions.

Turning on his heel, Sam reentered his office. It bothered him that he had to lie to Tory. The subterfuge and falsehoods, the intrigue and mystery surrounding Jon and his dream were beginning to affect him. He also had to contend with the curious manner in which Marie had behaved. All of it ate at him like a cancer. He preferred being open and above board, especially where Marie was concerned. Not wanting to dwell on the enigma any longer than he already had, he shook his head as if to loosen the ideas from his mind. Knowing he would be rudely reminded of these same distressing thoughts later in the day when Jon kept his appointment, he busied himself preparing for his next patient.

A few minutes before three o'clock, Sam readied the recorder, placing a blank reel of tape on the machine. Checking the controls for remote operation from across the room, he returned to the chair he normally used when with a patient, and waited for Jon to make his appearance. At three o'clock Tory announced his arrival.

When he entered the room, he appeared fresh and relaxed from his long walk around the Loop. "How are you, Doctor?" he asked, placing the recorder on his lap.

"I'm fine, Jon," Sam said, smiling. "I'm the one who's supposed to be concerned with your well being. How are you?"

"From the standpoint of working, quite well." He hesitated, looking away from the doctor when his pretense of ease disintegrated.

After several seconds passed clumsily without either man speaking, Sam broke the silence. "I don't understand, Jon."

"I had the most peculiar experience Friday—" he began.

"This past Friday?"

"Yes. It's bothered me ever since. However, I don't think I alerted Trina through anything I did or didn't do over the weekend."

"I see," Sam said, reaching to the desk to start the tape recorder across the room. "Go on."

"Well, I tried something new for me—recording dialogue. I hadn't slept well the previous night—ah, trying to solve a problem in my novel. I guess I dozed off while I was sitting on the couch in our living room. I had the recorder running and it continued operating until it turned itself off automatically. That's when I woke up."

Sam closely studied his patient, repressing

the urge to ask him if his new book could be so dull that its writing put the author to sleep. His professional aplomb and concern for his patient prevented him from being facetious during a consultation. Considering the different aspects of Jon's hypnosis to this point in his treatment, he eagerly anticipated hearing of the man's experience.

"At first," Jon continued, "I wasn't aware I had dozed off. But when I found the cassette completely exhausted, I knew I had slept about fifteen or twenty minutes. When I rewound it, I heard the dialogue I had recorded, and then my voice, faltering as I fell asleep. Let me play it for you." He punched a button, activating the machine.

"You can never be honest with me again, Karen," Mike snapped vehemently.

"Mike, you're a fool if you thin—" His voice drifted away as he dozed. Then, the sound of steady, even breathing filled the office. After several minutes, during which Sam watched his patient apprehensively waiting for some development other than the gentle snoring, the rhythm changed abruptly, becoming more rapid. The labored gasping grew in volume, accompanied by the sounds of someone thrashing about.

Sam held up his hand, indicating Jon should stop the machine. When the room was quiet, he said, "Were you experiencing your dream at this point?"

"I'm not certain. I don't recall anything about it and I didn't have a headache when I was awakened by the machine turning itself off. However, the thing that disturbs me is about ready to play. Do you want me to continue?"

"By all means," Sam said, pulling himself to the edge of his chair.

Jon punched the button, the sound of his disturbed sleep once more coming from the small machine. Suddenly, it stopped. A low moan began, growing in intensity until a choking, heaving scream gashed the space between them. Then a voice, unfamiliar to him but known to Sam as the one which had spoken German during the last session, cried triumphantly, *Ich lebe noch!*

Stopping the machine, Jon sat back, staring at the psychiatrist. "Well?" he said after several minutes passed.

"Well, what?" Sam asked in return, hoping to buy a little more time before attempting an explanation that would satisfy his patient.

"Explain that, for chrissake! You asked me last week if I had ever spoken German, if my mother had ever spoken German around the house. I think you were trying to find out if I might have been exposed to the German language when I was a kid, when I could have subconsciously picked up some of the words. What the hell gives? Is that what you were looking for when you asked those questions? Did I speak German last week while I was under hypnosis?"

Sam knew it was too soon, too premature, to tell Jon the possibility existed of another personality dwelling within him. A dissociative type of hysterical neurosis would be difficult enough for the psychiatrist to accept, to control, under the right conditions. Usually patients affected by such a neurosis were women of high intelligence. It had only been within the last decade or so that definite confirmation of a man being affected had been documented. Through research, since Jon had become his patient, he had found the condition in men to be extremely rare. No established treatment had been found except to work patiently with all of the personalities involved, make an attempt to have the original individual become aware of, and gradually accept, the other beings residing within his body. Jon's body in this case. Deciding the best course to follow for the present would be simply bypassing the question, he cleared his throat. He would have to be evasive and at the same time maintain Jon's confidence.

"I want you to try and follow what I'm going to say," he began slowly. "I hope you aren't trying to tell me you have never once in your entire life ever heard the German language spoken. There are literally hundreds of ways you could have been exposed to the language. Through movies. Television programs. Overheard conversations on buses or elevators, or just walking downtown or through a store. Any one of these instances could have made an impression on you and under the right conditions, a complete recollection of a few words or a phrase could be made. For instance, being tired and falling asleep when you least expected could have triggered this phenomenon. The words you spoke while apparently dreaming might actually have been words you inadvertently picked up someplace, retaining them in your subconscious."

"But, did I actually speak them? It certainly doesn't sound like me."

"Under the circumstances, I feel the voice sounds familiar to me," Sam said, turning away. He hoped his lie would escape detection.

"Are you leveling with me, Doctor?"

Jon's direct manner warned Sam he was on thin ice concerning his patient's trust.

"Actually, Jon, it is too soon to tell if such is the case. I'd like to reserve opinion, if I may. When we have all the necessary information, we can make an intelligent decision concerning your particular neurosis. If you like, leave your tape and I'll have it translated to help put your mind at ease. Is that fair enough?"

Jon frowned for a moment before answering. It's not unlike, he thought, trying to write about something obscure without doing the necessary research. If he cooperated, giving all the information he could, the psychiatrist would be able to tell him what the nightmare concerned. Then all of his questions would be answered in due time.

"I guess," he said, handing him the cassette, "I'll be patient and play the game with you, Doctor. Let's get on with it. I've had the dream for twenty-eight years and what's another week, month or year when it's been that long?"

"I'm glad you've decided," Sam said, silently breathing a sigh of relief and placed the small tape on the desk.

"Other than the German speaking incident, have you had anything unusual take place?"

Jon bit his lip for a moment. "No. None that I can think of. I find it a little strange that there are no apparent repercussions from this—this thing."

"That's true. You don't seem to be suffering in any way because of the dream. The only incidents I can think of that are not in keeping with the norm, are this last one Friday, when you went into the hospital—and, of course, the time in Galena."

Sam thought back to his patient's folder. He knew he harbored doubts concerning Trina's ability to observe. The blood had been seen by her alone and all evidence, if indeed it had existed, had disappeared by the time the ambulance attendants arrived. He hoped to get to the bottom of that experience before releasing Jon as a patient.

"I'll admit," Jon said, smiling, "the recording of me speaking German threw me a bit, but I do trust you, Doctor Dayton. I guess I just don't want to lose my appointment to be hypnotized."

Sam smiled thinly. "Very well. Now, you don't recall having the dream occur since our last appointment—other than the incident you accidentally recorded, which may or may not be related to the dream?"

"Not once."

"That you remember," Sam corrected.

"That I remember," he agreed.

"Does the word *Zozobra* mean anything to you?"

Jon's forehead puckered at the sound of the strange word. "No. I don't believe I've ever heard it before. Why?"

"No reason that's important right now. What language would you say it is?"

He mouthed the word silently for a moment before shrugging.

"It's not important, Jon. However, *blue trees* are."

Jon instantly relaxed, entering a state of hypnosis.

"Are you comfortable, Jon?"

"Very comfortable. I'm very relaxed."

"Do you recall our having talked about your dream before?"

"Yes." His voice quickly became unvaried in its inflection.

"Would you like to discuss it some more? Explore it more?"

"Yes."

"Do you remember the part where you describe yourself as swimming?"

He began wringing his hands, shaking them as though they were wet. "Yes."

"Why are you swimming, Jon?"

"I must swim to survive. I must live. No one else."

"What do you mean by no one else?"

"None of the others must live—only me!"

"Are the other swimmers just like you, Jon?"

"Yes. No. Not really like me. I'm different from them."

"How are you different?"

"Something—or someone—is with me. There are two of me—only one of them."

"I thought you said before when we talked there were many others."

"There are. Individuals. There's something or someone with me."

"Can you explain that to me, Jon?"

"I can't. I don't understand it. But I must live," he said softly, each word failing until his mumbles were devoid of meaning.

Sam knew, if the other personality were to manifest itself as it had before, the moment had come. Sitting forward, he said firmly, "If you are there, whoever you are, speak and let me know."

Jon's face began heaving as it had during the last session until he looked like someone else, someone Sam felt he would not like as a person. Jon's eyes blazing brightly, stared straight ahead, past Sam, toward the ballerina.

"*Guten Tag, Herr Doktor!*" the voice said in a higher pitched timbre.

Swallowing hard, Sam cleared his throat, speaking slowly and distinctly. "*Wie heissen Sie?*" What is your name? What are you called?

The sinister laugh coming in answer sent a chill down his spine. He tried again. "*Wie heissen Sie?*"

Again no response, other than the awful laugh.

Sam fumbled in his jacket pocket for the slip of paper on which Marie had written the phonetic pronunciations of several German questions and statements. Pulling it out, he first checked the question he had asked. Repeating it to himself to make certain he had spoken it correctly, he voiced the query again.

Still nothing.

His eyes scanning the list, Sam found one he thought might help the situation. If the personality were told he did not speak or understand German, perhaps the cooperation which the doctor wanted would be given. Rehearsing it for several seconds first, he cleared his throat. *"Ich spreche nicht Deutsch! Wie heissen Sie?"*

Jon's eyes, focused on the statuette since the tumefaction began, suddenly moved, riveting themselves to Sam's. The psychiatrist recognized madness in the stare. A low, evil chuckle replaced the laughter and slowly, Jon's mouth opened. *"Adolf Hitler!"*

The two words brought drops of cold sweat to Sam's forehead. Impossible! It was completely, irrevocably impossible for Jon Ward to have said and meant what he had just heard. Had his question been answered properly? Had he pronounced the words correctly? He sat back heavily under the malevolent gleam pouring from the eyes fixed on him. Silence in the room pounded loudly in his ears. The only noise he could hear other than his patient's and his own breathing came from the tape recorder, taking down every sound made in the office. Its hum seemed to be slowly growing louder.

Dabbing at his forehead with a handkerchief, Sam studied the slip of paper, quickly mouthing the words that would ask in German if the personality could speak English. *"Spricht Sie Englisch?"*

Perniciously reflecting malice, depravity, hatred, Jon's eyes remained fastened on Sam for several long seconds before his mouth moved again. *"Ja! I could not when I was alive —in Germany. But now—I can speak English."*

"You say you are Adolf Hitler. How do I know you are who you say you are?" His throat felt rough and dry. He could scarcely believe the words he had just spoken.

"Does Jon Ward speak German?" the voice asked slyly.

"He says he can't," Sam countered.

"Well, doesn't that prove it? If he doesn't speak German and I do, doesn't that prove I am who I say I am."

"That proves nothing," Sam sneered. "You're not dealing with an idiot. You could be anyone, or anything." He blanched again at what he had just said, unable to understand why he had added the last word.

"You are most curious, are you not, Herr Doktor, as to the meaning of Herr Ward's dream?"

"Yes. Yes, I am."

"Wouldn't you like to know how it is I inhabit his body with him?"

"Yes." Sam watched the face slim back a little until he appeared almost normal. "Jon? Can you hear me? Jon Ward, answer me!"

"Nein! I am here yet. I have not left. *He* is the one who is gone."

"Is he gone for good? Will he come back?"

"He will be back."

"Where is he? Where is Jon Ward?"

"You hypnotized him."

"I know that. Is it only when he is hypnotized or asleep that you are strong enough to make your presence known?"

"Ja," the voice answered reluctantly. "When he sleeps, certain memories of mine invade his thoughts, disturbing him deeply."

"The dream is *yours?"* Sam wheezed in a hoarse whisper.

Jon's facial muscles grew rigid, unmoving. The voice did not answer.

"Is the dream Jon Ward has experienced since childhood, your dream?" He could not bring himself to address the new personality by the name it had chosen.

"Ja!"

The single word carried a sharpness that caused Sam to flinch momentarily. "Tell me about it," he said firmly after several minutes passed.

"No! *Nein!* Never!"

"Why?"

"It is too painful—*too painful!"*

"I know," Sam said with a touch of sympathy. "Jon has suffered a long time with it!" He felt as though he might be gaining an advantage over the new personality despite its sudden appearance.

"That is not my concern," the voice said

haughtily.

"You have no right to—"

"I have every right! Am I not Fuehrer of the Third Reich?"

The strong voice, precisely clipping the last words, sent an involuntary shudder through Sam. The thought couldn't be more horrible, more terrifying. If this really were— He stopped, mentally chastising himself for having formulated the thought. It's not possible, he told himself repeatedly. He would not be able to dwell on any one aspect of the conversation at this point. Later he would study the tape before beginning an analysis of it. "That part of history is over!" he said.

"You are right," the voice agreed without the alarm he had anticipated. "But it is only over for now. Not forever."

"What do you mean?" Sam asked, trying to smother the panic he had experienced just seconds before. "How will you rise to power if you are dead?"

"I will use Herr Ward's body. I will direct it, and it in turn, will be followed by all true Nazis in the world."

"What happens to Jon?"

"Who cares? *I must rise to power again!*"

"I care. Jon Ward especially cares what happens. His wife cares."

"And I care about me. The world cares about me."

"The world *hates* you, Adolf Hitler, if that is who you are."

"Nein!"

"Your public, your countrymen, your fellow Germans, all despite you. They loathe the memory of your very name!" he said loudly.

"NEIN!" the voice screamed, unable to accept the truth.

"Tell me about the dream, if you do not want to talk about yourself," Sam said, bearing in to find the truth.

"Nein. It is too painful. It is not good for me to remember it. It is bad enough when *he* experiences it through the dream."

"What does it mean?" Sam persisted.

"How I came to be with him in his body—in his mind—in his soul."

"Tell me about it. Perhaps I can help you forget it. That is my job, to help people. I can't help you unless I know all about your problem."

Sweat beaded on Jon's corpulent face as he rolled his head from side to side. "After I killed my body," the voice began after several long minutes of indecision, "I found I still existed. I sensed, rather than saw my surroundings, but I existed. I floated up and out of the bunker where I had hid for so many days. I wanted to scream to those faithful few who had remained with me that I was still alive. I tried, but I could not make a sound. I passed through the ceiling and earth separating my underground fortress from the fresh air and for a while, hovered over Berlin in all its ruination. I could feel death and destruction all about me but I did not care—I still existed. Somehow, I instinctively knew I must survive long enough to solve my dilemma by acquiring a new body. Something like highly excited feelings of emotion attracted me toward an underground railway that was not too far distant from my bunker.

"There I found a crazed soldier about to rape a woman. I had no control over what happened next. I was drawn to the soldier, absorbed into his spermatozoa. When he ejaculated his seed into the woman, my spirit passed along with that particular seed that was to become Jon Ward." The voice fell silent.

Many times in the past, Sam had thanked modern technology for the tape recorder when things happened quickly and words or phrases could have been missed during an analysis. He knew he would have failed miserably at taking notes and would have had less than half of what had been said. Now, he couldn't be grateful enough. Knowing he had every sound on tape, he'd have the leisure of time to study each word, each syllable if necessary. "Would you explain the first part of the dream to me now?"

"*NEIN! NEIN! NEIN!*" the voice screamed. "It is too painful."

"What did you say in German the first time you spoke while Jon was in a trance?"

"You don't understand German, Doctor?" the voice chuckled. "That is my little secret. Only I know what it means and I shall keep it my secret until the time is ready."

If the information given the first time was so highly confidential, Sam did not want the entity to be aware of the fact he already knew its content. It would be better to be on good terms with the other personality if Jon were to be helped at all. He made a note to check with the library to see if they had found the meaning of the word *Zozobra*. They were also checking the coordinates for him and hopefully the two riddles when answered, would explain the cryptic message.

"Can I bring Jon back now? I believe our conversation is ended."

"You may if you want. I shall be back. Back to stay. Soon." The voice deteriorated with each word.

The tumescent features shriveled, disappearing as the voice weakened and Jon's face reappeared. Sam looked at his watch, calculating he had more than an hour of tape remaining on the unused reel. An idea flashed in his mind. Without thinking, he acted immediately. If wrong, he would be able to undo it the next time Jon came in. However, if it proved to be correct, his patient would be able to solve his problem in degrees each time he had the dream in the future.

"Are you relaxed?" he asked when Jon's eyes returned to the ballerina.

"Yes. I feel very good."

"When I touch you on the shoulder, you will awaken refreshed and well rested. Do you understand, Jon?"

"Yes."

"However, the next time you have the dream, Jon, I want you to study it closely. Take your time with it. Examine it in its minutest detail. Allow it to develop in slow motion so you will be able to look at each scene more than once and be able to tear it apart as you experience it. Do you understand?"

"I understand."

"Fine, Jon," he said, reaching out to touch him. "Wake up, Jon. How do you feel now?"

"Great. Simply great," he said, noticing the look of delight on the doctor's face. "What happened? What did you find out?"

"I don't want you to get your hopes up about anything. It may be nothing, and again—" His voice drifted off. If would be wrong to tell Jon too much and have him be too aware. "Just trust me a while longer. As soon as I know something absolutely concrete, we'll talk. Is that fair enough?"

"I've gone along with you this far, Doctor, and I guess a little more trust isn't going to hurt me. See you next week?"

"Sooner if you feel you should need or want to talk with me, Jon." Sam had deliberately let the door remain open for his patient to call him between appointments. He seldom, if ever, had done that in the past. He was jealous of his free time. He felt he needed space about himself, to keep his patients as independent as possible. But Jon had an exceptional problem. He was convinced of that. If Jon needed him during the week, then, as a psychiatrist, he should be available. "Here's my card with my unlisted private number. Call anytime. If I'm not there, my answering service will be able to locate me."

"Fine, Doctor," he said taking the card and

slipping it into his shirt pocket. "I'll see you next week."

Jon left the office, making an appointment for the following Monday with Tory. A wide smile masked her real feelings of anticipation for the tape she knew would be more than interesting. The cries of *"NEIN! NEIN! NEIN!"* she had overheard piqued her curiosity. She wanted to get her hands on that tape as soon as possible. Something pretty awful must have happened today and it might be worth something. If she were right, Howie would be more interested in Jon Ward.

When the door closed behind Jon, Sam quickly looked up the number of the library he had called previously. He had requested their reference librarians to search for the meaning of the word *Zozobra* and to locate the spot indicated by the coordinates as given by Jon in German.

When the nasal voice of the library's switchboard operator answered, Sam said, "Betty Renard, please."

Tapping his fingers impatiently while he waited, he dwelt on the latest aspect of Jon's analysis. Could the spirit of Adolf Hitler be cohabitating in the same body as one of his patients? Unbelievable! Totally impossible. Or was it?

"Betty Renard, please," he repeated when the reference department answered.

"I'm sorry, Betty isn't working today. Can I

help you?"

"Who's speaking?"

"Ann Shepherder."

"This is Doctor Sam Dayton. I had asked Miss Renard to do a little research for me. Would you know if she has completed it?"

"Pertaining to what, Doctor?"

"I wanted to know the meaning of the word, *Zozobra*, and the location indicated by the coordinates 109 degrees West, 37 degrees North."

"Yes, Doctor. I worked with Betty on that. We haven't found the meaning of the word yet. Do you by chance know what language it is?"

"I have no idea. What about the coordinates?"

"I believe they're here on Betty's desk—someplace. Just a moment, please."

He forced himself to breathe normally. For some reason he felt closer to solving the dream than at any time since Jon had walked into his office for the first appointment.

"I've found them, Doctor," the girl said. "They locate the Four Corners area in the Southwest, exactly."

"Four Corners? Oh, yes. Where four state boundaries form right angles. Is that correct?"

"Yes, it is. The spot indicated sixty kilometers south and sixty east, is almost the center of a town called Cistern. Do you still want us to continue looking for the meaning of the word, Doctor?"

"By all means. If you find anything, could you call me immediately?"

"Of course."

Sam gave his office number, adding, "If I'm not here, leave any messages with my secretary."

"Fine, Doctor, and thank you."

"Thank *you*, Miss Shepherder," Sam said and broke the connection. Shaking his head, he returned the phone to its cradle, looking at the piece of paper where he had scribbled, "four corners—exactly. Sixty S., Sixty E.—Cistern." Now, what the hell could that mean? And what did this bit of information have to do with Jon and his dream, or more precisely, with Adolf Hitler's dream?

CHAPTER 12

A single bare bulb hanging from the ceiling lighted the squalid apartment in the harsh flood. If Tory ever noticed the ugliness of her life she never mentioned it for fear of incurring Howie's wrath. Watching him read Carole Nelumbo's file, she waited for some indication that her choice proved suitable for their next endeavor. The tension resulting from having stolen confidential records slowly eroded her nerves. A word of thanks, a compliment, a smile from him, would serve her well now.

"Hmph!" he snorted, grinning broadly. "Maybe *I* ought to offer to throw a fuck into her."

"Howie!" She pouted at the thought of her lover having sex with someone else.

"I'm only kidding. What I meant was, this broad is unhappy with her husband because of a—the—*Frohlich's Syndrome.*" He held the folder up to the light so he could read the unfamiliar words.

"The what?"

"Frohlich's Syndrome. I gather from the way she describes her husband and from the way the doctor explained it, it means he's pretty fat and ain't gót much in the pecker department."

"Oh."

"I guess that's why she went out looking for a little strange stuff and found a lover."

"I see." She looked expectantly at him, hoping he would say something that would resemble praise or a thank you.

"Get your pen and paper. I'm ready to dictate."

"I've got them right here, honey," she said eagerly, picking up the tablet she had brought home from the office.

"Dear, Mrs. Nelumbo, or may I call you Carole?" he began.

Tory recorded each word and syllable with a squiggly line that would be transformed into typed words the next day.

"I believe I know why you enjoy screwing good old Ed as much as you do. He's nothing like your old man, is he? Poor Guido with his big fat belly and little itsy-bitsy, wee-wee maker just doesn't do right for you. You must like big cock or you wouldn't play around with Ed the way you do. I strongly suggest you play my little game or I will see to it that Guido gets a letter in complete detail telling all about your meetings with his lieutenant and how you've decorated a sleazy apartment

into a regular sex den for the two of you
on the near north side."

"Do you want to sign it, Howie?"

"Naw. I'll be right there and explain how a
real letter will be going off to her husband
within forty-eight hours unless she comes up
with the amount of cash I ask for."

"How much?"

"I haven't decided yet. Five, maybe ten
thousand. Depends on how she reacts to my
offer to keep quiet about her love life."

Rereading her shorthand, she closed the
tablet, certain she had no questions concerning
the letter's content.

"I noticed you brought another file home
tonight," he said, motioning toward the folder
on the bed. "What did you bring this time?"

"I—I brought the transcription I did of Jon
Ward's session from last week."

"Is there something in it this time? Something that can make us some money?"

"I don't know."

"You don't know? What the hell is that supposed to mean? Haven't you got a fucking brain
in your goddamn head? You know what the hell
you're supposed to look for," he yelled.

Lowering her head at the unexpected
diatribe, she said quietly, "I think you should
read it. There's—"

"Why? Why should I read the goddamn thing
if there's nothing in it?" He stormed about the
room, slamming a fist into an open palm.

"That's just it. I think there might be, but I don't know what."

"What the fuck are you talking about?" Stopping, he turned to face her.

"This morning, Doctor Dayton said I should make absolutely certain the tape was not erased. That it should be labeled and put with the recording of his first session."

Howie studied her face for a moment and said more quietly, "So? Is that unusual? Has he ever done it with any other patient?"

"A few. He has several bookshelves with recordings that are never to be erased. But most of his tapes are erased as soon as they're transcribed to typewritten notes."

Picking up the folder from the bed, he leafed rapidly through the thin stack of papers. "What makes you think there's something worthwhile in these?"

"There was German on the tape today."

"German?" he said and stopped flipping pages.

"Yes, and Doctor Dayton had the translation all written out. I had to insert the English words when Mr. Ward started speaking in German."

"What'd he say? In German?"

"A bunch of goofy things. I thought they sounded sort of like directions for something or other."

"Directions?"

"Well, you'll have to read it to see if I'm right."

"You still haven't told me why you thought this was worth something."

"I guess it was the way Doctor Dayton explained how Mr. Ward could speak German when he apparently doesn't understand the language."

"What'd Dayton say?"

"Something about—I forget the word—how Mr. Ward could have picked up the words when he was young. His mother came from Germany and he was born there, too."

"Well, shit, that explains it. What got you so interested other than the fact you got hot pants for this Ward character?"

"That's not true, Howie," she said, feeling her face redden at the accusation.

"Okay. Okay, already! So you're not hot. What made you interested in it?"

"I think Doctor Dayton wasn't telling me the truth. I think he lied about how Mr. Ward could speak German when he claims he doesn't.'"

"So he's lying. What right have you to know everything?"

"He's explained different things to me and he's always been straightforward. But this time, it wasn't the same. I think he was trying not to tell me the real reason behind the different language."

Turning the folder over in his hands, he glared at her.

"Read it. Please?" she whispered. "Maybe you can figure out why Doctor lied and why Mr. Ward can speak German while he's hypnotized. I just don't believe what Doctor told me."

As he sat down on the bed, he made no effort to camouflage his disgust for the indecision and lack of imagination she had revealed. Why did he have to make all the decisions about their intended blackmail victims?

His eyes quickly flitted across the pages while he read the transcript of the second hypnotic trance. Nothing impressed him until he came to the notation concerning the subject's mumblings being indistinguishable and the heading: "Translated from German." He slowed his reading until he came to the coordinates. "They sure sound like directions for something," he murmured more to himself than to Tory.

He continued reading before suddenly leaping from the bed. "*Zozobra?*" he cried. "What the fuck is *Zozobra* doing here in the middle of the German translation?"

"Is—is that important, Howie?"

He ran his fingers through his hair, shaking his head. "I don't know. It sure as hell doesn't make sense. Does the doctor or this Ward know what it means?"

"I—I don't know. Why?"

Pacing the room like a caged animal, his face screwed up in thought while trying to fit the puzzle together. Periodically, he would stop to smile in a way that frightened her. "Naw," he mumbled under his breath, "that doesn't make sense. No sense at all." He continued his route around the small table, to the side of the Murphy bed, over to the curtainless window and back without deviating from his course. After twenty minutes, he stopped, shrugging at the same time.

"What is it, honey?" she pleaded. Concerned he was going into some sort of reaction from drugs they had taken in the past, she stood, confronting him. "Tell me what's wrong!" she demanded. "What's the matter?" She grabbed his beefy arms, barely stopping him before he walked over her.

"Nothing! There's nothing the matter with me. I just can't figure out what *Zozobra* is doing in the translation." Sidestepping her, he continued his pacing.

"What does it mean?" she asked, releasing her grip.

"Huh? Oh, Old Man Gloom."

"What?"

"Every September there's a fiesta at Santa Fe and they burn a big figure they call *Zozobra* in the middle of a huge bonfire. They have to get rid of Old Man Gloom before they can have a good time, or some goddamn thing."

She picked up the folder, studying it for a moment. "What does this mean? '*Zozobra* took the people away. No one was there because of *Zozobra*"? She wrinkled her forehead thoughtfully.

"You got me there," he said. "When does this Ward guy come in again?"

"He was in today. Why?"

"Apparently you haven't typed his session from today. Or is this it?"

"No, this one is last week's. I'll probably type today's within the next day or two."

"When you do, I want to see it."

"Then there *is* something there?" she asked

hopefully.

"I doubt it. I just want to know what the hell this dream of his means and why *Zozobra* was mentioned. It just doesn't make sense."

She suddenly felt dejected. For some reason, she had decided that Jon's folder would interest him for the same reasons Sterling Tilden's and Carole Nelumbo's had. Now, he was just curious.

"Get your goddamn clothes off!" he ordered roughly. "I want to get to sleep early so I can go to the library tomorrow and check out the coordinates Ward mentioned. Maybe I can solve the puzzle before your doctor can." He reached out, tearing her blouse open to expose her well formed breasts. Pulling her to him, he kissed her roughly, exploring her mouth. He ran his tongue down her chin and attacked her breasts, evoking a scream of pleasure when he roughly bit her taut nipples.

Thankful for what she took as his show of gratitude, she responded in kind. The couple fell to the Murphy bed, tearing at each other's clothes.

Although their lives as husband and wife had been an emotional puzzle, Millicent Tilden found, soon after her marriage to Sterling, diverse outside duties to perform. Countless charities held her attention, taking the place of his apparent lack of interest in her as a woman. She loved him despite his indifference to having sex with her. The few times they had made love during their twenty years together, she had found rewarding, and Sterling had been a kind and considerate man in every other aspect. Now, for some inexplicable reason, he had died by his own hand.

The shock of his death had anethesized her feelings since Friday when the bank president called. Following his cremation early Monday afternoon, the weight of tears she had held back broke through her thin veneer of control, washing away her composure. He was dead. He was gone—forever. She would survive without him in her societal functions as she had done in the past. But the gnawing question she could not answer was, why? Why had Sterling killed himself?

Following the memorial service, Millicent left the chapel with Charles and Jennifer LeMay, the only people Sterling had ever allowed to enter their married lives as close friends. Charles drove in silence, concentrating on traffic as he made his way toward the Tilden home.

"Are you certain you'll be all right tonight, Millie?" Jennifer asked, squeezing the widow's hand.

"Yes. I feel much better since I was able to let my sorrow out at the funeral home," she said, her voice soft but controlled.

"Jennifer could stay with you tonight, if you want," he offered, breaking into their conversation.

"I appreciate everything you two have done but I'll be all right. I can't ever expect Sterling's death to be explained to me in a way that I will understand. But I do realize I can't mourn him forever. The sooner I adjust my way of thinking to being alone, the better off I'll be." She stared through the windshield, not focusing her eyes on the dancing lights which flitted past.

"Well, I'm glad we took you out to dinner and had a chance to talk," Charles said. He and Jennifer had practically spirited her away from the funeral home following the service. The bank officials and acquaintances, people who had come in contact with the Tildens because of charitable undertakings, had descended on Millicent, about to smother the grieving woman with their expressions of sympathy.

"I think you two are the most precious commodity in the world," Millie said when Charles eased the car to a stop in front of her home. "You're friends and totally irreplacable. Will you come in and have a nightcap? It's really quite early. Only nine-thirty."

"Of course we will," Jennifer said, opening her door.

The threesome walked to the front entrance and as Millie unlocked it, Charles shot a furtive look at his wife, slowly nodding his head. He knew their friend would not allow the loss to change her in any way.

Entering the wide hallway, Millie said, "Why don't you make yourselves comfortable in the living room and I'll get three brandies. Will you pick up the mail, Charles, and put it on the table?"

He bent down, gathering the half dozen envelopes that had scattered when the postman dropped them through the mail slot earlier in the day. Absently, he thumbed though the mail stack, finding two utility bills and a thick envelope from the bank containing their monthly checking account statement. Two small missives, containing sympathy cards, he surmised, and one with Millicent's name typed across it without a return address, held his interest momentarily. With the exception of the bills and the bank envelope, he retained the rest, offering them to Millie when she brought the drinks.

"Just put them on the coffee table if you will, Charles," she said, sitting down after giving her guests their drinks. "I don't feel much like reading mail right now. Were there any bills?"

"I left them on the hall table," he said.

"I'm to meet with our attorney in the morning. He advised me today to bring any outstanding bills along so he could pay them for me." She raised her glass and said, "To Sterling, who was not the happiest man in the world and who will hopefully find peace in the death he has chosen."

The LeMays slowly lifted their glasses, drinking the macabre toast. Having chatted amiably for almost an hour, and after a second brandy, they departed.

Millicent turned out the lamps in the living room by means of a master switch in the hall. Just as the room plunged into darkness, something caught her attention. The envelopes resting on the coffee table were framed in the light spilling through the hallway arch. Retrieving them, she found names on the backs of the two smaller envelopes. Expressions of sympathy from the Hackgens and the Helbarths. She studied the larger one for a brief moment and laid it along with the unopened cards on the table. Her exhaustion prevented her from confronting the condolences, to read the saccharin messages contained within. The next day would be plenty of time. Tomorrow, after she returned from the attorney's office, she would sit down and open every one of the letters, circulars and advertisements. Slowly, she walked up the staircase to her bedroom.

An errant, cool breeze wafted through the open window, immediately losing itself in the humid atmosphere of the fourth floor apartment. Howie lay on his back staring at the shadowy ceiling. Next to him, Tory's even breathing told him she slept soundly. Propping himself up on an elbow he studied the woman's naked body, finishing his appraisal with a study of her face. What the hell did he see in her? She had been a good meal ticket but now she suddenly burst into his thoughts as a possible millstone he would have to rid himself of in the near future. She didn't have the class to go along with the possibility of being rich.

Rich! He rolled the word around his mouth, enjoying the feel of it. He would soon be rich because of his plan for people like Sterling Tilden and Carole Nelumbo. Since Tory had to type the letter to the woman, he'd go to the library and locate the spot indicated by the coordinates Jon had mentioned in his trance. Perhaps there would be something in future sessions with the psychiatrist that would be worth the trouble to write a letter seeking additional funds from the Wards.

Refocusing his eyes on her body when she began moaning in her sleep, he trailed one fingertip across her breasts. He encircled her nipples in an imaginary line before tracing it down her stomach, around her navel, ultimately to her hairy triangle. She writhed at his touch.

Once she had served her purpose, now that she had one other than merely satisfying his sexual needs, he knew it would be smart to replace her. "You just ain't got it, baby," he mumbled softly. "As soon as I get enough bread together, you'n' I are splitting."

Opening her eyes, she groggily sat up. "What'd you say, honey?"

"I'm glad you woke up." Encircling her shoulders with his arms, he lowered her back to the thin mattress before rolling on top of her. "I'm horny again."

Smiling, deliciously sleepy, Tory spread her legs before wrapping her arms around his body.

Despite the fact that she had won two out of three racquetball games, the feeling of elation she should have experienced escaped Trina. Unlike the times in the past when she had defeated Jon in the game he had taught her, she felt weary. Not of body, but of spirit—almost morose. He had been quiet most of the evening, ignoring her questions about his hypnotic session earlier in the day. Normally, they played racquetball on Wednesday nights but because of a meeting Trina wasn't certain would be over early enough for them to play that evening, they had moved their midweek game to Monday night.

When they arrived home from the indoor tennis club, he had gone directly to the shower, then to bed. Although she followed a short while later, he feigned sleep when she slipped between the sheets. Now, she lay on her back, eyes wide open, wondering if she should say something. She could tell he was awake. He, too, lay on his back when normally he turned on one side or the other to go to sleep.

"Are you awake?" she asked.

"No."

"Is something bothering you?"

"In a way." He knew he shouldn't tell her about Friday's incident when he had fallen asleep and spoken German in a voice that didn't even sound like his.

"Want to talk about it?"

"No."

"Is it something to do with this afternoon's appointment with Doctor Dayton?"

"No. And I thought I said I didn't want to talk about it," he snapped.

Trina didn't answer.

Turning his head to see if she had been insulted or hurt by his cutting answer, he offered, "I'm sorry. I've got something bugging me and as soon as I figure it out, I'll fill you in. All right?"

She nodded. "Are you sure I can't help? It might do you good to talk it out with me."

"You'll be the first to know—when I have it solved." He smiled reassuringly. "Are you happy?"

"Me? Happy? Yes, I'm very happy." Her voice held a touch of sarcasm at first but softened immediately. Why shouldn't he have a private problem to solve? He didn't have to consult her about everything. Ultimately he would tell her about it.

"About everything? About me having to go to a psychiatrist to get my head straightened out, are you happy about that?" His voice, carrying a decided edge, cut through the darkness.

"I'm mostly happy because of you," she said. "I'm happy because you're finally going to have an old, old question answered for you. If you weren't going to Doctor Dayton, we'd both be disturbed over your dream—"

"Oh, it's all right for me to be disturbed. But now that I'm going to see a shrink on a regular basis, you've dropped the concerned role and are happy. Is that it?"

"Are you disturbed over something that happened today?" she asked, impulsively sitting up in bed.

"No. I thought—"

"You thought I didn't care anymore since you're going to the doctor? Oh, darling. I'm interested in everything where you're concerned. I didn't mean to imply I'm not worried about you. I'll worry until you're given a clean bill of health."

"I'm glad that's what you meant." He sat up next to his wife.

She reached out, taking his hand. "How do you feel? Are *you* happy?"

Hesitating several seconds, he finally said, "I was just taking mental inventory and I guess I'm about as happy as anyone could be." *Except*, he thought, *I want a dog.*

"Are you happy, even about seeing the doctors and having spent time in the hospital?"

"I guess I am. Yeah. I am." *But a dog would make things absolutely perfect.*

"Then," she said dramatically, "let's go out Saturday night. What do you say? We haven't been out to dinner since our anniversary in April, other than in Galena."

"It's been a while," he agreed before voicing the thoughts that had intruded several seconds before. "I want a dog."

"You want a *what?*" she exclaimed, studying her husband's shadowy figure.

"Yeah," he said, bounding off the bed. "I've been thinking about it for a long time. An Alsatian bitch, and I could call her Blondie."

"You're serious, aren't you?" she said, smiling to herself in the dark.

"*Ja!*"

"Are you forgetting the landlord has a rule about no pets allowed?" she asked, misinterpreting his one word answer for slang instead of German. After groping for the lamp on the stand next to her side of the bed, she turned on the nightlight.

Limping up and down the half dark bedroom

in a slow, almost painful manner, he bellowed in English, "Who does he think he is, anyway? When I regain my power, he'll be the first to go. It is very important for me to have a dog."

Huddling back toward the headboard, she pulled the sheet around her bare body when the high pitched voice slashed out, sending a chill through her.

Despite his nakedness, he went to the window, opening it to the top. Breathing deeply, he turned to face her. Startled by her appearance, cringing behind the sheets, he said in his normal voice, "What is it, darling? Will the opened window be too much?"

She fought the tears struggling for release and coughed to rid her throat of the lump forming there. "It might be. Why not just leave it open a few inches and come back to bed."

"All right," he said passively, closing the window to within a hand's breadth of the sill and returned to bed. When he lay next to his wife, he looked up at her. "I love you."

"I love you, too," she managed, sliding down next to him. Within minutes, he breathed deeply but his eyes remained fixed to the shadowy ceiling. If Jon were to be helped, Doctor Dayton would have to be told about this latest incident of personality change.

CHAPTER 13

The hum of the copying machine automatically stopped and Tory scooped together the duplicate pages of Jon's third session. Placing the material in a manilla envelope, she returned to her desk, quickly concealing it in the drawer over the kneehole. She straightened the original copy, slipping it to the back of the file the doctor had asked for when he came in. Picking up the reel of tape, she went to the door of the psychiatrist's office and entered quietly.

"Yes, of course you did the right thing, Mrs. Ward," Sam said, not noticing his secretary coming through the door. He paused while listening to Trina. "It may be helpful. At this time I wouldn't be able to say. However, I will put it in his file." He paused again. "Thank you, Mrs. Ward. 'Bye, 'bye." He laid the phone in its cradle.

Perhaps it was Sam's haggard appearance, or the way he sat behind his desk staring at nothing in particular while he talked on the phone, that told her something out of the norm bothered her employer. She wondered if he suspected something about her activities. A quick mental check of her covert methods convinced her that such could not be the case. At least, not at this point. She knew of no clue she might have left. She was certain. Maybe the psychiatrist needed a psychiatrist, she mentally giggled.

"Doctor Dayton?" she said softly, approaching him. "Here is the complete file on Jon Ward."

Looking up with a start, Sam forced a tired smile. "Oh, thank you, Tory. Do you have the tape of yesterday's session, too?"

"Right on top," she said, laying the items on his desk.

He opened the file, inserting the information about Jon's wanting a dog. What could that have to do with his dream? he wondered. Still, he knew from his own professional experience that many times it was the insigificant clue or item that had gone overlooked for a long time, that held the solution to a patient's problem. Right now, he couldn't think straight. He'd wait to attack the meaning when he was with Marie that evening.

"I'll be leaving right after my three o'clock appointment today," he said, rubbing his face. Even his skin felt tired. Earlier in the day, he had fallen asleep on the couch in his living room at five-thirty, awakening with a sense of panic at seven. He had played Jon's tape so many times Monday night he had lost count. After a quick shower and shave, he still had not arrived at any conclusion concerning the strange turn of events when the other voice proclaimed itself to be Adolf Hitler. The brief walk to his office had been refreshing but with barely an hour to wait before his last appointment, his exhaustion closed in with a vengence once more. The morning appointments had gone smoothly but fatigue began rapidly overtaking him after lunch. Only the opportunity to talk about this Hitler thing with Marie would revive him to the point of being efficiently alert.

As she left Sam's private office, Tory wondered what Mrs. Ward had wanted. When she got her hands on the file, she'd read the note Sam had scribbled hurriedly, then stuck in the folder. She smugly realized that Howie would find the latest episode in Jon's hypnotic revelations more than interesting. Hoping the information she pilfered would be worthy of their scheme as well, she resumed her work. Five minutes before three, the attractive but troubled Carole Nelumbo entered the office.

Marie never looked better to Sam. Once they were together, his exhausted faculties quickly rejuvenated, the cloak of weariness peeling from his tired body. She told him how she had waited apprehensively to see him since her own musings about Jon had turned up nothing but more confused thoughts. Still, the idea that his dream seemed somehow familiar, constantly, persistently gnawed at her. It was just begging to be recognized.

"I think I'd better just have coffee for now," he said when she offered him a martini.

"Why?" Noting his tired appearance, she wanted to know the reason for his fatigue.

"You said we should be eating before settling down to play Ward's tape from yesterday's session. I'll tell you why I'm beat though. I only slept about an hour and a half last night."

"Out running around while I'm working my you-know-what off?" She smiled teasingly, re-entering the living room with filled cups.

"I wish," he said, taking the coffee, "that was the reason. I played Ward's tape over and over last night—"

"Must be interesting," she broke in.

"I think you'll find it a little more than interesting. But we'll wait. I'm hoping dinner perks me up."

"You've really got my curiosity aroused." She turned to leave for the kitchenette.

"Wait a minute, Marie. I want to play one little thing for you," he said, taking Jon's cassette from his jacket.

"What is it?"

"You'll see." Flipping the door shut on the cassette, he turned his portable machine on. He had set the tape so it would be a minute or so before Jon spoke the brief German statement. "Jon fell asleep Friday afternoon and had his dream manifest while his recorder was running. He spoke German and I want you to translate."

"Is it much?"

"Only three or four words."

As though on cue, the strange, high pitched voice shouted, "*Ich lebe noch!*"

He stopped the tape and turned, waiting for her translation.

"I still live!" she said simply.

"He seems to be stuck on that one idea, doesn't he?" he suggested, ejecting the cassette from the deck.

"Was that all? There was nothing more?" she called over her shoulder from the kitchenette.

"Just labored breathing before and after. If you liked that number, wait 'til you hear yesterday's session."

"Why, Sam? After Jon began speaking German unexpectedly during the one meeting, and now again when he fell asleep, what else has happened that could top it?"

"I won't say. I want you to hear it for yourself," he said, mentally cursing the habit of taking food for bodily sustenance. He wanted to get on with playing the tape. "You say he stated in German, 'I still live,' right?"

"That's correct." She brushed past him to the dining area with the salad.

" 'I still live' seems to be a kind of theme, doesn't it?" he said, thinking back to when the voice identified itself as Adolf Hitler.

She nodded, indicating he should sit down and begin eating. Reluctantly taking his seat, he toyed with the leaves of Romaine lettuce. They had talked about her trip when he first arrived and she had insisted, because of his exhausted appearance, that they have dinner before devoting the evening to Jon Ward and his dream. Suddenly, she found herself wondering what Jon Ward was like as a person since she had previously thought of him and his dream as being one complete entity. The dream's strange scenes had crossed her mind more than once in the last few days when she tried linking it with her own memory. For now, she would allow Sam to have his secret. After a decent meal, they would listen to the tape together.

Purposely avoiding the subject of Jon and his dream, they indulged in more small talk about her trip. When they finished, he seemed more alert. Leaving the dinner table cluttered with the debris of their meal, they went to the far end of the living room where stereo equipment stood against the wall. Threading the tape onto the machine, he adjusted the volume before sitting down on the couch. He kicked off his shoes, looking across the room where she sat curled up in a large chair.

The tape inched toward the moment he anticipated, all the while watching Marie intently to see her reaction. She smiled at his more than passable albeit rote German, when he said, "*Wie heissen Sie?*" The dark laughter, which met the query, froze her lovely features in a questioning mask.

Again, Sam's voice asked in German, "What is your name?" The laughter filled the room again and when it died away, silence crushed in on the two psychiatrists. He remembered fumbling for the paper in his pocket. The intensity of the void brought Marie's eyes up to glance at him. He tiredly stared at her. She was just about to speak when Sam's voice sounded from the speaker. "*Ich spreche nicht Deutsch! Wie heissen Sie?*"

She held her breath and sat forward as though knowing this time there would be some response other than the laughter. The only sound in the living room was the quiet hum of the recorder's motor as it turned. Then, "*Adolf Hitler!*" came out of the speakers in a voice dissimiliar to Jon Ward's but exactly like the one that had previously spoken German.

Marie gasped. "My God, Sam," she managed when he stopped the machine. "What do you make of that?"

"What do *you* make of it, Marie?" he shot back.

She leaned back, silent. After several minutes she asked, "Is there more?"

"Yes."

"In German?"

"No. Surprisingly enough, he cooperated, agreeing to speak English. Want to hear it?"

"By all means."

He flipped the machine's control bar forward, listening once more to the unfamiliar voice. Having heard the tape so many times the previous night, he mouthed the words as they were spoken. When it finished, he stopped the recorder before turning to confront Marie. Her ashen face brought the freckles out more boldly than he had ever seen.

"What do you believe at this point, Sam?" she

asked after several minutes of silence passed. "Do you believe what you've heard?"

Shrugging, he walked to the large window overlooking the outer drive and Lake Michigan. Lines of cars fled past hurriedly, seemingly to escape his detection from above. "I've listened to that tape at least eleven or twelve times and I still don't know what to believe. Are we dealing with another personality—a personality so devious as to assume a well known person's name? Could it be a wildly complicated Oedipus complex? Could it be—" and his voice trailed off.

"Could it really *be* Hitler?" Marie quietly finished for him. They stared at each other.

"Come on, Marie, you don't believe that, do you?" he scoffed.

"At this point, with what little we know," she said, smiling in a reassuring way, "I think we should keep our minds open to most anything."

"I can't accept it," he said curtly. "I can't accept a male Bridey Murphy who thinks he's Adolf Hitler. Do you realize what you're saying? That this is Adolf Hitler manifesting in the body of my patient!"

"I didn't say I believed it—not yet, at any rate. There *are* a couple of points going for that particular argument, however."

"What? I don't believe the direction you're taking. Where's my cool headed, unflappable, Vienna-trained psychiatrist?"

"I'm right here, Sam. That's primarily why I'm being so open to the idea."

"You'll have to explain yourself. You've lost me someplace."

"You remember how I kept saying something about the first part of the dream seemed somehow familiar to me?"

"I remember," he said, sitting on the ottoman opposite her.

"When I was going to school, I did a thesis on the psychology of mass hypnosis. In fact, it was the subject matter of my talk the first time we met. Remember?"

He smiled, acknowledging the pleasant recollection.

"While I was doing my research," she continued, "I naturally gravitated to a study of Hitler and his ability to sell his ideas so convincingly. In essence, he was mesmerizing thousands of people at once. His record, I think, speaks for itself."

"So far, I agree with you. But I don't understand the connection to what you're saying now and what it has to do with Jon Ward's dream."

"All right, Sam. Listen carefully because I'm not certain I'm right about this. Let me have his folder."

He retrieved the file from the coffee table in front of the couch. Handing it to Marie, he sat down again, watching while she carefully went through the papers.

"All the pieces," she said while scanning the neatly typed sheets, "at least for the first part of the dream, fell into place for me when the voice said it was Adolf Hitler. Here it is," she said, withdrawing his notes on the first and second sessions. "Remember now, the voice said he didn't want to recall the first part of the dream because it was too painful for him to do so."

He nodded.

"The reason I felt it seemed so familiar was because I had studied him closely. Now I believe the first part of the dream is a reliving of his career in vivid symbols. He simply can't bear the thought of how his grand plan failed."

"You're serious, aren't you?" he said, shifting forward on the ottoman.

"I'm very serious. I'm not saying I believe it completely at this point, but I do see similarities between his career and the first part of the dream."

"Go ahead."

"First, the dream always started with the sound of cheering. 'Screams of adulation,' to use Jon's words when describing the sound. The *dee-hah* rhythm of the cheers could be '*sieg heil*' cried over and over. I'm not certain about that aspect, but I've seen a Nazi propaganda film showing thousands of people gathered at a rally. The cries of the people had a definite '*dee-hah*' beat to it. Just as he describes."

"Score a point for the 'other voice,' then," he said quietly. "What about the running, and being all alone?"

"Hitler felt as though his generals had deserted him toward the middle of the war. By the end of it, he trusted absolutely no one. The running in a vacuumlike situation could be his interpretation of being deserted by those he trusted. Toward the end, he made all the decisions concerning the war."

Sam shook his head. "What about the trees turning into people and then burning? Have you got an answer for them?" His voice, ringing with disbelief, quavered.

"Probably the Jews he ordered murdered. I'm not sure. They were the obstacle he had to overcome to gain purity in the German super race. He probably feared retaliation at their hands toward the end of the war, as much as defeat at the hands of the Allies."

"The whole thing is unbelievable," he said. "The way you're describing it, it sounds plausible and incredible at the same time."

"The woman," Marie continued, "in the first part of the dream, could be Eva Braun."

He shook his head slowly before nodding in mute agreement.

"It's been reported she commited suicide at the same time Hitler did, but she didn't shoot herself. She supposedly took poison," Marie said.

Sam's eyes brightened. "That would explain her clutching her throat and collapsing without the gun going off—the one Hitler tried to kill her with. Hey, wait a minute. If she killed herself with poison, how come he tries to kill her in his dream?"

Shrugging, she said, "Perhaps he feels responsible for her death. For all we know, he insisted she commit suicide."

His tanned complexion paled a bit. "I suppose," he said softly, "the recurring statement about being alive, or still living, or whatever the hell was said, strengthens the argument?"

Marie thought for a moment before speaking. "I suppose it does. If Adolf Hitler suddenly found his spirit still existed after he shot himself, he would naturally relish the fact that he had beaten death as he had anticipated it to be. *Ich lebe noche!* I still live! He said it the first time Jon spoke German. In fact, he said it directly to you, Sam. Then, when Jon fell asleep and accidentally recorded himself having the dream, the same gloating boast—I still live, was said. Now, in the third hypnotic trance, it's the same theme, over and over. I think it reinforces the idea but we should examine the whole of the dream."

"I was just going to bring up the second part of the dream," he said. "The part the voice was willing to talk about. Do you believe that's on the level?"

Thinking for a moment, she pursed her lips before speaking. She riffled through the pages, pulling one of them out to study before continuing. "It could be. Listen to this. This is from the translation I made the first time the voice spoke in German. *I have been very weak—every day I become slowly stronger. My host has been difficult to conquer. Soon I will control him!*"

"I see what you're driving at, Marie," he said. "The second part of the dream was never experienced by Jon because each time he had the dream, he woke up at the suicide of—of—of Hitler. Christ! I can hardly bring myself to say it, much less say it in a way that lends credence to the theory. Apparently the only way the other voice—Hitler—had any degree of control over Jon was when he was either asleep, or very relaxed, or—or hypnotized. He was able to *live,* if you will, or experience the second part, when Jon was on the angiogram table in a very relaxed state. The hypnotizing speaks for itself. I removed his inhibitions where control over his mind was concerned. I left the door wide open for this—this thing to happen. The incident in Galena was the first time he didn't have enough resistance. Or the other one had too much strength. Whichever, the result was the continuation of the dream under so called normal conditions."

Marie nodded, understanding what he said, but held up her hand in a gesture bringing him to a stop. "Don't get too optimistic, Sam."

"I'm not. I'm not even certain I can buy any of this, even if all the proof indicates that such is the case. The entire idea seems just a little preposterous." Snorting, he rumpled his curly hair.

"Why? Why does the possibility seem preposterous?" she asked, sitting forward.

"What's the purpose of it? Why would Hitler's spirit—no, make that personality—suddenly surface here in Chicago after all these years? It doesn't make sense."

"If you discount the second half of the dream as it was explained by the voice while Jon was under hypnosis, it doesn't. But if you take what was said in truth, it almost makes good sense."

Fumbling through the folder, she withdrew a sheet and said, "Here's more evidence of a sort: his sudden, spasmodic abhorrence of alcohol. His limp. His apparent sore arm. What's this?" She held up the memo he had written that morning about Jon's change in personality the previous evening and wanting a dog.

He explained what Trina had said and wondered about Marie's reaction when she merely nodded. "I don't understand about his arm, though," he said, shaking his head.

"When the assassination attempt on Hitler's life failed, he was injured slightly but retained stiffness in an arm and one leg. As a result, he limped."

"The same arm and leg?"

"The same." The expression on his face told her she should continue. "Let's deal with the facts as they are and not as they appear to be. If what the other personality said is true, then the *why* is readily explained. The *how* and *who* and *where* are more or less taken care of. We know *who* the other voice says he is. We know *how* and *why* he came to be locked into the same body as Jon Ward. The physical evidence concerning the sore arm and the limp seem to verify it. The unknown factors at this point I would say, are what happens next and *where* do we go from here?"

He digested her evaluation for several moments. "I think we could expand on *what* a little more than 'What happens next.' What does he want? What is he after? We could also extend the *how*. How does he intend to accomplish whatever it is he is after?"

"How do we know he wants to accomplish anything, Sam? For all we know, the spirit of Hitler, or this particular personality, may be a victim of circumstances just as Jon is."

"Are you saying he had no choice in the matter, Marie?"

"Perhaps."

Reaching for the open folder, he took it from her lap. He thumbed through the stapled sessions, withdrawing the second hypnotic trance. Scanning the contents for a moment, he stopped short, looking up at her. A confident smile played on his mouth. "Then how do you explain what he said in the second trance when he spoke German? *Soon I will control him.* He means his host—Jon Ward. Then he said, *Then, I can claim what is rightfully mine.* He has a purpose all right, an intent of will that seems as though it was almost planned before he died—or formulated soon after death."

Her face whitened as she sat back in the easy chair. "He also said something about retaining information—the coordinates and directions to something," she added quickly. "If your theory is correct, Sam, these aren't the ramblings of a recently freed spirit. They're the plans or the most important memories Hitler retained when he died."

"You mentioned the coordinates," he said. "I had them checked. They pinpoint the Four Corners in the southwestern part of the States."

The questioning look on her face brought further explanation from Sam. "I have no idea what the connection is," he finished.

"Did you find out anything about *Zozobra?*"

"They're still looking."

She frowned and said, "I'll call a friend of mine at the University. Maybe he can help."

While both doctors ruminated their deductions, a lull fell over the room until Sam began to chuckle.

"What's so funny?" she asked.

"I was just thinking that we sound like a couple of ghost chasers. I'm sure we're overreacting to the tape. Parapsychology isn't my bag and it's not yours, either."

Her face brightening noticeably, she jumped from her chair, pacing about the room, her forehead furrowed in thought. He watched, fascinated as the woman he loved suddenly displayed facial expressions showing puzzlement, successful recall, wonderment, joy, sadness and discovery. She stopped her perambulating in front of the large bookcase that covered one wall of the living room. Scanning the titles she reached up, selecting a thick volume.

"I don't want you to think I'm forgetting the topic we've been discussing," she said, plopping down in the easy chair again, "but I've got to do some research right now. In the meantime, you get all of Jon's health records together and I will put some questions to you in a little while that might help us."

Bewildered, he picked up the file containing Jon Ward's medical and psychiatric history and sat on the couch. Studying the detailed outlines, he periodically raised his eyes to study Marie who was lost in the book lying open on her lap. He hadn't caught the title and after several minutes of overpowering curiosity, decided he would know in time when she had found whatever might be the object of her search.

Thirty minutes stretched into forty-five and when an hour had almost elapsed, she cleared her throat. "I think I've got some corroborating material here that might help us make a decision about the other voice."

"What book is it?" he asked, purposely waiting until she answered.

"John Toland's *ADOLF HITLER*. It's probably the most comprehensive work ever done on his life. At any rate, I've been able to find most everything I've wanted by using the index. This information, and Jon's folder, will corroborate my findings even more—I hope."

"You hope?"

"We'll see, Sam. First, how old was Jon when his mother died and what did she die of?"

Having read the file history several times while Marie was poring over the thick volume in her lap, he knew exactly where to find the answer. "Ah, he was nineteen and she died of cancer—four days before Christmas."

"The same," she said curtly.

"What?"

"Exactly the same as in Hitler's case."

"Unbelievable! Wait a minute. Why did you pick that particular item?"

"There are several points in Jon's case that

stuck in my mind for no reason I can fathom."

"Would you say the two points are coincidental?"

"If that's the only similarity, it could be nothing more than coincidental. However, I think we might have more to work with. Next, Jon was devoted to his mother, was he not? Very broken up when she died?"

"I know that from his sessions with me."

"Again, it matches Hitler's. But that would be possible in most instances. For the time being, we'll count it but not rely on it. Now, are the dates April twentieth or thirtieth mentioned any place in either set of records?"

Dayton quickly scanned the medical records, finding the date Jon had been admitted to Presbyterian Medical Center. He looked up into Marie's inquisitive face.

"Well?" she asked.

"The thirtieth of April was the day he was admitted to the hospital as an emergency case. That was the day Mrs. Ward called me about the blood. She raved he was bleeding from the eyes, ears, nose and mouth when she arrived home from work. After she hung up, she claimed all traces of the blood had disappeared and he was merely suffering from the headache that normally followed his dream. What's the significance?"

"Hitler killed himself April thirtieth, 1945," she said slowly, deliberately. "Perhaps the trauma of experiencing the dream on that date, the anniversary of his death, caused the blood to appear momentarily. Perhaps this incident triggered the strengthening of Hitler's personality.''

"Oh, Christ," he whispered in a low, disbelieving voice. After several long minutes passed, he said, "I've got the twentieth, too. I made a notation in my pad about his having a few drinks the night before his initial examination, which was on the twenty-first. He and his wife had been celebrating their wedding anniversary the night before. Now, don't tell me Hitler got married on that date."

"I won't, Sam. It was his birthday, though."

"I don't believe any of this," he said, throwing the folder down next to him on the couch.

"I know you're tired, Sam, but do you recall the type of dog his wife said he wanted to get? And what was the name he wanted to call it?"

He fumbled through the file, withdrawing his hastily scribbled note. "He wanted to get an Alsatian bitch, of all things, and wanted to call her Blondie. Why?"

"According to Toland, and I've read about Hitler's dog in many different books, he had an Alsatian bitch named Blondi."

"If everything about Hitler is in that book, wouldn't it have been possible for Jon to have read it and absorbed the information—" He stopped. "Of course not," he said. "He's had the dream since he was five and I suppose the book is only a few years old."

Marie said nothing.

He looked at her. "If this could be true, and that *if* is a mighty big one, how, no make that *what* the hell do we do next?"

"We don't run off half-cocked accepting it right away, do we, Sam?"

He studied her before speaking. Would she make fun of him? He didn't want to believe that of her and after thinking about it for a moment, he knew it could not be.

"No, of course not," he said simply. "What I meant was, how do we go about ridding Jon Ward of Hitler's spirit or personality or whatever you want to call it? Is there a precedent we can follow? Do we treat it like a dual personality? Just what the hell do we do?"

"We continue investigating—confirming or eliminating parallels until we are absolutely certain. Maybe you've already laid the groundwork for a solution."

"Wha—? Me? What did I do?" Struggling to understand the avalanche of ideas beating at his mind, he found his fatigue refusing to allow him a clear memory or perception.

"You gave Jon the suggestion, while he was still hypnotized, to examine in minutest detail each facet of the dream the next time he experienced it. You may have created a situation wherein Hitler's spirit will voluntarily leave, if the dream, especially the first part, becomes too traumatic."

His face brightening, he recalled his spur of the moment proposition as a last ditch effort to get the other voice to tell him more of the beginning segments of the dream. "Do you think that's possible?" he asked.

Shrugging, she stood, crossing the room to return the book to its place on the shelf. "It could be. I don't really know."

"Would that be harmful to Ward?" he asked, concerned for the immediate well-being of his patient. Would a severe trauma for the spirit of Hitler be equally devastating for Jon? He knew the aspiring author to be a healthy, well adjusted person. But who could foretell the consequences of such a situation? He doubted if he could, and Marie appeared to be acting strangely again, as she had earlier, before consulting Toland's book.

Ignoring his question, she stopped to face him. "I had an electrifying chain of ideas take place before I began reading. I know you were watching me, trying to understand and anticipate my thoughts at the time. I believe I can explain to you in correct order what I was thinking. First, the whole chain was triggered by your reference to something about parapsychology not being our bag." She closed her eyes for a brief instant and could see Helmut Rosenspahn as clearly as she had the day she left Vienna. She'd refer to him but wouldn't offer any more information than Sam needed to know.

"An old friend of mine, with whom I went to school in Vienna, went into the field of parapsychology after we graduated. He studied in Bonn for a while. If you recall, he is the friend I referred to as wanting to call in Vienna for some information if we couldn't solve this problem ourselves."

"Are you saying that you suspected last week this was something totally out of the ordinary?"

He began laughing. "Did I say out of the ordinary? God, how odd and unusual can a case get? Dual personality was the front runner last week right up until the other voice said yesterday he was Adolf Hitler. What else are you holding back from me, Marie?" He thought his voice sounded hysterical but when he finished speaking, he knew he hadn't overreacted to the woman's surprise announcement. Maybe she was a better psychiatrist than he.

"Just hear me out, Sam. Then you can question me all you want. Is that fair enough?"

He shrugged, waiting for her to continue.

"While we were students, we worked together on an assignment that led to an interesting, and for the time, curious discovery. I'm sorry I don't recall everything about it but I feel it is vital we contact Helmut in Vienna. He can look up the manuscript he and I discovered in the archives at the University."

"Slow down, Marie. What the hell are you talking about? What manuscript?"

"We had to do a thesis on hypnotists and their different methods. One man we were researching had taught at the University before the war. This man, Dr. Hans Mattiges, had supposedly written a book but no one knew of its whereabouts. Helmut and I, quite by accident, found the manuscript of his memoirs in the basement of the library. It had never been published. He had died suddenly, or something. At any rate, I'd like to have Helmut look up some information in it that might shed more light on the German spoken while Jon was under hypnosis."

"This is crazy, you know," Sam said, immediately regretting his choice of words. "You know what I mean. What could this dead professor's manuscript tell us about Jon and Adolf Hitler that would be pertinent to helping Ward now?"

"All I will say at this point, Sam, is that the coordinates sound familiar, now that we have uncovered so much confirmatory evidence. I want Helmut to find it so we have the information without error or conjecture on my part. If what he tells us is completely irrelevant, we'll dismiss it and go at the problem from another angle. Besides, you'll have another, more important question, answered for you if the call is made," she said, smiling coyly.

Confused by the twist the woman wanted to give the case, he could not comprehend the meaning of her last statement. His brain was tired. His body was tired. The case was tired. He needed sleep and if she wanted to call Vienna, he would not object.

"What time do you have?" she asked.

"It's a little past ten-thirty," he said, looking at his watch. "Why?"

"There's seven hours difference between Chicago and Vienna. It would be past five-thirty tomorrow morning there. It'll take some time to locate Helmut and get the call through. Besides, it won't hurt him to wake up early one morning," she said lightly, more to herself than

Sam when the thought of hearing Helmut's voice again entered her mind.

Crossing the room to the telephone table, she sat down, dialing the operator to place the call. After she had given what scant information she still had on Helmut, the operator told her to wait for a return call. Replacing the phone in its cradle, she found Sam sound asleep on the couch. She went to the next room to get him a light blanket. After covering him, she returned to the phone table to look up the telephone number of Dr. James Nash, chairman of the linguistics department at the University of Chicago. He would be able to tell her the meaning of the word *Zozobra*.

Howie and Tory sat crosslegged on the Murphy bed facing each other. "Does this nut think he's Hitler or what?" he sneered after reading the third transcript she had brought home.

"I don't know. I just thought you'd find it interesting. What did you find out at the library about the coordinates?"

"Shut up and let me think," he growled. There was something here he felt he should know—recognize—but for some reason it kept evading him. What was it? The coordinates as given in the second trance were the location of the Four Corners area in the Southwest. He had taken the time to check out several maps and had been as precise as possible. His double checking placed the exact spot sixty kilometers south and sixty kilometers east to find the virtual center of Cistern, New Mexico.

Running his fingers through his hair, he shook his head. "I don't know. It sure as hell doesn't make sense. Does the doctor or this Ward guy know what any of this means?"

"I don't know, honey. I don't think so. Why?"

Suddenly, the missing pieces fell into place. "Of course!" he cried. How many times had he heard some of the prospectors and old sourdoughs who roamed the western part of New Mexico looking for the lost Adams Diggings speculate on other hoards of gold lost in the area? Among the stories he had heard was one of gold supposedly smuggled into the United States by Hitler sometime in the thirties. The story said it was a sort of nest egg to fall back on in the event things didn't work out the way Hitler planned in Europe. The Four Corners area had been looked at more than once but each time someone had searched, nothing had been found. Could this be the location?

His eyes flashed brightly in the garish light of the single bulb. Smiling, he said loudly, "If—" and began laughing wildly. "If—if it is—oh, wow!" he whooped, clapping his hands.

"What is it, Howie, honey?" she begged, frightened by his strange behavior. Grasping his face in both her hands she shook his head. "Tell me what it is!" she begged. "What's wrong with you?"

"Nothing! There's nothing the matter with me. If—if this is what I think it is—our troubles are over!" He got off the bed and walked to the window.

"What? Tell me, Howie!"

"If what I'm thinking is right, baby, we're rich! Filthy, stinking, fucking rich! And Jon Ward is going to show us how to get it!"

"What? I don't understand anything you're saying," she said, following him to the window.

"This guy, Jon Ward, is going to lead us to a lot of fucking money," he said, slowly walking toward the door.

"How can he? Why would he do that for us?" She shadowed him like a puppy.

"He'll do anything I ask. Especially when I kidnap him and have him in my power." His voice had a strange, tinny ring to it.

Trembling, Tory moved to the window and rested her back against its frame. She watched Howie sit on the bed and pick up Jon's folder.

He went through the papers, throwing them aside one by one until he found what he had been looking for. Running a dirty-nailed index finger along the neatly typed lines, he stopped when it rested beneath the words, *blue trees*.

Howie looked up, staring unseeing at Tory, through the open window into the dark beyond.

CHAPTER 14

Despite the clouds, thin, reedlike shafts of sunlight broke through on occasion, spilling into the kitchen where Jon lingered over his morning coffee. When Trina laid her handbag on the table, he snapped out of his brown study.

"I didn't mean to startle you, darling," she apologized, sitting down. Pouring a half cup of coffee, she thought back to Monday night when her husband had acted out of character again. She shuddered inwardly, trying to negate the memory with the fact that he had acted normally ever since. Last night he had been particularly enjoyable and restful—one of their soft music, reading, talking, and eventual love-making evenings.

"I was just thinking about the trip we want to take," he said flashing his toothy grin. "When are you completely through with your job for the summer?"

"June fifteenth. That's a Friday. Now, let me

ask you a question. Will you be far enough ahead on your writing schedule to enjoy a vacation without worrying about working?"

"I should be. I have to admit that I feel more relaxed since beginning my visits with Doctor Dayton."

"I'm happy for you, darling." She felt relieved about her husband's admission, considering how upset he'd been about going to see a doctor first, then to the hopsital before seeing the psychiatrist. It could not be easy concentrating on his work while having the worry of analysis hovering in his thoughts. "Will your manuscript be good enough to be published?"

With a look of mock indignation, he stood. "When have I ever produced anything that wasn't?"

They both laughed before he continued. "I really think it might stand a chance."

"That would be wonderful."

"And because I feel so good about it, I think we should plan on leaving for our vacation the Monday following your last day. What do you say?"

She thought for a moment, then said, "The eighteenth?"

"Right."

"How long will we be gone?"

"I've still got a long way to go, so I think no more than a week or ten days."

"Is that long enough?"

"It'll have to be, won't it?"

"What about your appointment with Doctor Dayton?"

"I'll clear it with him," he said quickly. What difference would one appointment more or less make? He simply knew he had to go west, or southwest, for—for something. But what? What made him feel almost obligated to go there? He wondered if moths experienced the same curious attraction when a flame beckoned. He shook his head when reasons refused to form.

"Fine," she said, missing his head shake when she moved to put her cup in the dishwasher. "We are agreed now on going out west—someplace?"

Standing, he said, "I hope you understand. I just feel I have to go there. It's almost like a compulsion."

"No reason?"

"None that I know of."

A look of concern briefly crossing her face, she turned to leave, remaining silent rather than pose another question.

"What time will your meeting be over this afternoon?" he asked.

"Probably not before five. I don't think it'll run beyond that. What have you got planned for today?"

"I want to get away from the typewriter for at least a day. I'm going to the library to do a little research on an idea I'd like to incorporate in the book." He took her outstretched hand and they walked to the front entrance.

"You'll be home when I get here, won't you?"

"I should be. Probably between two and three."

"Do you want me to drop you now?"

"It's too early. Besides, a walk'll do me good."

They kissed and she left. Locking the door, he limped to the kitchen to pour another cup of coffee. Bringing it to his lips, the aromatic fragrance suddenly turned his stomach. Dumping the liquid into the sink, he retched for several minutes, dry heaves pumping his abdomen.

The gentle chimes of Marie's telephone rang through the quiet apartment. Fluttering his eyelids at the intruding sound, Sam stretched, rising from the couch where he had slept all night. Stumbling to the phone, he lifted the receiver and managed, "Hello?"

"Dr. Von Kelzer, please," the man's voice rasped in his ear.

"Who's calling?" he asked, stifling a yawn while he scanned the room to find evidence of her presence in the apartment. He saw her curled up in an easy chair. "One moment please. Who's calling?"

"Dr. Nash."

A quizzical expression forming on his face, he yawned again. Crossing the room to where she slept, he gently shook her shoulder. "There's a Doctor Nash on the phone for you," he whispered, not wanting to wake her too abruptly.

Opening her eyes at the sound of his voice, she comprehended what he had said when he repeated the message. She quickly stood, running to the phone. Watching her, he wished he could wake up as easily.

In several minutes, she replaced the phone in

its cradle and turning, discovered he had left the room. Hearing noises from the kitchenette, she hurried to the tiny room where she found him making coffee.

"That was Doctor James Nash, a linguistics expert at the University of Chicago. I called him last night after you dropped off to sleep, to have him find the word *Zozobra's* origin and meaning."

"And?"

"It's Spanish for anxiety. He also told me it's used as a name for an effigy burned each year in Santa Fe, New Mexico to begin the *Las Fiestas de Santa Fe*. The word *Zozobra*, as they use it, means Old Man Gloom. The burning allows the celebrants of this fiesta to experience unbridled joy."

Moving past her once the coffee was made, he went to the living room and began thumbing through Jon's folder. Several minutes later he said, "Here is it. *Zozobra took the people away —no one there because of Zozobra.* That means *anxiety* took the people away? No one was there because of *anxiety?* That doesn't make much sense, does it?"

"Try using the other meaning," she urged.

"*Old Man Gloom* took the people away. No one was there because of *Old Man Gloom.* What do you think?"

Entering the living room, she said, "It makes a little more sense than using anxiety. I see it possibly meaning that people were drawn to this fiesta, and a certain place was deserted because of the celebration. What do you think?"

"Assuming that's what it means—what does it mean?"

She shrugged.

"Did you get through to Vienna last night? And forgive me for falling asleep, but I was completely shot."

Marie thought back to the early morning hours when her call finally had been put through. The fact Sam had fallen asleep had been fortunate since she could speak more freely with Helmut. When she learned that he was married and the father of a daughter, she managed to control her frustrated emotions. Then she explained the purpose of her call and they agreed he would call back as soon as possible with the information. She hung up, and alone with Sam sleeping on the couch, gave vent to her feelings and cried. Not because of Helmut. She had accepted his loss when leaving her home five years before. She wept for her own stupid, romantic notion of assuming the role of the injured woman where her family was concerned. That and the fact she had wasted three years keeping Sam at a comfortable distance.

"Yes, I did. And yes, you are forgiven," she said. "First, I'll tell you about the conversation and then about a discovery I made."

"A discovery?" His eyes searched her face, waiting for an explanation.

"Be patient, Sam," she said quietly. He'd been noble for so long. She breathed a silent prayer that he would bear with her for a few more minutes. "Helmut recalled the manuscript vividly and agreed to find it and check out certain bits of information."

"Such as?"

"These coordinates seemed somehow familiar to Helmut, too," she said hesitantly. "At first, they didn't seem to ring a bell with him. But after talking for a while, they began sounding familiar. However, I guess, based on what I told him of Jon Ward and the other voice, his mind began working at a furious pace. He seems to accept the fact Hitler's spirit could be locked in with Jon's. He believes that shortly after Hitler committed suicide, his spirit transmigrated, becoming linked with Jon's."

Sam snorted. "You're kidding!"

"He seems to think the explanation you managed to acquire from Ward, or Hitler, if you will, is too plausible to be the product of a dream. He also agrees about the first part being too traumatic for Hitler to dwell on while his spirit speaks through Jon. However, Helmut warned me to make certin Ward is not allowed to manifest the dream while he's alone."

"What do you mean—alone?"

"He believes that under clinical conditions we might succeed in forcing Hitler's spirit from Jon. He suggested examining the dream very slowly. That way, it might become unbearable to relive the trauma of his career."

"What about the post hypnotic suggestion I planted?"

"He merely said we should try to induce the dream in your office. It might be dangerous for him to have Hitler's personality irritated, so to speak, under any but the most stringently controlled conditions."

"What do we do? Christ, Jon could have the dream and go bonkers without us having a turn at bat."

She approached him, slipping her arms around his neck. "I think we're safe until tonight. If anything would have happened last night, we would have heard by now. As long as Jon Ward is awake and not sleeping or hypnotized, the dream should remain dormant. Right now there's something I want to talk to you about."

He looked into her eyes before pullng her arms from around his neck. "It'll have to wait for a minute. I just thought that no one knows where I am. I didn't tell my secretary where I'd be."

"Don't, Sam." Her eyes pleaded for the chance to make amends for three years of aloofness.

"Don't?"

"Don't tell her where you are. Check with her and tell her if she hears from Jon, she should call your answering service and you will check with them from time to time. All right?"

Puzzled by her attitude, he asked, "Why are you being so darned mysterious? Why don't you want me to tell Tory where I am?"

"Because I want to spend as much time as we have until Helmut calls back, telling you how much I really love you and—"

He didn't wait for her to finish, instead

kissing her deeply on the mouth. He would check with Tory in a little while.

The gray skies reflected Millicent Tilden's spirit. She had awakened early to find the sun battling clouds for possession of the skies over Chicago. Feeling more depressed than at any time since Sterling's suicide, she elected to return to bed, hoping to feel better when she awoke from an extra hour's sleep. Soon, after she had arisen the second time, the gray skies began weeping gentle tears of rain, in apparent sympathy with the grieving woman. The full impact of his death had not sufficiently impressed her to cause more than surface depression during the first few days. After spending all day Tuesday with their attorney, G. Carlton Hughes, going over his will and papers, everything crushed in on her spirit. Mentally exhausted, physically worn out, she cried herself to sleep well after midnight. She knew certain joyless duties remained for her to perform following his death. Acknowledging sympathy cards. Making personal phone calls to those few people who had gone out of their way at the funeral home to be especially nice. The closet full of his clothing to be disposed of and— She began weeping again, amazed that tears still existed in sufficient quantity to flow. Throwing herself across the bed, she resolved to get up, shower, dress, and start the cards of thanks as soon as she went through the mail. Tears continued flowing until they dried, deep sobs convulsing her body long after she dropped off to sleep once more.

When Howie accompanied Tory to Sam's office Wednesday morning, he found it impossible to think of anything other than Jon Ward, his dream, and the riches waiting to be found. If he displayed any outward nervousness, Tory had not mentioned it. To keep him occupied and out of her way while performing her duties, she gave him access to the files containing the histories of the doctor's patients.

Shortly after nine o'clock, she placed a call to Jon Ward but received no answer. Instantly upset, Howie paced back and forth mumbling under his breath. She caught only a few words whenever he pivoted in front of her desk to retrace his route.

"It's gotta be today—During office hours— Logical to hear from the shrink—Absolutely vital or it won't work—"

She still trembled, frightened whenever recalling his facial expressions the previous evening when he first began raving about suddenly being rich. Too timid to pursue the topic then, she still found it impossible to ask him about it now. Perhaps when they reached Jon he would be in the right frame of mind to explain his plans. Until then, she accepted the fact that he knew they would soon be wealthy.

At ten o'clock she placed another call to Jon. Still no answer. Throughout the day, whenever attempting to complete the call, she could feel Howie's resentment building against her. It must be her fault that the man didn't answer.

Other than two phone messages for the psychiatrist, there had been a wrong number before noon but no other incoming calls. At one-thirty, when the phone rang again, he jumped nervously when the bell broke the silence.

"Doctor Dayton's office," she said tersely. "Oh, yes, Doctor Dayton."

Leaping from his seat without a sound, Howie hurried to her side, trying to hear the psychiatrist's voice.

"No, he hasn't, Doctor."

Again, he strained to hear.

"I see, Doctor. Yes, I will. Bye, bye, Doctor."

"What the hell was that all about?" he asked anxiously.

"S'funny. He was inquiring if Mr. Ward or his wife had called in."

Running his hand through his straggly hair, he quickly paced around the room. "Why? Why would Dayton want to know if Ward had called? Is that normal for him to call on his day off and ask if a patient has called him for something?" he asked.

Shaking her head, she watched him. "Not really. It might be he arranged for Mr. Ward to call."

"Maybe," he said, his voice trailing off. "Try Ward again. The sonofabitch can't stay away from home forever. What are you supposed to do if he does call in?"

"Notify Doctor Dayton's answering service. He didn't say where he was and probably doesn't want to be disturbed. He said he'd check every now and then with his service." She dialed the number again from memory, waiting while the phone rang on the opposite end. "Nothing," she said, fearful the one word would anger him.

Instead of becoming upset, he leaned on the desk to look at the digital clock. "That was an extra one we threw in for the fun of it. I think you'd better start calling every half hour. We gotta get him to come down here this afternoon. Without the shrink here, it'll be easy."

She stared at him dumbly. *What* would be easy?

The call at two o'clock echoed the day's efforts but when Tory called at two-thirty, Jon answered, and she panicked. Accustomed to hearing the ring without anything happening, she nervously sat up when it stopped and he said, "Hello?"

Clamping her hand over the mouthpiece, she squeaked hoarsely, "It's him. He answered. He's home. What do I do?"

"Tell him to get down here right away. Tell him the doctor has discovered something important. About his dream. Go ahead," Howie ordered sharply.

"Ah, Mr. Ward? This is Doctor Dayton's secretary, Tory Worthington. Doctor asked me to call and see if you could come to the office this afternoon."

"What's up?" he asked excitedly.

"It seems he's found something concerning your dream or—something. He said it was most important for you to come in this afternoon.

What time should I tell Doctor you'll arrive?"

"If it's that important, I guess I could be down there within the hour. Is that all right?"

"Just a minute, Mr. Ward," she said, placing her hand over the mouthpiece again. "He says he can be here within the hour. Is that all right, Howie?"

He nodded vigorously.

"That'll be fine, Mr. Ward. We'll see you then. Bye, bye." She laid the phone in its cradle, smiling triumphantly. "Now will you please tell me what you've got planned?"

"Not yet. Let him get down here first," he said, knowing she might refuse to help further if she were cognizant of his entire plan. "After he gets here, I'll fill you in. All right?"

"Okay," she said, pouting.

The minutes crept by, each one seeming to take longer than its predecessor. At three-fifteen, the door to the outer office opened. Jon walked in, striding briskly.

"You may go right in, Mr. Ward," she said shakily, betraying her fear.

If Jon noticed any tremor in the secretary's voice, he ignored it. Finally, he would find out something concerning his dream. Entering the plush office, he didn't see Sam in his usual chair.

The coarse voice behind him sounded frightened, almost choking when it said, *"Blue trees!"*

Jon stopped walking, frozen in position as he went into a hypnotic state.

PART IV

CISTERN, NEW MEXICO

June 6, 1979

CHAPTER 15

Excited because of the results of his attempts to place Jon in a trance, Howie rubbed his hands together. Not once had he considered the possibility that his efforts at hypnosis might fail. Nor had he reflected on the consequences had his plan not succeeded. He had Jon Ward in his power. Consequently, he held Adolf Hitler in his control and if his theory and conjecture proved correct, Howie would gain knowledge of a hidden cache of gold. He laughed aloud.

Easing the door open, Tory peeked into the room hesitantly. "Is everything all right, Howie?" she whispered hoarsely.

"Fine! Come on in and take a look at what ol' Howie's done."

White-faced, she timidly entered the office. "What's wrong with him?" she asked, pointing toward Jon who stood stiffly in the middle of the room, a blank expression in his normally animated features, his eyes staring vacuously.

"I've hypnotized him," he gloated.

"You've what?"

"I put him in a trance just like the shrink does."

"How? How did you do it?" Her voice trembled when she spoke. What if Doctor were to suddenly come in? She knew it wasn't likely but the possibility existed. An overwhelming urge to urinate swept through her lower body. In what sort of plot had Howie entangled her?

"Just like Dayton does. I read it in those files you brought home. If this turkey hears the words *blue trees*, he goes under. I figured he'd be easier to control if he were hypnotized."

"Control? Howie, you gotta tell me right now what you're doing or I'll leave. I think you're getting into something that's way over your head. Something that's going to get us both in a whole lot of trouble," she said, her voice firm, the tone of which surprised even her.

"You're in so deep right now, you could run all you wanted and you'd still end up in hot water." He strutted to the other side of the room to sit on the edge of Sam's desk. "Ain't nothing here I can't handle. What do you want to know?" He folded his arms, demeaningly staring at her.

"Everything. I want to know everything you're planning to do or I won't help you anymore."

"Okay." He leaned back on the desk with both hands, his left one accidentally depressing the button that activated the concealed tape recorder. "First, I just want to say it's too goddamn bad your boss with all his fucking education can't figure out what's wrong with this jerk, here." His head motioned toward Jon, laughing arrogantly.

"What do you mean, Howie?"

"I know what's wrong with him. Ward's got the ghost of Hitler locked up inside of him somehow. The spook wants to control him to claim a treasure in gold."

"Gold? How do—? Where is the—?" She blustered partial questions, vainly trying to comprehend.

"It's easy if you know all the answers. Apparently the shrink doesn't—and I do. That's why I'm smarter than he is right now."

"I haven't got the slightest idea what you're talking about."

"Okay. Shut up and listen. When I was a kid, there was lots of talk about some Nazis burying a hoard of gold somewhere around the Four Corners area."

"Four Corners?" she asked quietly, afraid to voice questions but seething with curiosity at the same time.

"Where New Mexico, Colorado, Utah and Arizona come together. It's the only place in the country where four states form right angles with their boundaries."

She vaguely nodded, not quite certain if she understood.

"At any rate, the story was that a plane or planes loaded with gold, flew into the area and a treasure was buried. Why? I suppose maybe to be a cushion to fall back on if Hitler had to leave

Europe in a hurry. At least, that's what I remember hearing. Anyway, a lot of people spent a lot of time looking for some sign where it could be buried. As far as I know, nothing was ever found. At least if it was, nothing was said. I guess I wouldn't say anything about it if I found it, and now it looks as though I have. Any way you cut it, Mr. Ward here, is going to show me where to find all this Nazi gold."

"How do you know, Howie? There wasn't any mention of gold in any of the transcripts I typed."

"There was, and there wasn't. The coordinates given when this clown talked German, are the coordinates for Four Corners—right on the money. He said something about being able to control his host—this guy standing here like a dummy—and claiming what is rightfully his. Well, the gold ain't at Four Corners at all. It's sixty kilometers south and sixty east of Four Corners. I looked it up carefully on several maps and it should be right around Cistern, a ghost town. All I gotta do is find a landmark shaped like a swastika."

"What about that funny word—ah, zoz-something or other?" she asked excitedly, her pulse pounding at the thought of becoming wealthy.

"*Zozobra? Old Man Gloom?* It's my guess the Germans made a study of the area and found out about the fiesta at Santa Fe and how it draws people from all over. They probably figured the best time to fly the gold in would be during the fiesta. They wouldn't have as many people around to hear the plane motor or see them digging."

"So what are we gonna do? How are we going to get the gold if it's out of the country in New Mexico and we're here in Chicago?"

"Christ, you're stupid! First of all, New Mexico is in this country, not out of it. And we're going to go there."

"Go there? When? How?"

"As soon as possible. Like today."

"Today? How? Has Mr. Tilden come through with some money?"

"Naw! That's chicken feed compared to what we got waiting for us in New Mexico."

"How are we going to get there, then?"

Turning to Jon, he said, "Give me your bill-fold, Jon."

Jon reached to his hip pocket without flinching and pulled his wallet out, handing it to him.

"See?" he said, taking the proferred pocket-book. After opening it, he snarled at the thin stack of bills. "Sixty-two bucks? Is that all?" Suddenly, he found himself wishing that his blackmail victim had come through with the ten thousand. At least he would be able to finance his new venture without concern for funds. Fumbling with the billfold, he opened the card file and yelped. "Here we go! American Express and Diner's Club charge cards. We got it made, Tory!"

"Do you think this is right? Trying to get money from people like Mr. Tilden was one thing but kidnapping somebody—?"

"Who said anything about kidnapping?"

"Didn't you say Mr. Ward was going to show us where it was hidden?"

"Yeah. I did. But that ain't kidnapping in the general sense. We haven't abducted him, you know, knocked him out and taken him by force, or tied him up and gagged him. We haven't demanded ransom from his old lady. Let's just say he's going on a business trip with us and he'll be free to leave when we're finished conducting our little transaction."

"Oh," she said quietly. To her, it sounded as though they were going to kidnap Jon but Howie knew more about these things than she did. And, because she wanted to be included in his future, Tory decided against questioning his plan any further.

"You'd better call O'Hare and find out about flights to Albuquerque. See how much two tickets will cost."

"*Howie Lieman!*" Tory shouted, stamping her feet. "You'd better be taking me along or I'm going to make you sorry."

"Huh? What'd I say? Oh. Make it three and tell them they're going to be charged." He smiled broadly, completely self satisfied, and called after Tory who was almost out of the room. "Better call Hertz and have them get a car ready for us at the other end. Make it a big one! Once we get down there, I want to be able to move fast. Got it?"

"I got it, Howie, honey!" she said cheerfully, hurrying to her desk.

322

Twenty minutes later, she reentered the office to find him sitting behind Sam's desk, his back to the room, staring out the window. "We're on TWA flight 449."

"What time do we leave?" he asked without turning.

"Five-fifty this afternoon. We get there at 7:44, local time."

He leaped from Sam's chair, moving around the desk to the middle of the room. "Come on. We gotta get going. The plane leaves in a little over two hours. It's ten to four already."

"Wait a minute, Howie. I want to know if we're going to get married once we get all this money?"

"What?" he shouted. "Look, you dumb fucking cunt, we gotta go now if we're going to get out there tonight. We'll talk about that some other time. Okay?"

"I'm just trying to be practical where my rights are concerned. I wouldn't want to help you get all that money and then have you dump—"

"Come on," he growled, turning to Jon who rigidly stood in the center of the room. "Come with me, Mr. Ward." He spoke softly to avoid waking him.

"You talk nice to him. Why can't you talk that way to me?"

"Because him I don't want to wake up. You? I wish you'd go to sleep."

"Howie!" How could he be so nasty? Especially now, just when they were going to be able to retire with loads of money?

"I'm only kidding. Come on, for the last time."

"What if he wakes up? What then?"

"I'll just say the magic words again and, *poof!*
—he goes to sleep."

Moving to the door, he turned to address Jon
again. "Come on, Mr. Ward. We're going for a
nice airplane ride."

Jon turned mechanically, following Howie to
the outer room. Tory lingered for a moment
before turning the lights off, then left Sam's
private office.

Behind the louvered doors, the tape recorder
quietly continued running.

While they waited for the elevator, Howie
whispered, "Just act normal, Mr. Ward. Keep
your eyes open and do what I say."

"All right," Jon said flatly.

The doors opened and in minutes they were
standing on the street in the light rain, watching
for a cab. When one swooped to the curb,
momentarily clearing the gutter of water,
Howie threw open the door. He ordered Jon to
get in after Tory, placing the hypnotized man
between the conspirators.

"Where you going?" the cab driver asked
from the front seat without turning.

"O'Hare!" Howie said, settling back for the
long ride to the terminal.

Glancing about, Tory found Jon staring
passively ahead. She shivered, leaning back
once the taxi sped onto the Northwest tollway.

Looking at the hands of her watch through
more tears, Millicent Tilden could not read

them until she blinked, sending a fresh torrent down her cheeks. Her eyes cleared momentarily and she could make out the time. Four o'clock. God! Why had she gotten out of bed? She had felt safe there. Her hands perspiring, she shifted the phone from her left to the right hand.

Shortly after two, she had showered and dressed. While having a cup of tea, she had begun attacking the stack of mail. One by one the cards of sympathy were opened and answered immediately. She knew her responses would be more spontaneous that way, rather than open them, read the message, and later write a thank you card. Toward the bottom, she found the long, business envelope without a return address, her name neatly typed across the front. Opening it, she screamed when she read the contents. Frightened, then angry, then enraged, she picked up the telephone, dialing the police.

What kind of sick animal would send something as obscene as this letter to her? While she waited for her call to be put through, a persistent thought kept surfacing. Could the statements be true? Might the letter have actually been written before Sterling destroyed himself? She checked the postmark on the envelope and found the missive had been mailed the same day he had died. Whoever had written it wanted to blackmail her and her husband into giving the anonymous author ten thousand dollars to keep quiet about—about— She found it difficult to think of her husband performing the perverse acts outlined in the letter. Still, he had been undergoing analysis for almost a year for something he refused to discuss with her. Too, he had never been overly attentive to her. Not in the manner for which she had longed.

"Lieutenant Jules Hongisto speaking," the raspy voice sandpapered into her ear, destroying her chain of thoughts.

"Lieutenant," Millie said bravely, "this is Mrs. Millicent Tilden. I want to report an attempt to blackmail my late husband and me."

Pulling on a sock, Sam hesitated, peering through the bathroom door where he could see Marie's body outlined through the steamy glass door of the shower. One thought predominated. Finally. She had finally expressed herself totally and he knew it would not be too long before they would marry. A warm, secure feeling of fulfillment seeped into his body, sending a fresh tingling sensation through him. Could this be love? If feeling good all over while studying a surrealistic, flesh-colored silhouette in a steamy shower could be love, then Samuel Dayton truly loved Marie Von Kelzer. He had seen her in the shower many times but never had he experienced this type of excitement.

The splashing stopped when she turned off the water and opened the door. Stepping out, she saw Sam sitting on the edge of the bed, his legs crossed, frozen in the motion of pulling one sock on. "Sam?"

"Huh? Oh, hi!"

"Are you all right?"

"I'm fantastic. How about you?"

"I'm very much in love with you, Sam Dayton. I hope you will forgi—"

"Hey, stop," he broke in when he heard her voice cracking as though she were about to cry. "Look, you had your reasons for waiting until now. Whatever they were, you can tell me when you're ready."

She rushed from the bathroom, still dripping, to encircle his neck with her arms, kissing his cheek, eyes and mouth. "I do love you, Sam," she murmured, tears of happiness and relief intermingling with the shower water dribbling from her hair.

After dressing, they alternately paced or sat in the living room waiting. The phone had to ring. When they considered the seven hours difference between Chicago and Vienna, the thoughts of failure on Helmut's part repeatedly crossed their minds. Would he find the old manuscript? Was he having difficulty completing the transoceanic phone call?

The chimes sounded too loud when the phone finally rang. Marie and Sam both jumped to their feet.

"You take the phone in here, Sam, and I'll use the bedroom extension so we both can talk with Helmut," she said, leaving him.

He waited until he heard her say hello before picking up the phone in the living room. When he did, he heard an operator explaining that she had a phone call from Vienna. He breathed a sigh of relief.

Making the necessary introductions quickly and advising Helmut to speak English for Sam's sake, Marie began. "What have you found? Did you locate the manuscript?"

"Yes, I did, Marie. It was just as you suggested. The coordinates are the same. Some rather intriguing things have been found, as well."

She had been right about that part of the mystery. But were they truly dealing with the spirit of Adolf Hitler? His personality? Sam still had gigantic doubts and it would have to be crystal clear proof if he were to accept it. Half listening as Marie and her friend rehashed how the odd directions had stuck in both their minds, he wondered about the "intriguing" things Helmut had mentioned.

"Perhaps you'd best tell the whole thing for Sam's benefit, Helmut," she said. "Begin with Dr. Mattiges being called to meet with Hitler."

"Very well," he said, his English more heavily accented than Marie's. "It was because of this particular job which Dr. Mattiges was asked to perform, that he went into hiding for the duration of the war.

"Mattiges refers to a method of hypnosis rather sketchily in the first part of the manuscript. He implies he discovered the means to keep someone in a hypnotic state for a very long time, 'a matter of years was feasible,' he said."

"Years?" Sam broke in. That seemed impossible. With the use of drugs and mechanical devices, long periods of control were possible today, but over forty years ago such means had not yet been discovered.

"I know it doesn't seem likely, Sam," he offered. "I wish he would have gone into further detail but apparently the incident I'm about to relate caused him to decide against any implicit information.

"Around the middle of May, 1938, he was summoned to Berlin where he was informed the Fuehrer wanted to meet with him at Berchtesgaden. When Mattiges arrived at Berghof, Hitler's villa, he was advised that he was to put on a demonstration of his new hypnotic technique for Hitler, himself. An army captain was placed in a trance and given post hynotic suggestions, which were to be carried out at certain specific times in the future over the next three months. If the experiment succeeded, then Mattiges would be recalled and his technique further utilized."

"Did you find out what the post hypnotic suggestions were, Helmut?" she asked.

"No. It was just an experiment for demonstration purposes. However, the experiment apparently worked since Mattiges was again called back to Berghof the first of August. I gather from bits and pieces in the manuscript that the method he discovered was capable of going deeper into the subconscious than any method before or since. Mattiges claims in his manuscript that he was able to order people to perform tasks absolutely contrary to their nature. We all know a person who is hypnotized normally, as is done today, will usually rebel against suggested actions they would not perform if they were conscious."

"The thought is staggering," Sam agreed. "It would be a powerful weapon during wartime, or peacetime, for that matter. Go ahead, Helmut."

"When he was ordered back to Berghof, Mattiges was told by Hitler himself, and with no one else in the room, that he was to hypnotize four men. He would be given the post hypnotic suggestions by the Fuehrer. The men were brought into the room one at a time and the first, a sergeant, was placed in a state of hypnosis. Mattiges was told to order his subject to be totally subservient to a Colonel Köenig. No matter what was asked of him by the colonel, he was to execute the commands directly, explicitly and without hesitation. You can see what a powerful ally a man so hypnotized would be in any type of situation."

"It is almost frightening when one thinks of the potential," Marie said softly.

"I agree," Sam concurred, "but what has all this to do with Jon's dream and its solution?"

"Please be patient, Sam," she said.

"I understand your concern," Helmut said slowly. "I'm positive that if you listen to this story you will have the understanding and answers you need."

"Okay. I'm sorry," he said, running a hand through his hair.

"The next man brought in after the sergeant was an S.S. captain who had been trained as an agent. His orders were to locate the precise spot given in the directions based on the coordinates. He was to transmit a radio signal on a prearranged band and provide fires to guide a plane in for a landing. He, too, was to be totally subservient to this Colonel Köenig.''

Helmut hesitated as though waiting for questions. During the lull, nothing could be heard but their quiet breathing mixed with normal phone noises.

He continued. ''The colonel, a Luftwaffe pilot, was next after the S.S. man. From what Mattiges says in his writings, the men would appear to be normal, except they would react to certain commands or stimuli. Granted, this is no different than methods we use today but post hypnotic suggestions are limited the way we currently use them. Several months at the longest and suggestions will be very weak at best. When he implanted the orders in the colonel's subconscious, the coordinates were mentioned again. He was to fly to the exact spot, sixty kilometers south and sixty kilometers east of the coordinates. There, he would see the fires the agent would have lighted and would have been able to find them because of the radio signal being sent. The plane was to carry a cargo of gold, which was to be buried near a landmark of some sort resembling a swastika. When the sergeant and the agent were finished with their digging, the colonel was ordered to kill them and bury their bodies with the gold. All evidence of their having been there was to be obliterated.''

"This landmark, Helmut," Marie broke in, "did Mattiges say what it was?"

"He doesn't say if it is a natural or man made formation. It isn't really important, unless you want to hunt for the gold," Helmut said, his voice lifting in a good natured jibe.

"I don't think we'll have time. Do you, Sam?" she asked.

He grunted his agreement. Gold? What a shipment of gold, a landmark shaped like a swastika, or a few German soldiers, had to do with Jon Ward's dream remained a befuddled mystery to him. Unless—? Suddenly, the clouds began thinning and Sam felt he might be grasping the cryptic meaning of the dream.

"When the task was completed, Köenig was to fly back to the point of takeoff and report to a General Kleist. The General was the last of the four men brought in."

"I really don't see what all this has to do with ridding Jon Ward of his problem, namely the fact that his voice changed and he said he was Adolf Hitler," Sam said, breaking into Helmut's report. He wished the German would stop being so dramatic.

"I know it sounds farfetched considering this took place over forty years ago, Sam," he said, "but if you listen, I think you'll understand some of the things that were said while your patient was in a trance."

"All right, Helmut," he agreed reluctantly, "go ahead." He found himself wondering if his own thoughts would be close to matching the solution Helmut claimed to have.

"The general was hypnotized and given his orders which included overseeing the transport of the gold to Mexico by submarine where it was to be transferred to a truck, acquired by yet another undercover operative, who simply was obeying orders. The truck, general, colonel and sergeant were then driven over the Mexican border into New Mexico, to a town—ah, Lordsburg. There another agent had acquired the use of an airplane and the cases of gold were loaded. The colonel and sergeant flew to their preselected designation. Here's the—how do you say—clincher? The general was ordered to kill Köenig when he returned to Lordsburg after completing his mission. Then, the general was to report back to Hilter and finish his remarks by asking for a glass of wine. Mattiges guessed the wine was probably poisoned. Consequently, Hitler would be the only one cognizant of all of this information."

"But Mattiges was aware of it, was he not, Helmut?" Marie asked.

"Of course. Apparently, Mattiges thought if he could escape with his own life, he would be lucky, considering everything he had been told by Hitler. But, in order to make his plan completely secret and foolproof, Hitler had ordered the doctor to be murdered as well, once the hypnosis had been performed."

"Why wasn't he?" Sam asked, caught up in the fascinating tale.

"A captain of Hitler's personal guard was to drive the psychiatrist back to Vienna. When he stopped the automobile in which they were traveling, he pulled a gun. However, Providence stepped in to protect Doctor Mattiges."

"What happened?" Marie asked.

"The captain was apparently an epileptic and suffered a seizure just as he drew his gun. Mattiges watched as his intended murder choked to death. Then, free, the doctor went into hiding lest Hitler find him and finish the job at which the captain had failed. You know, of course, what the coordinates are?" Helmut asked.

"Yes," Sam said. "I had them checked out last week. The Four Corners area where four states' boundaries meet at right angles."

"What is your conclusion then, Helmut?" Marie asked.

"I feel your patient truly does have Adolf Hitler's spirit within him. I don't feel this is just one personality splitting into fragments, but two separate, distinct personalities. Not such as you find in cases of dual or multiple personalities. No. This is a case of soul transmigration wherein Hitler's spirit intermixed with the spirit that was to become your patient at the time of the rape mentioned while the subject was under hypnosis."

"And you say this because—" Marie asked.

"Because it is not possible for your patient to know of these particular coordinates in conjunction with these specific directions in any other way. Only two people knew of them ultimately—Mattiges and Hitler. Both are dead but the directions were evidently important to Hitler just as he died. Consequently, the memory and ability to recall them."

"Do you actually believe this is what happened, Helmut?" Sam asked.

"If there is a spirit in each one of us, and that spirit lives beyond the body's death, yes. I believe it without reservation."

"Why, or better, how, could this have happened?" he persisted.

"At the instant of the body's death, the spirit can become totally disoriented. Without being aware, it can refuse to acknowledge its own body's physical death."

"Are you saying this is the case here?" Sam wanted to fight the reasoning, but knew he had no alternate argument at this point.

"I believe you have a classic case of soul transmigration."

"It seems to all fit together, Sam," Marie said quietly.

"Yeah, I know," he muttered. "It also shows why I didn't see the solution, if this is the problem. I deal in more real problems."

"You'll find this all too real, Sam," Helmut said, his voice fading momentarily.

"Any suggestions, Helmut?" Marie asked, raising her voice.

"Just be certain you are the one to instigate the dream for your patient and help him examine every facet—every detail. Should it occur without the proper controls, I feel anything could happen. There is nothing else?"

"Not that I can think of," Marie said. "Do you have anything, Sam?"

"No. I think we've been given a lot of information to kick around. Thank you very much,

Helmut, for all the trouble you've gone through."

"It was my pleasure to be of assistance, Sam. I would do anything for Marie—and the man she loves," he said evenly.

"How did—?" Sam began, stopping when he remembered Marie was on the bedroom extension.

"Just the way Marie sounded when she mentioned your name when we talked the first time. You've very lucky, and I wish you the best in the future."

"Thank you, Helmut," Sam said, grinning. Could it be that obvious?

"Let me know the final outcome of your case, will you?"

"Of course," Sam and Marie said simultaneously.

They said their goodbyes and Helmut's voice disappeared when both phones were hung up. Sam turned and saw Marie coming through the bedroom door. "Well?" he asked. "Where do we go from here?"

Curling up on the couch, she motioned for him to sit next to her. "I think you should have a talk with Jon. Convince him to enter a hospital until we can rid him of this other personality."

"Why don't you call it what it is, Marie? Hitler's spirit."

He found it peculiar of Marie that, although she had solved the apparent mystery of the dream, she had difficulty handling the solution.

"That's pretty tough, Sam. Let me refer to it my way and I'll be fine."

"All right, darling," he said, mouthing the word again. He had never called her anything but Marie, and found the affectionate term most pleasant when he said it aloud. "I think I'll call Jon right now and have him come down to the office in the morning."

"I'd make it tonight. Remember, he's virtually defenseless when he's asleep or in a hypnotic state. The only thing we have to worry about is his going to sleep without some sort of supervision tonight."

"Okay. You're going with me to the office, aren't you? I'd like to have you meet Jon. I also believe he'll be more prone to accept the idea of being hospitalized if you're there."

"Of course I'll go."

Standing, Sam picked up the folder to find Jon's telephone number. Seconds later, Trina answered.

"Mrs. Ward? This is Doctor Dayton. Is Jon there? I'd like to speak to him, please."

"Why, no, Doctor. Isn't he with you? He left a message saying he was going to your office. What was it you found out about his nightmare? Is—"

"Mrs. Ward, I didn't contact your husband today," he exclaimed, suddenly aware that he shouldn't have corrected the woman. Something was wrong. Why would Jon tell his wife of an appointment with him at his office? He never went to the office on his day off. Only Tory had been there all day. "Will you read me the note, Mrs. Ward?"

"Yes. It says 'Dr. Dayton's secretary called.

He wants to meet me as soon as possible at his office. Be home when I'm finished.' Didn't you meet him, Doctor?''

Casting a look at Marie on the couch, he found she had caught the subtle change in his voice and content of the conversation. He said, ''Will you meet me at my office as soon as possible Mrs. Ward?''

''Has something happened to Jon?'' she asked, her voice a frightened whisper.

''I don't believe so.'' He spoke soothingly, trying not to upset her, hoping his own sense of panic would not telegraph itself to her through his voice. ''Will you meet me there by, say, six-fifteen? Can you be there by that time?''

''I—I believe so, Doctor. Can you give me the address?''

He quickly relayed the information and hung up. Turning to Marie, he said, ''Something's wrong someplace. Jon got a call from someone who claimed to be Tory. She said I wanted to meet him at my office as soon as possible. Does that make sense to you?''

She shrugged and stood. ''I have no idea what it means but I think we'd better get to your office and meet Mrs. Ward. I don't like the idea of not having Jon in a situation where he's safe.''

Both psychiatrists rushed to the door and were soon hailing a cab. Surrounding lights and buildings rested on their psychedelic reflections, mirrored in the streets, wet from the day long rain. The jumble of colors seemed to symbolize their thoughts as the taxi splashed its way to the Fuller Building.

CHAPTER 16

High above the clouds, delicately washing the middle United States with an all day June rain, a TWA 727, its nose pointed southwest, swept through the gold-splashed sky. Traveling at speeds to maintain an average of better than four hundred miles an hour, the plane's first stop would be Albuquerque, less than three hours after leaving Chicago's O'Hare.

Howie glanced at Jon sitting back in his seat, his eyes closed in deep sleep. More confident now than when they had left the Fuller Building, Howie felt in total control of the escapade. When Jon awoke from his trance during takeoff, the words, *blue trees* instantly reinduced the hypnotic state. Everything had gone smoothly until then.

To keep his mind off their objective, Howie thought back to the cab ride through the rain. The Northwest Tollway had been crowded with the normal late afternoon traffic. However, the rush on homeward bound commuters had just begun and they arrived with time to spare.

"Pay the man and give him a decent tip, Jon," he ordered after they got out of the cab.

The driver had tried to make conversation more than once during the trip to the air terminal, but had written off his passengers for any type of gratuity. His eyes bugged when Jon handed him a twenty-dollar bill along with the necessary fare. "Thank *you*, sir," he cried, cramming the bill into his shirt pocket before the passenger could ask for change. When the back door slammed shut, he floored the accelerator, fleeing the terminal lot.

"Now listen to me, Jon," Howie ordered. "When we get inside, I want you to walk right up to the counter and ask for our tickets."

"They're not in his name," Tory said, anticipating a rebuke from him.

"Whose name are they in?" he asked quietly.

"Yo—yours, Howie," she whispered.

"No problem. I'll just go with him in case there's any question," he said, smiling unpleasantly at her before turning back to Jon. "Pay for the tickets with one of your charge cards. Do you understand what I'm saying?"

"I understand," he answered obediently, following Howie to the ticket counter while Tory stayed back a few paces.

"Do you have tickets for—for," Jon faltered, staring straight ahead. Since he had not been told directly who Howie and Tory actually were, he did not know his captors' names.

"Yes?" the attendant asked, waiting for him to continue.

"For Howard Liemen," Howie interjected.

"One moment, please." Turning to consult the computer, the man looked up in several seconds and said, "Yes. Three first class to Albuquerque, New Mexico? Round trip? That'll be twelve-hundred eighty-four dollars."

Without hesitating, Jon handed the man his American Express Card. Waiting while the airline representative filled out the form to pay for the tickets, Howie turned to face Tory, who stood ten feet away looking bewildered. The dumb broad had ordered round trip tickets as if they wanted to come back to Chicago and run the risk of being arrested.

With his line of credit checked and the form signed by Jon, the counterman filled out the tickets in the names of Howard Liemen, Jon Ward and Tory Smith. She had protected herself but not Howie. They followed the directions as given, making their way to the correct concourse and gate. After a short wait during which Jon sat between Howie and Tory, the 727 taxied into position and the passengers were allowed to board.

Then it happened. After moving his plane to its position in line to await his turn, the pilot, at the direction of the control tower, thrust the throttles open, sending the ship roaring down the runway. The sudden noise filtering into the cabin aroused Jon from his trance. He sat up, straining against his seat belt. "Wha—where am I?" he demanded loudly. "What the hell's going on?" He turned to Howie who had a look of panic sweeping across his face.

"Ah, uh, *blue trees*," he whispered desperately and Jon immediately relaxed, sitting back. "Why don't you just rest, Jon?" he said softly, hoping the suggestion might work and he wouldn't have to worry about any more unexpected awakenings.

His eyes wide open, Jon stared straight ahead until the flight attendant approached. She first asked Tory, who was seated across the aisle from Howie, if she would like a cocktail before dinner.

Looking dubiously at Howie, Tory said, "I'll have a screwdriver," and dropped her eyes to avoid confronting him. To escape the risk of being reprimanded for having a drink, she turned her head, attempting to be nonchalant and stared out the window.

"Gentlemen?" the woman asked when she turned her attention to the two passengers opposite the blonde. "Can I get you a drink?"

His face distending, Jon glared at the attendant. "*Nein*," he barked.

The woman, taken off guard, forced a smile before turning her attention to Howie.

"Easy, Jon, old boy," he said comfortingly and patted him on the arm. "I'll have a Jack Daniels on the rocks. I guess my friend won't have anything."

After the woman had left to complete her round of the first class passengers, he growled into Jon's ear, "Knock that German shit off or you'll be sorry. Just sit back and behave. Do you understand me?"

Slowly, Jon turned to face his adversary, unblinkingly gazing at his captor. Howie could feel his skin crawl under his clothes.

"Just—just sit back and relax, Jon. Okay?" he said shakily. Abruptly, he began wondering if his idea would work after all.

Jon's face returned to normal and Howie breathed an inaudible sigh of relief. For the time being, things appeared settled. When the drinks were brought, he sat back to gain more than just the enjoyment the fiery refreshment would bring him. He felt he needed it if he were going to complete his plan. After a second drink, the attendant served dinner and he ordered Jon to close his eyes after they had eaten.

While the jetliner winged its way toward the southwest, a cab splashed to a stop at the curb in front of the Fuller Building sending a wave of gutter water to the sidewalk. Two people jumped out. After paying the driver, Sam joined Marie under the canopy extending from the front of the building to the curb.

"I hope Mrs. Ward is here," Marie said, hurrying beside him into the quiet lobby.

"There she is by the elevator," Sam said, rushing over to her. "Mrs. Ward. I'm glad you're here already."

"What's happened? I've been going out of my mind since you called." Stepping into the elevator after the doors swooshed open, Sam introduced Marie to Trina, explaining how she had helped analyze Jon's tapes.

"What have you found out that makes this meeting so important?" Trina persisted. "Why did Jon come to your office to meet you if you didn't know anything about it? How come—" Asking her questions rapidly, she stopped when Sam raised his hand.

"Wait until we're in my office. I think we'll want some privacy."

When the doors opened and they got off, she said, "Very well, doctor."

Two men who had stepped back to make room for the disembarking passengers, now moved forward, blocking their path. "Doctor Dayton?" the larger of them asked, flashing a badge. "I'm Detective Lieutenant Jules Hongisto, police. I have a few questions to ask you. Could we go to your office?"

Marie shot an uncertain look at Sam who returned one of his own. Had something already happened to Jon? In turn, the two psychiatrists looked at his wife, both wondering if she possessed stout enough moral fiber to understand, without breaking down, the information they would reveal to her.

"Let's go to my office," Sam said, indicating they should follow him. "Normally I'm gone by this time and today's my day off. What made you come by now?"

"We just started this case and we had to begin someplace," Hongisto said.

Once inside, Hongisto introduced his partner, Sergeant Mike Ross. "We received a phone call from a Mrs. Millicent Tilden this afternoon, saying that she and her late husband were being blackmailed by someone."

"Late?" Sam choked the word hoarsely.

"Sterling Tilden killed himself last Friday morning at the First Federal Security Bank."

"Oh, my God!" Sam said softly. "Poor Sterling. I didn't know."

"Mrs. Tilden informed us that her husband had been consulting you but she wasn't aware of the reason. The letter seemed pretty explicit in—ah, certain details and we thought it logical for us to question you first to find out why Sterling Tilden was consulting you."

"I'm sorry, Lieutenant, but that's privileged information. I couldn't possibly release my files on Sterling to anyone. Not even his wife."

Hongisto reached in his serge coat pocket, withdrawing a folded piece of paper. "If I allow you to read this and it happens to be the reason for his seeing you, will you tell me?"

"Just what are you getting at, Lieutenant? Are you saying whoever was attempting to blackmail the Tildens, might have gotten their information from me or my records?"

"I'm not saying anything, Doctor. I'm here to follow up on a possible lead where I might be able to gather some information. Information that will lead to the apprehension of the person or persons responsible. That's all. I don't accuse, I don't judge, or try people. I merely gather information and present it to the proper personages in charge. I'm not a difficult person to get along with and usually I'm most congenial where others are concerned. However—" Hongisto paused dramatically before continuing in a slightly ominous tone of voice, "I dislike anyone who stands in the way of a police officer performing his duty."

Mike Ross suppressed a grin. How many times had he heard the same type of thinly veiled threats? Hongisto's line of chatter got results more frequently with people hesitant to talk to them, than any other method at their disposal. Hongisto's size intimidated people. His six-feet four-inch frame carried two hundred sixty-five pounds molded in place in such a way that told everyone not an ounce of fat or out of place muscle existed anywhere on his body.

"Let me see the letter," Sam said reluctantly. The thought angered him. Only one other person had access to his files. Tory. What possible reason could she have to jeopardize her position by doing something so obvious and foolish as to blackmail his patients? He quickly scanned the letter. Swallowing hard, he slowed his brain to analyze the words. He finally acknowledged to himself that whoever had typed the letter must have read Sterling's file. He knew Sterling would never have mentioned to anyone his turbulent feelings of being discovered and what he would do if he were. Looking up, Sam blanched when he found Hongisto studying him with narrowed eyes.

"You don't have to say anything, Doctor," he said. "Tell me how they got the information.

Where do you keep the records of your analyses?''

"Are you all right, Sam?" Marie asked, stepping forward.

"It's just a little condemning, isn't it? You think you know someone. Then you find out, because of something like this, you don't really know them at all." He drew a deep breath and waited to see what happened next.

"What are you saying, Doctor?" Hongisto asked, knowing he had made the right decision in coming to the psychiatrist's office.

"I have reason to believe another of my patients may be in trouble because of this same person."

"Jon?" Trina cried, moving closer to the knot of people. "Has something happened to Jon?"

"Please, Mrs. Ward," Marie stepped next to her, placing an arm around the woman's shoulders. "We don't know anything for certain yet. Let's not jump to conclusions."

"Is Doctor Dayton talking about Jon?" she demanded, turning to face Marie.

"I—I'm not sure," she lied, hoping to keep Trina calm until the police left. Then, she and Sam could explain to her, in a carefully orchestrated manner, the problem at hand.

"Marie, why don't you take Mrs. Ward into my office and have her relax until I'm finished with these gentlemen," Sam suggested.

She showed Trina to the inner office. When Sam was alone with the two police detectives, he offered, "I didn't want to unduly upset her. I was referring to her husband, Jon Ward.''

"Really?" Hongisto asked blandly. "Now, since we're alone, why don't you tell me what you were about to, before the ladies left the room?"

"Dr. Von Kelzer, Marie, and I have been analyzing Jon Ward's tapes at her home—''

"Tapes?" Hongisto broke in.

"I record each session, with the patient's permission, naturally. It allows me the luxury of time to better study each case.''

"Would you show me your recorder and how this is done, Doctor?"

"Why?"

"Perhaps someone has placed a second microphone in your office and is recording at the same time you are," Hongisto said.

"I—I never thought of that. If that were the case then Tory wouldn't necessarily have to be implicated.''

"Who?" Hongisto asked, tenaciously hanging on each word the doctor uttered.

"Tory Worthington, my secretary. She transcribes each tape to written pages, enabling me to have a regular file in addition to those tapes I elect to keep.''

"Why did you suspect her in the first place, Doctor?"

Sam explained about the phone call Jon mentioned in the note he had left for Trina. "I still feel it was someone impersonating Tory.''

"Show me your office, Doctor."

Opening the door slowly to avoid alarming Trina, Sam entered quietly, motioning for the officers to follow him. He went to the louvered doors and opened them. "The machine can be run either locally here or by remote control from my desk. The first few times with a patient, I usually go through the motions of starting the machine from here rather than from my desk. It seems to reaffirm in their minds that I'm doing what I said I'd do. As a result I'm able to build trust and confidence in a secondary way. About the third or fourth time, I begin using the remote controls and they just accept the fact that they're being recorded."

"I see," Hongisto said, while absently running thick fingers around the shelves in search of a concealed microphone.

Mike Ross checked possible hiding places in other parts of the office, wherever small listening devices could be concealed.

"You realize," Hongisto said after examining the recessed area where the recording equipment rested, "if we don't find a bug of any type, we'll have to question your secretary closely. She's probably our number one suspect."

"I still find it hard to believe," Sam said obstinately and began closing the louvered doors. "Wait a minute," he exclaimed, throwing the shutters open again.

"What is it, Doctor?" Hongisto asked.

"This tape," he said, pointing to the reel on the right, "it's been used."

"How can you tell?"

"I always place a new reel on whenever I take a recorded one off."

"So?"

"The machine records from left to right. This tape has been run through the machine and isn't even threaded anymore. Besides, the machine is on. See?" he said, indicating the dim glow behind the recording meters. Sam pursed his lips in thought. Mentally picturing his actions after Carole Nelumbo left the previous afternoon, he remembered specifically placing a blank reel on the machine. He also recalled having to return to his desk to retrieve the recorded tape of her session, which he almost forgot to give to Tory.

"One way to find out, you know," Hongisto said.

"Huh?" he asked snapping out of his recollection.

"Rewind it and play it," Hongisto offered.

"What? Oh, right! Yeah, why didn't I think of that," he said, quickly rethreading the tape before he rewound it. When it was ready, he punched the play button.

First, I just want to say it's too goddamn bad your boss with all his fucking education can't figure out what's wrong with this jerk, here. Howie's voice filled the room with its coarse tones.

What do you mean, Howie?

"That's Tory" Sam whispered, running a hand over his face. But who was this Howie?

"Shhh," Hongisto cautioned, motioning silence with a stocky finger to his lips.

Hurrying across the room, Marie and Trina

joined Sergeant Ross who had been examining the bookcases. Standing behind Sam and Hongisto they were able to hear the conversation. The five people listened intently to the two conspirators outlining their plan. Trina wept at the mention of Jon's name when Howie asked him for his billfold and Tory referred to him respectfully as "Mr. Ward." Convinced that Jon had been abducted for the information he genetically possessed, Sam and Marie covertly shot concerned looks at each other.

When Tory left the room to call the airlines and the twenty minute silence began, Hongisto said after several seconds of quiet, "Shut it off. What the hell kind of soap opera was that? Hitler's ghost? Lost gold? Kidnapping? What's going on here, Doctor Dayton?"

Sam quickly explained about Jon's dream and what had happened during the three hypnotic sessions. Trina listened in rapt amazement. "It appears," he concluded, "as though Tory and her boyfriend, this Howie Liemen, had begun blackmailing some of my patients. Somehow, Liemen was able to figure out what Jon's dream meant and is taking action to find what he believes is a hidden treasure of gold."

"Amazing. Simply amazing," Hongisto said detachedly. Turning to his partner, he shook his head. He thought he had heard everything in his nineteen years on the Chicago Police Force but this topped it all.

Turning the machine on fast forward, Sam let it run until a high pitched gabble of speeded up voices burst forth from the speakers. He stopped it, resetting the speed to normal and they listened again as the flight number was given.

"Well, I've never had law breakers give such a detailed account of their misdeeds before, but as soon as these two are apprehended, they'll have a tough time arguing against this tape. May I have it, Doctor?" Hongisto asked, holding his hand out.

"I suppose this is evidence?"

"It'll play a big part in obtaining a confession."

"What happens next?" he asked surrendering the reel after he took it from the machine.

"We'll call the Albuquerque Police Department and have them apprehend the three as soon as they get off the plane."

"No!" Sam shouted adamantly.

"What?"

"Absolutely not! My patient's consideration has to take precedence over the arrest of these two—" His voice died away when he tried to think of an appropriate term for the woman he had trusted and the man she apparently loved.

"Why? All care would be exercised for his safety."

"You don't understand," he said feeling totally circumvented. "Tell them, Marie."

Trina stood rooted in the same position she had assumed while listening to the tape. Jon was in danger, but the revelations she had just heard frightened her even more. Hitler's spirit inside Jon? Jon kidnapped for whatever purpose the man and woman involved had in mind? Lost gold? Her mind spun. What would happen now? Could they still help Jon? Would Jon be in even more jeopardy with the doctor not wanting the police in New Mexico to arrest the kidnappers and rescue her husband?

When Marie cleared her throat, Trina looked up. What little the psychiatrist had told her had been enough for Trina to establish a beginning rapport and she found herself drawn to the German-born woman. Trina quietly turned, leaving the office without being detected.

"You must understand, gentlemen," Marie began, "if Mr. Ward were merely hypnotized there would be virtually no danger. He would simply wake up as though he were asleep if too much noise occurred around him. However, I'm positive this man who induced the hypnotic state doesn't know Mr. Ward should be talked with and given directions carefully while he's hypnotized. If he allows him to remain unattended, the possibilities of his awakening are very good.

"Since we must contend with the fact that Mr. Ward is not alone as an individual personality, we must take into account the fact that the spirit residing within him is a malevolent one. We have absolutely no precedence to base a decision on at this point. Mr. Ward should be approached by Dr. Dayton and no one else."

"I think I understand what you're saying," Hongisto said, "but for the life of me why you believe it, is beyond me. Why I think I understand—?" He shrugged his wide shoulders.

Marie quickly explained several of the

incidents wherein Jon's personality had changed drastically. Re-emphasizing the importance of not having anyone interfere with Jon, other than Sam, when he arrived in Alburquerque, she finished.

"My only concern," Sam said, rejoining the conversation, "is for Jon. You have your evidence to convict this Liemen character and Tory anytime you want. All you have to do is arrest them. The only thing I'm asking you to do is wait until Jon is safely away from them. Is that really impossible?"

"I suppose I could put the APB out for them in the normal channels," Hongisto said slowly, conceding to himself that this was no ordinary case. "But how are you going to get Jon Ward away from them in the meantime? I mean, they're evidently on their way to New Mexico."

"We can catch up to them," Trina said from the doorway before anyone answered the question.

"What?" Hongisto asked, turning.

They all faced Trina. "While Doctor Von Kelzer was explaining things, I took the liberty of calling O'Hare to find out the next flight to Alburquerque."

"What time?" Sam asked excitedly, admitting a high degree of admiration for Trina's cool thinking under stress.

"There is a flight leaving at seven-thirty that is non-stop. It gets there at nine-thirteen local time. We'd only be an hour and a half behind them if we could take that flight. But it's full," Trina said.

"Besides, we're here in the heart of the Loop and not at O'Hare," Sam said dejectedly, looking at Marie. Were they going to be beaten so easily by time and distance?

"There is another flight at seven thirty-five that makes one stop enroute, at Wichita, I think she said," Trina continued. "It had room. I made reservations for the three of us."

Sam grinned broadly before sobering immediately. "But how do we get to O'Hare on time? It's a couple of minutes to seven." A stillness quickly enveloped the room.

"There's a heliport on top of the Stradler Building," Hongisto said brightly. "I think we can convince them to get you there on time. Ross, you call them and tell them it's police business. Then call O'Hare and ask them to have the tickets at the gate. It'll be close but I think we can make it. Have them hold the plane until they get there in case they're a couple of minutes late, Mike."

"Right, Lieutenant," Ross answered and went to the phone.

"The rest of you, follow me," Hongisto ordered. Now, that he had a plan of action to follow, he wanted to waste no time in executing it since everything depended on the three people getting to O'Hare within the next half hour.

"I'll have the Albuquerque police meet you people, however. That is, if you don't mind, Doctor," Hongisto said, hurrying toward the door.

"Fine! Anything if you can get us on board

that plane," he answered.

Marie tugged on Sam's coat sleeve, motioning for him to hang back. "When you first hypnotized Jon," she asked softly, "and gave him the command words *blue trees*, did you qualify the order by telling him he would go into a trance only if it was your voice he heard?"

A troubled look clouded his face. "That thought has been condemning me as a therapist ever since I heard the tape. No! No, Goddamn it! I didn't, and I should be chastised no end for slipping up."

Studying him with a sympathetic expression, she wanted to ask him why he hadn't. But she knew he was punishing himself sufficiently without further questions from her.
her.

"I guess," he said, taking her arm to guide her toward the door, "I felt since no one else was in the room and the words were an uncommon combination, it wouldn't be necessary. Only Tory and I were supposed to know. After all, Jon wasn't consciously aware of them. A small mistake with big consequences. It'll never happen again, I can assure you."

"I'm sure it won't, darling," she said squeezing his hand on her arm.

Half walking, half running, they hurried to catch up to Trina and the huge policeman who were just entering the elevator.

CHAPTER 17

The rain stopped shortly before the helicopter settled gently onto a landing pad at O'Hare. The pilot, apprised of the urgency of their flight, turned to his passengers and said, "You've got thirteen minutes, folks. I believe the Security Police are meeting you to take you to your flight."

"Great," Sam shouted above the *chop, chop, chop* of the rotor as he opened the door. "Thanks a lot." He jumped to the ground, turning to help Trina, then Marie to his side.

"Doctor Dayton?" a voice yelled from behind them.

Turning, they saw a Security Police vehicle and a burly, blue uniformed man motioning for them to hurry.

"We don't have much time but we'll make it," he said, throwing the gear shift into drive when Sam had followed the two women into the back seat. Tires spinning on the damp concrete, the car lurched forward, speeding toward the concourse where TWA flight 347 was being loaded.

With eight minutes remaining, the guard slammed on the brakes, careening to a stop at a ground-level door of the terminal beneath the wing of the 727.

"I'll lead the way!" he shouted, leaping from the car to be followed by his passengers. They rushed up a flight of stairs, bursting into the main level of the concourse. "Here're your passengers the police called you about," the man said to the girl behind the check-in desk.

"Thanks, Steve." Smiling professionally, she turned a charge card form to Sam who already had his Visa card and pen out.

Thank God for Hongisto's efficiency, he thought. The lieutenant had told them as they rode the elevator to the Stradler Building's heliport that he would call any instructions to O'Hare and TWA if Sam would give him a charge card number. The necessary forms could be filled out and waiting for them when they arrived. If ever a policeman would be revered in Sam's memory, it would be Lieutenant Jules Hongisto.

After he had signed his name to the form, the girl handed him three tickets and boarding passes. Sam, urging Marie and Trina to hurry, ran down the boarding tube to the plane.

One of the flight attendants, Kate Manrey, met them at the door. "A few minutes to spare, Doctor." Accepting the passes, she indicated they should take their seats and buckle their belts. Once the door closed, the 727 jerked backward as a tractor towed the plane out of its position at the concourse. The jet's whine began building and the ship turned smoothly toward O'Hare's maze of runways. Then, a few minutes later, the departing jetliner raced down the wet runway to which it had been directed.

Howie Liemen looked at Jon's wristwatch. A smile crossed his unshaven face when he thought that less than an hour would pass before they touched down at Albuquerque International Airport. Looking at his captive, he saw that Jon appeared to be asleep. He turned, facing Tory across the aisle.

"It won't be long now," he said softly.

"How much longer?"

"Less than an hour. Are you excited?"

"Naturally. Why wouldn't I be? It isn't every day I get a chance to fly away from everything to pick up a fortune in gold," she said dreamily.

"Jesus Christ! Hold it down," he spat, looking about the cabin to see if anyone had heard her. "Do you want the whole fucking plane to know about it?"

She cast her eyes to the floor. "I'm sorry, honey. Really I am. I won't say anything to anyone about this—ever."

He turned away. She had no idea how close to the truth she had come. She had become a liability. She had outlived her usefulness. His forehead creased in thought as the expression ran through his mind. It was just an expression—a saying. But could it be the answer he wanted? He knew she wouldn't fit into his plans once he had the gold. And he certainly didn't want her in a position where she could blab to the authorities about his blackmail activities, or the treasure. So what was the answer? Elmination? The furrows on his forehead smoothed out, a calm, sagacious tranquility seeping into his thoughts. Why not? Who would ever find her in New Mexico? He knew a little about the area around Cistern. Her body would never be found if he disposed of it properly.

Turning his head, he studied Jon for a moment. Another liability. Once Jon had led him to the gold there would be no logical reason to release him. Even though the chances of his remembering anything were practically nil, the possibility that he might, nevertheless, existed. No sense taking chances at this stage of the game. It looked as if Tory would have company in her lonely, New Mexican grave.

Howie smiled evilly. Nothing left to chance. Every contingency, every little thing that could go wrong, taken care of in advance. The only way he liked things. Neat. All loose ends tied up. Settling back in his seat, he closed his eyes, dozing contentedly.

The thin, tinny voice of the captain awoke him from his nap a short time later. "This is the captain," the voice said. "We'll be landing at Albuquerque International Airport in approximately twelve minutes and we have already begun our approach. Please fasten your seat belts and when the *No Smoking* sign comes on, please extinguish your cigarettes. The temperature is seventy-two degrees Farenheit and the skies, as you can see, are completely clear. For those deplaning at Albuquerque, thank you for flying TWA and we hope to be able to serve you again in the near future."

A soft "bong" accompanied the flash of the *No Smoking* sign when it went on. Tory, alert as she peered out the window watching the ground rush up to flash alongside the jetliner, grinned expectantly.

A squeal of rubber touching concrete, the plane's weight settling on its landing gear, brought a smirk to Howie's face. The 727 slowed when the jet's baffles were turned, diverting the plane's thrust to the front with a roar. After taxiing for a few minutes, it stopped at the small satellite terminal several hundred feet distant from the pueblo style main building. When the plane stopped, Howie turned to Jon, touching his shoulder. "Come on, Mr. Ward. Time to get off."

Jon's eyes opened, bright, clear, taking in the interior of the plane in once glance. "Where in the hell am I?" he demanded.

Without raising his voice, Howie muttered, *Blue trees!*

Jon's eyes glazed again, his face easing into a passive, slack expression, and he returned to the hypnotic state he had been in practically from the moment he had arrived at Doctor Dayton's office over five hours before.

"Just be ready to follow me," Howie ordered softly.

Once Tory left her seat, Howie commanded Jon to stand and move into the aisle. Sand-

wiched between his abductors, he left the plane.
Entering the satellite building, they hurried
down to the tunnel leading to the main
terminal.

"What a beautiful place," Tory exclaimed,
slowing her pace to look at the Indian mosaics
set into the walls of the tunnel.

"Come on. We got no time for sightseeing,"
Howie growled, prodding Jon to a fast shuffling
walk.

In less than five minutes, the trio stood at the
Hertz Rent-a-Car counter, Jon mechanically
signing his name, displaying his driver's license
as he had been instructed.

"Your Impala is out front," the blonde who
had registered them said, pointing to an unoc-
cupied car. "There, the blue one. Here are your
keys. Have a nice trip."

"Thanks," Howie muttered, taking the keys
from Jon who had studied them, unable to
understand why he held them.

The car, roaring to life when Howie turned
the ignition key, pulled away from the curb
slowly. He steered the Chevrolet toward the
Yale Boulevard exit once they had left the
terminal area.

"I thought you were in a hurry, honey?" Tory
said from the back seat.

"I am, but it ain't gonna do any good to get
picked up for speeding in town. We'll make
tracks once we hit the freeway and get out of
the city."

"Oh," she said, sitting back.

He turned right onto Yale, carefully main-

taining the speed limit and, once he entered
Gibson Boulevard, began accelerating. Several
minutes later he shot up the approach ramp to
the Pan American Freeway, heading north.
Holding the car's speed to fifty-five, he concentrated on driving at the speed limit. Within a
few miles they sped onto the Coronado Freeway
at the interchange and the Impala began
picking up speed as they flashed past buildings
and housing developments which became fewer
and farther between. By the time the sun dipped
behind the volcanoes on Albuquerque's western
skyline, they were well out of the city and the
car raced westward through the encroaching
New Mexican night.

TWA flight 347 lightly touched down at
Wichita. Sam, impatient at the delay, squirmed
in his seat. Marie and Trina, across the aisle,
discussed the whole of Jon's predicament.
Watching the people who were deplaning, Sam
motioned for Kate Manrey.

The tall, light-haired flight attendant moved
gracefully down the aisle to Sam's seat. "Yes,
Doctor? Is there something I can do for you?"

"Is there time for me to get off the plane? I'd
like to make a long distance telephone call from
here. It's quite urgent."

"Normally we don't like passengers to get off
unless it's their destination. However, I think it
might be arranged. The terminal is quite close
and we do have almost twenty-five minutes
before take-off. You'll find a bank of telephones
to your left when you enter. I'll give you a

boarding pass so you won't have any trouble getting back on," she said, returning to the front of the plane.

"I thought of a telephone call I should make," Sam said to the two women sitting to his left before following the attendant. "I'll be back in plenty of time. Don't leave without me." He smiled reassuringly at Trina.

"Hurry back, Sam," Marie called after him. Turning back to Trina, she said, "Now where were we? Oh, yes. You had asked something about why—"

"Why," she cut in, "this—this thing—hadn't happened sooner."

"You mean—?"

"Why Hitler's spirit," she shuddered, "didn't make itself known before. Why now?"

"I think it's because your husband has such a strong personality and mind. The spirit probably had difficulty in trying to make itself known. In fact, that was one of the things he said the first time he spoke through Jon to Sam. *My host has been difficult to conquer.* The only way the other personality could get through was while Jon slept. Then, only the dream would manifest. But, because of the traumatic experience of committing suicide in the dream, Jon would wake up screaming. The rest lay dormant.

"What triggered it now that enabled the rest of it to come through so loud and clear?" she asked, turning to face Marie.

"Probably the hypnosis. It removed all of Jon's defenses against being overcome."

"My fault," Trina said simply, resignedly, a tear meandering down one cheek. Looking out the window she murmured, "If Jon is all right and comes through this thing, I'll never ask him to do anything again."

"What?" Marie asked.

"It was at my insistence that he went to a doctor in the first place, and that ultimately led him to see Doctor Dayton." She turned her back to Marie.

"You can't blame yourself, Trina. Not for something that was to be inevitable sooner or later. Be thankful we know what the problem is and that we know where Jon is going. Don't chastise yourself. It's not fair. Ultimately, it would have happened with or without Jon's involvement with other doctors and Sam. If you want to do anything, pray we get to Jon before anything adverse happens."

They continued talking. Shortly before the door closed, Sam reboarded the plane to sit across the aisle from them, a wide grin creasing his face.

"What's pleasing you so much?" Marie asked.

"I got thinking about the police meeting us," he said softly. "I feel it would only be so much delay, don't you?"

She hesitated before answering. Of course she knew how precious every minute, every second, could be now. Any needless setback they could avoid would mean that much more possibility of success. Nodding she said, "Probably. What have you done?"

"I called ahead to Albuquerque and was put

in touch with a charter helicopter service. The man who owns and operates it, Chuck Bergan, is going to meet us in an airport vehicle at the satellite terminal."

"The what?" Marie asked.

"It's an auxilliary terminal building TWA usually uses that's some distance away from the main building. He'll pick us up and take us to his helicopter that'll be a short distance away."

"I hope it's the right thing to do, Sam. We might have need of the police if this Liemen character tries to get rough."

"Personally, I don't think he will. He doesn't sound like the type who would face up to anything really tough. Besides, we'll cross that particular bridge when we come to it," he said, buckling his seat belt.

"I hope you're right," she said, knowing Sam had probably drawn the correct conclusion about Howie's strength of purpose and intent if he met any opposition.

"I also checked with this Bergan guy about distances. Cistern's about one hundred thirty air miles or so from Albuquerque and we can get there in under an hour. He also happens to know where it is, which is lucky. From the way he described it, there's only a few crumbling buildings at a crossroads and that's it."

"How far is Cistern if you're driving? I assume Liemen will drive with Jon and your secretary," Marie said.

"A little over two hundred. Bergan says they should average sixty miles an hour pretty easily on the wide open roads they have there. If they do, they'll get there just about the same time we do. Of course, they could arrive a little ahead of us."

"Then," Trina said, cutting into the conversation, "we should be able to help Jon before anything happens. Liemen will need Jon to show him where the gold is. Isn't that correct?"

"From what we know, that's exactly right," he agreed.

Taxiing to the end of the runway, the plane swept into the night. Within ninety minutes, it would touch earth again at Albuquerque.

Fifty miles north of Gallup, the blue Impala sped through the blackness. Howie, clutching the steering wheel, stared straight ahead at the broken white line dividing the blacktop road. His normal, haggard appearance had long since been replaced by a wild, intense expression.

Mumbling under his breath for the last hour, the only comprehensible words Tory had caught were, "Gold—all mine—no one else's." She had given up trying to make conversation with him and now found herself wishing she were back in her studio apartment where she had lived before meeting him. Her reflections convinced her she had been a fool to live with him, working for him, doing whatever he had ordered. Never had he made a request or suggested something she might like to do. Everything she had done since meeting him had been for him at his demand.

She felt a growing terror spreading through her body, not unlike a chill. She had no concept of his plans at this point. Would he include her? She hoped not. She didn't love him anymore. Suddenly, she found herself wondering about her own safety. Cowering back in her seat, she fought her natural instinct to cry. Did he plan something awful for her? Oh, God! She sniffled once before tears ran down her quivering cheeks.

Ramming the car into the night, Howie chose to ignore the woman in the back and the man who sat next to him in the front seat. Jon's face, illuminated by the eerie halflight of the dashboard, slowly swelled, an iniquitous smile twitching the edges of his mouth. His eyes darting about, he turned his head to study the driver of the auto.

CHAPTER 18

As TWA flight 347 rolled to a stop close to the satellite terminal at ten-twenty-one, Sam, Marie and Trina loosened their seat belts, quickly standing to leave. Making their way to the back of the cabin, they waited until Kate Manrey had supervised the lowering of the steps from beneath the plane's rear. She stepped out onto the top of the stairs, signalling Sam to come forward.

"Doctor Dayton, this man says he's to meet you," she said, indicating a tall, muscular man dressed in a leather jacket and billed cap who stood several steps down.

Moving up a step, the man said, "I'm Chuck Bergan, Doctor. I have a Jeep waiting for you and your party on the other side of the building. Are you ready?"

"Let's go," he said, turning to his women companions. Hurrying down the steps, they followed the pilot around the building and got into an open Jeep.

Bergan wrenched the gears into low and floored the accelerator. Turning in a half circle, the car raced away from the jetliner and the terminal. "You really want to go to Cistern tonight?" Chuck yelled above the roar of the Jeep's motor and the rushing air that swept over them.

"Absolutely," Sam cried. "It's of the utmost importance. A man's life could depend on you getting us there in time."

"But Cistern's a ghost town. Deserted. Nobody's lived there for over fifty, sixty years." Slowing the Jeep, he approached a helicopter parked near a low, flat-roofed building. The pilot leaped from the driver's seat, motioning for them to follow, and ran to the Bell Helicopter. Opening the door, he climbed aboard with Sam following him into the front seat. Chuck motioned for the women to sit behind them.

"The man we're trying to help is being taken there against his will," Sam explained while the engine turned over. The huge blades on top of the fuselage began turning, slowly speeding up. Taking advantage of the moment, he quickly explained those details necessary to have Chuck assist them to the best of his ability. He avoided mention of Hitler's spirit, stressing instead Jon's mesmerized state.

Chuck shook his head. When the blades whirled faster and faster over their heads, he said, "I don't understand, but I'll help you in any way I can, Doctor." He picked up the mike.

"Fine," Sam said above the increasing volume of the motor and swooshing rotor. Turning, he found a look of relief on the women's faces.

"Here we go," Chuck said, the helicopter rising gently from the concrete apron. When he had attained sufficient altitude, he pitched the rotor and the helicopter moved forward over the pinpoints of light below.

"I wish there were a moon tonight," Sam said.

"There will be later on but not much of a one. Why?"

"It would help us see better, wouldn't it?"

"I've got a pretty powerful spotlight under the fuselage. I use it to light neighborhoods whenever the police department presses me into night patrol. They've got several of their own but utilize me and a couple of others whenever they need us."

Sam and the women watched Albuquerque passing beneath them. From four thousand feet, the lights resembled stars against the blackness of space. Solid bars of light marking main thoroughfares interrupted the upside down universe like densely populated Milky Ways.

"It's quite a town," Chuck said. "Lots of transients moving in and out, but a good place to live. I'm kind of a rare bird. I was born here. Wouldn't think of living anyplace else."

The chopper continued flying in a north-westerly direction. Thirty minutes after leaving the airport, Albuquerque lay behind them and only occasional, lonely pricks of light twinkled forlornly against the gloomy sea of night below. Overhead, the canopy of stars beckoned, reminding them they were not alone.

"How did Cistern become a ghost town?" Sam asked, breaking through the *whump, whump, whump* of the rotor.

"Most of the deserted towns in the southwest petered out and died when the reason for starting the town petered out and died. Like a mine would stop giving ore, or an industry would be moved."

"Industry?"

"Yeah. For instance, the railroad started a lot of little towns to care for their locomotives, and people offering different services would move into the area. But when the engines were able to go longer distances without stopping for fuel or water, those facilities were let go to hell. Eventually, the stations were the only thing keeping a town on the map. Oh, maybe a house or two."

"What about Cistern?" he asked Chuck, who seemed to revel in talking about his home state.

"Cistern was named Cistern because of a deep hole in the ground a few yards north of the town. Because of its location, it naturally collected rain water and snow runoff from the mountains, but it was primarily fed by underground streams."

"So?"

"The damned thing went dry about seventy or eighty years ago and when that town's main water supply went, so did it. The hole is about two hundred feet deep with straight up and down walls. It's almost a perfect circle, too. Just like a—"

"Cistern," Sam finished.

The helicopter continued through the night, the pilot checking landmarks he knew he could rely on in the dark.

Seventy miles ahead, the Impala's headlights struck through the dark like bright knives slicing black velvet. Once the car passed, the tear repaired immediately. Howie's eyes, wide open, glancing from side to side, studied the road passing beneath the automobile. According to his calculations and the odometer, they should be reaching the remains of Cistern soon. Burnham, the last outpost of civilization they would pass through before reaching their destination, lay ten miles behind them. Off in the distance, at the extreme edge of the headlights' beam, a post appeared, apparently racing toward the Chevrolet. Slamming on the brakes so he would be able to read the sign hanging from it, he brought the car to a swerving stop fifty feet beyond. Throwing the gears into reverse, he backed up. Squinting to read the shadow of paint remaining in the form of letters that spelled, *Cistern, New Mexico*, he smiled.

"We've arrived," he said triumphantly. "Not bad time either. What time you got, Jon, old boy?" Howie grabbed his arm, turning the face of the watch right side up to him. "Ten past twelve in Chicago, huh? That's some pretty fancy moving." He dropped the gear shift into drive, sending the car forward until he reached the crossroads and stopped.

"Wait here," he ordered, getting out. Moving to the front of the car, he looked around. Where should he begin looking? Someplace around here he knew he would find a landmark shaped like a swastika. If he couldn't find it right away, he'd wait until sunup. Cursing the fact he didn't have a flashlight, he returned to the car. He steered onto the road to his right, which led north, moving forward slowly.

"Will we be able to find the marker in the dark?" Tory asked from the back seat, breaking her self-imposed silence since chastising herself for her involvement with him. Maybe she would be able to get some of the gold, steal it, and somehow get away from him. She knew she had to if she were to survive.

"If we're lucky," he growled, looking at Jon who stared straight ahead, "old *Schicklgruber* here will show me!" Moving off the road, he slammed on the brakes a hundred feet from the blacktop. He killed the motor and jumped from the car. Racing around to the front of the vehicle, through the splash of brilliance from the headlights, he went to Jon's door, tearing it open. "Out, Ward," he snapped.

Jon mechanically obeyed, getting out of the car while Tory slipped from the back seat to move around behind Howie.

"Show me where it is," he demanded, staring at the hypnotized man.

Jon's face, puffed since leaving Gallup, reflected the evil contained for twenty-eight

374

years. "I have no idea where the marker is," he said harshly, his voice changing to that of Adolf Hitler.

"You do, you sonofabitch!" Howie screamed, not noticing the difference in voices. "You're trying to ace me out of it. I'll be goddamned if that's gonna happen. Now tell me before I beat the fucking piss out of you."

"If I knew where to look, I'd probably show you. But I don't. I've never been here before. I was told of the landmark resembling a swastika by an agent many years ago, but I have no idea how to find it. I was the one who devised the plan to bury gold. I was the one who manipulated the execution of the plan and made certain everyone involved died so I would ultimately be the only one with the information. But, as far as knowing where to look, I have no idea," Hitler's voice said, distinctly forming each word.

"Show me, goddamnit," Howie shrieked. "Tell me what to look for."

"Look for a landmark in the shape of a swastika," Hitler said, smiling pitilessly. "That's all I know."

"Yeah!" Howie cried. "I'll find it and then it'll be all mine. All mine!" He continued shouting, "All mine," running around in circles while he searched for the marker.

Stifling a sob, Tory ran into the flood of light at the car's front end. "Howie! Howie, come back! You can't find the marker in the dark. Move the car and look in the light of the head-lights. Please, come back, honey."

She could still hear him shouting as he moved

laterally away from the car, the words, "all mine," filtering back to her through the still night. Turning to Jon, she shuddered when his eyes, burning into her very soul, locked with hers momentarily. She gasped, tearing her gaze from his, and moved out of the light toward the sound of Howie's retreating voice.

Then she stopped. Scarcely breathing, she listened intently. Had she heard a noise? An animal? Some animal breathing, stalking her this very minute? Her eyes darted from side to side. Each time she moved them, her peripheral vision made out grotesque shapes and shadows. Where were the buildings, the man-made canyons, to which she had become accustomed?

A shudder ran through her frame when she realized she had never been in almost total darkness over which she had absolutely no control. In the city, whenever she had been afraid of the nighttime, all she had to do was flick a switch to be bathed in light. Revealing, truthful light. Light that showed her no ghosts or monsters existed, lurking in her room to destroy her.

But here—out here in this God-forsaken wilderness—there were no switches to turn on. No flood of welcome brightness to put her frightened mind at ease. Only blackness. A blackness hiding the monsters of her imagination. Beasts ready to devour her at any moment.

Forcing one foot to move ahead of the other, she stopped, holding her breath again. She could only hear the pulse in her own temples pounding. She moved the other foot and stopped. Again, she heard the fast surf of her own heartbreat.

Feeling cold sweat ooze from her clammy skin, she moved slowly back toward the car. At least there she would be able to hide in the automobile if attacked. Jon had made no indication of harming her since they had called him to the office. When? When had they done that? It seemed like a lifetime ago. Forcing herself to determine the time, she gasped, realizing it had been only nine hours before. It seemed more like nine days.

"All mine," grew in volume as Howie made his way back toward the car. The noise she had heard before became louder. Looking about wildly, she saw a pinpoint of light moving out of the sky toward her. She sucked in her breath, holding it to hear better. It sounded like a helicopter.

"Howie!" she screamed. "Come on! Someone's coming! Hurry, honey. Please?"

"We're almost there," Chuck said.

"How the hell can you tell?"

"Besides instruments helping, I know the state like the back of my hand. That group of lights we flew over a few minutes ago was a little town, Chaco Canyon. Cistern is almost dead in the middle between it and Shiprock. I'm flying a heading that would take me to Shiprock. By watching the time and airspeed, and drifting a degree or two to the west, I'll be able to set you down in the middle of Cistern. All four buildings of it."

"How come they only had four buildings in town?" Sam asked.

"There were more but these four were made from adobe. That stuff lasts forever and three days. There's adobe ruins around the state that are hundreds, maybe thousands, of years old. Just sunbaked earth in the shape of whatever. It lasts."

"Do you know of, or have you ever heard of, a landmark around Cistern that might be shaped like a swastika?"

He turned to stare at his passenger. "A swastika?"

"Supposedly there's one around Cistern someplace."

"I've flown over that place lots of times. I've never seen anything remotely resembling one."

"You're positive?"

"Absolutely. If I say it's not around there, believe me. I know practically every square mile of New Mexico. How big is it supposed to be?"

Sam shrugged.

"If it's bigger than a small house, I'd know it. Of course, if it's small, it wouldn't serve too well as a landmark, would it?" His eyes twinkled good naturedly.

Sam nodded when he realized that the swastika landmark was probably non-existent. Pointing ahead to a tiny splotch of light, he said, "What's that?"

The pilot peered into the night and said, "You got me. It's just about where Cistern should be. Might be a car. Think it's your people?"

"If it is, we'd better land and go some of the way on foot. I wouldn't want to startle them into doing something at the last minute that might be harmful to my patient."

"I'll put my spotlight on," Chuck said, reaching for the switch.

"Don't, if you don't really need it."

"Why?"

"Again, we might alarm them. Can you land in the dark?"

"It's risky!"

"Can you?"

"I'm willing to take the chance if you are."

Sam turned, studying him for a moment. His finely chiseled face showed laugh lines that had worked their way into the sculpture over the years. A thin, delicately trimmed moustache displayed the apparent pride he took in his appearance. Glasses, edged in metal, had been chosen to complement his overall appearance rather than serve merely in a functional way. Sam guessed him to be a rare type of man. "If you think we can do it, go ahead. I feel we should be as unobtrusive as possible at this point."

"Okay, Doc—tor." Chuck added the last syllable, obviously electing not to offend his customer with an abbreviated title. "I'll drop down to about a thousand feet and try to land as close to the town as possible. I'll set her on the road since there's too many pine trees around to land any place else. Too risky." He changed the pitch and rpm's of the rotor and the helicopter began descending.

Sam turned to the women behind the front seat. Smiling confidently at Trina, he said, "It won't be long now. I'm sure we'll be able to have Jon with you in a matter of minutes. Are you doing all right?"

She nodded. "As soon as Jon is with me, I'll be super," she said quietly, more to herself than to either of the psychiatrists.

Leveling off at one thousand feet, the helicopter slowly approached the intersected roads that quartered Cistern.

While Tory cowered behind the car waiting for Howie to return, Jon, momentarily suppressing Hitler's spirit, could hear him yelling, "All mine! All mine!" in the distance. Then he caught the same beating vibrations Tory had heard minutes before as the helicopter landed. Somehow the sounds intermingled, the peculiar rhythm of the two hammering at his mind. He knew this rhythm, this chanting sound coming at him from a distance. Steadily the cadence grew. The voice of Hitler screamed. He concentrated for several minutes, trying to locate the source of the cries. With his hands thrown over his ears, he darted through the path of the headlights into the utter dark surrounding him.

Running wildly, blindly, he could hear the far-off distant voices screaming their maddening cry of *Dee-hah! Dee-hah! Dee-hah!* until it grew into *All mine! All mine! All mine!* Slowly it became, *Sieg Heil! Sieg Heil! Sieg Heil!* growing louder and louder until he stopped abruptly, covering his ears even tighter. A half-crazed smile wrenching his mouth, he recognized for the first time in his life, the words being shouted. A bewildered look held his face while he tried to understand the connection. With Sam's posthypnotic suggestion triggered, he obediently began trying to analyze the meaning of the shouts.

Continuing through the short pinons, he found himself completely alone. The black vacuum! He was actually running through it. But what did it mean? Sensing bursts of German words within his mind, he stopped, focusing his concentration on the idea of being alone in the oppressive gloom. The German voice ranted, raved, screaming shrilly within his mind until he spun on his heel to continue his flight through the trees.

Too late, he saw the trunk of a pinon tree, long ago felled by lightning. Unable to avoid the hazard, he tripped, sailing through the air after his foot struck it. He prepared to fall without being hurt but sprawled on the ground. Picking himself up, he brushed off his pants. Suddenly, his eyes saw movement to one side. Then someone called out. Jerking his head in that direction, he stifled a scream when the trees began turning into people.

The headlights, acting as a beacon, allowed Chuck to set the helicopter down in the middle of Cistern's only intersection. Leaping from the cabin, Sam, followed by the pilot and two women, dashed into the night along the road leading to the north, toward the car and his patient.

"Hurry!" he cried over his shoulder.

As the rotor coasted to a stop, the crescendoing silence sweeping in was broken only by the sound of their running footsteps and the cry, "All mine," filtering out of the night. Approaching the car, Sam saw Tory hiding behind the car. He also caught sight of Jon running away just out of range of the headlights. Tory would have to wait. His first responsibility had to be Jon. Hearing Chuck's heavy steps behind him, he didn't turn to see if the women were following but sensed they would not be too far away. Thoughts of Howie Liemen flickered through his mind bringing him to wonder for an instant where he might be. Then he saw Jon trip and fall. He stopped quickly, allowing Chuck and the women to reach his side.

"Sam!" Marie whispered excitedly. "Look at Jon! What does all this remind you of? Listen! Do you hear it?"

Tory watched her employer run past, wildly hoping he didn't see her. Frightened, she wondered who the man following Sam might be and immediately generated questions as to the identity of the two women chasing after them. Where was Howie? She could still hear him madly yelling off to the right looking for that damnable swastika. She wished she had never met him, had never laid eyes on him. But what could she do now? She had met him and slept with him and served him for the last— How long? A lifetime? Now she found herself alone. She must get away from here before Sam discovered her.

Crawling on hands and knees, she made her way to the driver's side of the car, opening the left front door. Slipping in, she fumbled for the keys but found only the empty ignition switch. Howie had taken the keys with him.

Now what could she do? If she went back in the direction from which the doctor had come, there might be more people waiting there to arrest her. She couldn't follow Howie. She didn't know exactly where he had gone, although she could still hear him yelling in the distance. Maybe, if she followed Sam and these other people, she could hide when they came back. Then she would continue in that direction after they left. She'd be able to get away after all. She moved away through the dark.

Sam strained his eyes to see his patient splayed on the ground next to the small upended pinon pine. He hushed the other three, motioning for them to get down behind the stunted trees. Working his way over to Marie, he said, "What do you mean? Listen? Look at Jon? Do I hear it? Do I hear what?"

"The dream! It's like the dream, Sam. Don't you hear someone crying *all mine* over and over? It sounds like the same *dee-hah* rhythm of *sieg heil*. And Jon, running through the trees, it's like his dream forest. Now he's fallen. All of it might prove to be too much for Hitler's spirit,'' she whispered excitedly.

''If that's the case, the spirit might willingly leave him,'' he said, motioning for the rest to stand. ''Jon! Jon Ward!'' he shouted at the bewildered man.

Jon had already gotten to his feet when he heard the cry but didn't recognize his name. Standing, he looked about and then screamed.

The trees appeared to be turning into people. The German voice babbled incoherently. The dream took a firm hold of Jon but he felt compelled to stand, to study the phenomenon. He counted them. Four. Four people staring at him. The German voice screamed maniacally but he steadfastly obeyed Sam's order.

Then, from behind the threatening people, he saw another figure. The blond woman ran out of the night toward him. At last, he would see the woman of his nightmare face to face.

Tiptoeing so she wouldn't make any sound, Tory didn't see the place where Sam and the others had crouched out of sight. Startled by their sudden appearance when they stood, she bolted toward Jon.

Entranced by the figure of the woman running toward him, Jon turned, following her departure as fascinated as he had been by her sudden appearance. He returned his attention to the people behind him and found them shaking their fists, waggling their fingers at him.

Terror-struck, the German voice continued hissing.

Tory swept past Jon. When she felt it safe to

do so, she slowed her pace. Afraid of falling in the inky blackness, she watched constantly for a decent hiding place. She finally turned when she saw a clump of trees looming out of the blackness, slowly making her way toward it. Just as she hunched down, she heard a crashing approach from the same direction she had just left. Her eyes widening, her heart pounding wildly, she waited.

"I know what you're doing, Sam," Marie said, shaking her fist at Jon. She followed suit while Trina and Chuck watched in shocked amazement. The psychiatrists knew the more real and terrifying the dream could be made for Jon, the better the chance of Hitler's spirit voluntarily abandoning his host.

"Do as we do," Sam ordered the startled man and woman.

"Wh—why?" Trina gasped.

"Just do it," Marie exhorted. "We'll explain later."

The four people swayed back and forth among the trees, clenching their fists, threatening Jon Ward.

Jon felt a tightness within him as though an unseen force were constricting his head, his limbs, his body. He wanted to scream but found his throat tight, dry. He opened his mouth. A choking gurgle burst forth. Bubbles of moans mixed with German curses vomitted out in screaming disarray. While spinning about in a clumsy pirouette, dizziness and nausea swept through him in waves. The cacaphonous stream of shouts and groans crescendoed to a deafening roar. Could this be reality or a different aspect of the dream he didn't know? Could the monotony of his nightmare suddenly change after all these years?

Thick spittle built in his mouth until, overflowing, it gushed down his chin, clearing his throat and windpipe. Alone at last, Jon Ward screamed. The figures of people and trees danced before his eyes and he willfully succumbed to the whirling spin in which he had been flailing about.

When he collapsed, he caught sight of Trina and Sam standing behind the low pinon trees, next to a strange man and woman. Staring at them while the landscape stopped spinning, he tried calling to his wife but his throat ached. He suddenly felt stronger than at any time before in his life. His face tingled as it returned to normal. The screams and cries and curses dissipated in the night when a sense of elation, of joy, of freedom, overwhelmed him.

Lying in a twisted heap, he felt a great weight lifted from him more quickly than the dream had manifested. He wanted to laugh and sing and cry.

Unexpectedly, out of the gloom, Howie dashed past him. Jon turned to watch the stranger he couldn't recall ever having seen. Looking about, he cried, "Where the hell am I? Hey? Who's around here who can answer a few questions? Hellooo?" He clumsily got to his feet, turning when he heard more running footsteps approach. He saw Trina's tear-streaked face coming at him out of the darkness and held his arms open. Leaping into the warmth of his embrace, Trina smothered her husband's face with kisses.

Unnoticed by the reunited couple, Sam and Chuck ran up. Deciding Jon was in no apparent danger, the psychiatrist continued running after Tory and Howie. The pilot indecisively followed him.

Jumping up from her hiding place when she saw it was Howie running toward her, Tory cried, "Over here, Howie!"

The sound of her voice brought him to a halt. "Where are you?" he asked hesitantly.

"Over here," she repeated, moving toward him.

"We gotta get outa here. There's people crawling all over the fucking place looking for my gold. Come on. We'll lead them away from here and then double back later to find my gold," he whispered hoarsely, trying to catch his breath. Grabbing her hand, he pulled her after him.

Walking faster and then breaking into a slow trot, he did not notice the blackness of the yawning hole stretching before him. Two paces away from the edge, he tried to stop but lost his balance, slipping over the edge, slamming Tory to the ground at the same time. He clung tightly to her hand.

"Don't let go," he screamed to the girl who lay on her stomach, struggling to keep him from falling. "Don't let go, Tory. For Chrissakes, don't let go!"

The words rang hollowly over and over, across the natural cistern, bouncing from one smooth wall to the other. Then, like the water held there for so long, they, too, evaporated.

"My hand's slipping," he hissed. "Help me!"

She reached down with her free hand, smothering the scream she felt rising in her throat when her breasts dragged across the rocks and dry, hard ground. When he slowly brought his other hand up, she grasped it tightly with her left but he released his hold from her right hand, and slipped, her fingers barely holding him.

"Jesus Christ!" he screamed as he dangled below her, suspended by her left hand only. "Don't let go until I get a grip with my other hand. Hang on to me."

"I'm trying, Howie," she grunted. "I won't let you go, honey. I love you." Sobs racked her body from the strain of holding him and from the thought of losing him. She had been wrong. She *did* love him. Now she must prove it by saving his life. But could she?

"Let us," Sam said when he and Chuck ran up.

They grabbed at Howie's forearm just as Tory's fingers, numb with pain, released her precious cargo. His scream echoed through the cistern, continuing to reverberate for several long minutes after the three people at the brink above heard his body thud when it struck the bottom.

No sound followed the death scream until Tory whimpered. "Oh, God! I killed him! My

God, I killed Howie. I killed him." She rolled over on her back, staring at the stars overhead, which writhed and danced through her tears.

Chuck on one side and Sam on the other, they reached down, helping the woman to her feet. Looking up at Sam's shadowy face, she mumbled, "I'm sorry, Doctor Dayton. I'm sorry for everything."

He put a comforting arm around her shoulder, leading her back to where Marie, Trina and Jon waited.

Howie's contorted face, hanging below her, persistently materialized in Tory's mind. Hearing his pleas, she sobbed convulsively each time he slipped from her fingers. Why hadn't she gone over with him? She had thought she didn't love him. She had thought he didn't love her. But they did. They did love each other. Now, she'd be punished alone. It would be easy if he were with her. But she was alone! He was gone! Howie was dead! She had killed him. She wanted to die, too. She wanted to be with Howie! She could not live without him.

Twisting free of Sam's protective arm, she spun about, racing headlong toward the cistern. When she reached the lip of the hole, her legs kept churning in midair while she fell silently, noiselessly, to the body of her lover below.

After their shock at Tory's suicide had subsided, Sam and Marie explained to Jon and Trina how Hitler's spirit could not tolerate the first part of the dream. "It was just too traumatic for him, I guess," Sam said. "At any rate, I think you're free of your nightmare, Jon."

"You know, that's the first time you've ever called it a nightmare, Doctor," he said.

"Normally, we don't think in terms of degrees for dreams. But after tonight I'm willing to make an exception in your case," the psychiatrist said, chuckling.

Marie slipped her arm around Sam's waist, pulling him gently toward the helicopter.

Looking down at her, he smiled. "When we get back to Chicago," he began, "I want to talk to you about possibly forming some sort of partnership."

"A professional or a personal one?" she asked, her eyes twinkling.

"Both." He winked and they walked toward the helicopter.

When Sam climbed in the ship, Bergan turned to him. "What the hell was wrong with the turkey who fell in the cistern?"

Feeling he could now reveal Howie's real intent, Sam told Chuck of the coordinates, directions, buried gold, and other details they had used to arrive at their conclusion.

When he finished, Chuck threw his head back, roaring with laughter. "Hell, I've heard that story ever since I was old enough to walk. Bunch of crap, if you ask me. Lots of people have wasted a lot of time and money looking for it. But it'll never be found—providing it was buried in the first place."

"What makes you say that, Chuck?" Sam asked.

"If it was buried near a landmark shaped like a swastika, the damned thing would have been found long ago. Believe me, Doctor, there's no swastika marking lost gold around here or any-place in the state. At least, not one big enough to be a decent marker. Remember, I know New Mexico like the back of my own hand."

"Are Jon and Trina coming?" Sam asked, turning to Marie.

"Yes. I think they're getting used to being alone for the first time," she said, laughing lightly at her own little joke. "What time is it, darling?"

"Ten before twelve, ah, Mountain time, that is. Why?" he asked.

"I don't know if the thought struck you or not, but today is June sixth, the anniversary of D-day," she said soberly.

"Oh, wow," he said. "That's heavy, isn't it?"

"It's quite coincidental, isn't it, Sam?" she said.

"Right, and I'm willing to let it go at just that," he replied, turning to watch the Wards slowly approaching the helicopter.

Jon, his arm around Trina, slowed their pace to be alone for an extra minute before reaching the others. "When we get home," he said, "let's make a baby."

"A baby?" she asked, smiling warmly.

"A boy baby."

"A boy baby," she agreed. "What about your book?"

"I'll finish it after we make the baby."

She hugged him.

"There'll probably be a few other changes in our lives, too."

"Such as?"

"No more sleeping late Sunday mornings. Going to church so we can set a good example for our son. Then, when he grows up, if he wants to be a priest like my mother wanted me to be," he said softly, "his mama and papa won't have to feel guilty."

"I think I'll like that," she said as they walked toward the others.

When they were in the helicopter, Bergan turned on the spotlight and lifted the machine off the ground. "We'll notify the authorities when we reach Albuquerque," he said, sending the dragonfly-like craft higher into the black night.

As they rose in the sky, the light from beneath the fuselage framed the intersection which had been the center of Cistern, New Mexico, in a splash of brightness. The higher the helicopter rose, the larger the pool of light grew until it embraced the crossroads and the ruins of four long, narrow buildings. Each ruin sat appoximately the same distance from the intersection, lending the ghost town the appearance of a huge swastika.

After a brief second, the craft headed for Albuquerque.

EPILOGUE

June 7, 1979
Shortly after midnight

The helicopter continued southeast passing over the tiny, isolated farm of Jose' Javier Romero, who wrested from the land the same meager living his father and forefathers had. No other person living in the county worked as hard or diligently as he did to provide for his young wife and the family they hoped to have one day. Confident that in the future he would be financially solvent, the man and his wife, Teresa Marie Alejandra, doggedly carved the hard ground, coaxing and begging from it the slight yield grudgingly given up by the earth.

At twenty-eight, he reflected the picture of health, his body as hard as drop-forged steel. His hands, calloused from hard work, became the gentlest of instruments when he lovingly touched and caressed Teresa. Exhausted most evenings, the young Mexican-American seldom reacted to his ardorous feelings. When he did, it was to satisfy his own bodily needs and to keep

Teresa happy and content to be his wife.

She responded to each touch, each caress, each kiss in fiery answer, every fiber in her exhausted body quivering deliciously. She considered herself fortunate to be married to such a man and always welcomed him whenever he wanted or needed her.

Today had not been any different for José and Teresa. They had worked hard and exhausted, retired shortly after the sun went down. Physically spent, they dropped off to sleep almost immediately.

When the helicopter passed over their house shortly after midnight, José began tossing and turning. He moved one hand until it brushed his wife's body. She turned to face him. "Are you asleep, Teresa?" he asked.

"I was, but—" she let her voice trail off.

His roughened hands carefully slipped the shoulder straps of her cotton gown over her arms.

"Let me," she said, sitting up.

When she drew the nightdress over her head, he watched her breasts jiggle in the half light when they came into view. Stroking the globules of flesh with one hand, he lowered his wife to the bed with his other.

Her nipples stood erect above the mounds of flesh, rising even more when his tongue caressed them. His body reacted when she lightly traced a familiar route toward his penis. He felt his manhood aroused to its fullest when her slender fingers intertwined with his hair.

Kissing deeply, the man and woman rolled

back and forth on the bed. "Now, Jose," she cried. "Do it now!"

He rose to his knees, positioning himself between his wife's outstretched, welcoming legs.

Then, he felt the sensation, first as a tingle at the base of his penis, close to the prostrate gland before it rapidly swept through him like a chill.

His erection grew larger before Teresa's widening eyes. When he flexed his muscles, he seemed more like a stone statue than her husband. His sinews bulged, swelling to extra-ordinary proportions.

Throwing back his head, he screamed, *"ICH LEBEN NOCH!"*

"EVERY TIME I HEAR THAT SOMEONE HAS BEEN UPSET BY SOMETHING I'VE WRITTEN— IT REALLY CHEERS ME UP!"

—SHAUN HUTSON

THE MASTER OF SHOCK HORROR